REGISTRATION FORM

Clip out and mail this card to:
Barr-Randol Publishing Co.
Box 4486
Covina, CA 91723

☐ Notification requested when supplements become available, expanding and updating the information in:
SMART TRUST DEED INVESTMENT IN CALIF.

Your Name _____

Address _____

City, State, Zip _____

ORDER FORM

Clip out and mail this card to:
Barr-Randol Publishing Co.
Box 4486
Covina, CA 91723

Your Name _____

Address _____

City, State, Zip _____

_____ more copies of SMART TRUST DEED INVESTMENT
  are requested @ $23.50 ea., total $ _____

California residents, please add $1.52
  sales tax for each copy   _____

Plus shipping and handling   1.80
                                    _____

Total amount due $ _____

☐ Payment enclosed

☐ Please charge my ☐ Visa ☐ Master Card

Acct. # _____ Exp. Date _____

Your signature _____

SMART TRUST DEED
INVESTMENT

in California

This publication is designed to provide accurate and authoritative information in regard to the subject matter covered. It is sold with the understanding that the publisher is not engaged in rendering legal service. If legal advice or other expert assistance is required, the services of a competent professional person should be sought.

— From a declaration of principles jointly adopted by a
   Committee of the American Bar Association and a
   Committee of Publishers and Associations.

SMART TRUST DEED INVESTMENT

in California

Second Edition
Revised

by

GEORGE COATS

ILLUSTRATED BY BETSY LAWBAUGH-ZACAVICH
COVER DESIGN BY BETSY LAWBAUGH-ZACAVICH

Barr-Randol Publishing Company
Box 4486 • Covina, CA 91723

Printed in the United States of America
95 94 93 92 91   6 5 4

Library of Congress Cataloging-in-Publication Data

Coats, George.
  Smart trust deed investment in California.

  Includes index.
  1. Deeds of trust—California. 2. Real Estate
investment—Law and legislation—California. I. Title.
KFC175.C6   1988   346.79404'3   87-33370
                      347.940643
ISBN 0-934581-01-0 (pbk.)

FORWARD

The Law Center
University of Southern California

A few years ago, while in search of material for our second and third year law students' class on Real Estate Transactions, I discovered George Coats' book *Smart Trust Deed Investment in California,* through an enthusiastic recommendation in the Los Angeles *Times* Sunday real estate pages ... To learn the practical application of real estate law, students need to know something about the business ... George's experiences in real estate lending, is reflected in the book's pragmatic approach and proved to be exactly what our class needed.

Since then, George has guest lectured our class from the standpoint of the private investor in trust deeds, to the delight of one and all. We have also incorporated portions of his book in our class curriculum and placed it in our law library as recommended reading.

The book is especially valuable because it is clear and easy to use. While there are many books about the real estate business, many of them are difficult for beginners, even skilled law students, too burdened with detail, too vague and hard to comprehend ... *Smart Trust Deed Investment* is vivid and an indispensable starting point for anyone entering the trust deed market place, or anyone already in it who wants a good overview. We are hugely in George's debt for this important work.

George Lefcoe
Henry W. Bruce Professor of Equity

Los Angeles
November, 1990

TO
JEANETTE

Acknowledgements

Thanks to

Leigh Robinson, author of Landlording, who has gone out of his way to provide much valued counsel at crucial points in the preparation of this book;

Vivian Davies, whose unflagging enthusiasm supplied the momentum needed to bring this book to completion;

Scott McReynolds of American Family Mortgage for his technical knowledge of TDs shared over many years past;

Phil Heib, owner of Hope Trust Deed Co. and discount trust deed broker of some 20 plus years experience, for his assistance even when I wasn't "buying;"

And to Douglas and Nancy Coats, Martin and Bella Shapiro, Doug Waide, Ursula Coats, Ted and Jan Randles, George Fuller, Maralyn McCracken, Stanley Cook, and Jon Coats, all of whom have contributed to this book.

Preface

The distance between the surface appearances of trust deed investment and its realities has always been a source of interest to this writer. Seemingly clear provisions in the loan agreement often mean nothing because they are voided by law. On the other hand, the law itself is also often meaningless because of impracticality of enforcement. And nothing gives an inkling of the tremendous amount of strategy and maneuver available to the investment, routinely employed by some professionals in the business. Only with actual experience does the investor ordinarily begin to gain some insight into such aspects of TDs.

This book aims to correct the situation and tell, not only the basics of the business, but also their real effect — the tricks of the trade, so to speak.

Because so many of the maneuvers described in the following pages are dependent upon state law, this book is written specifically with California investors in mind. State legislatures tend to copy each other with considerable fidelity, however, and investors in most other states will probably find it easy to translate the bulk of the information to their situation.

The wisdom contained in these pages wasn't achieved easily. During the author's 25 plus years of investment for himself and others, a lot of mistakes were made. Practically every cautionary comment, from warning of phony escrows to the need for prompt foreclosure is a product of some negative experience. Partly because of dumb luck, and sometimes because of failure to count the cost in time salvaging the deal, no TD losses were ever tallied. Partly because of dumb luck, less often by design, profits higher than normal — sometimes deliriously so — were also achieved, and these lessons too have been added.

A Word of Caution:

This book is not meant to be read straight through. Because it is intended for use by the layman investor, the material has been divided into two parts. Only the first half, the chapter portion, need be read for an understanding of the business. Non-recurring events such as maneuvers during foreclosure, have been relegated to an Appendix section, to be dipped into as the need arises.

Also:

A colored supplement section has been bound into the back of the book. It contains much valuable update information and is integral to the book's content. To aid in its use, each supplement section has been cross referenced to the affected pages in the book. For maximum use of the information, however, it is suggested that you in turn cross reference the affected book pages to corresponding supplement pages.

CONTENTS

CHAPTER 1

Trust Deed Profits

On October 6th of 1979, the Federal Reserve Board suddenly put a clamp on the nation's money supply in an effort to stop burgeoning inflation. A month later, Californians loosened restrictions on local interest rates by a constitutional amendment redefining the state's usury law. Previously suppressed interest rates were thereby freed to follow natural forces in the market place, and they took off like a scalded cat.

In California, most loans against real estate are called "trust deeds," after the name of the legal instrument used to pledge their security. The foregoing combination of events had a profound impact on the private lender portion of this market. Individuals with amounts as little as $3,000 had always been able to invest their money relatively free of the artificial restraints that afflict other businesses. Relaxation of the state's usury law removed the single greatest remaining obstacle to their ability to react to the laws of supply and demand. As the Federal Reserve tightened its grip on the supply of money, investors began to see trust deed yields of 16%, then 20%, and at one point 30%.

Interest rates went down after 1979, but the conditions which force inflationary changes will always be with us. And, thanks to the change in California's usury law, the ability of private trust deed investors to respond to fluctuations in economic conditions will also continue. As a consequence, private money trust deeds have become a nearly perfect investment for investors seeking to shelter their savings against the vagaries of inflation. If enough of the strategies described in the following pages are employed, investors also can gather profits as much as 50% above those of other investments of comparable safety.

SUPPLEMENTAL BENEFITS OF TRUST DEED INVESTMENT

Apart from their high profits and freedom to respond to the forces of supply and demand, private trust deed investments in California enjoy a number of additional advantages, some of which are unequaled elsewhere.

TRUST DEEDS ARE EASY

Anybody with a modicum of common sense can successfully invest in trust deeds. This contrasts with most other investments where extensive study and years of experience may be necessary before you can invest with confidence. In trust deeds, the skills necessary for success are present in any person of average background.

Trust deed investments also require little attention once the loan is in place. Most of the work of the investment is concentrated in its early stages while investigating various loan offerings — and much of that can be reduced if you refuse to waste your time on loans which appear only marginally acceptable. (In fact, as explained in the chapter on Filtering, immediate rejection of deals which are the least bit uncertain is the real secret to profitable TD investment.)

Trust deed investment can be made still easier if you are able to take advantage of the large and active brokerage profession set up for that purpose. A loan broker must necessarily charge a fee for such services, but a good one generally earns it. Many TD investors, especially those who invest only occasionally, actually profit more by using a loan broker. As explained in the chapter on Loan Brokers, a broker has certain strategic advantages which can lead to profits higher than those obtainable by unassisted investors who enter the market only once in a while.

TDS ARE SAFER

Because private money TDs have a reputation for exceptional profits, many people believe that they must be more risky than other investments. Not so. TDs are actually safer than other investments of comparable yield because all the risks are identifiable, and so are the procedures necessary to counter them. Though some investors have lost heavily in TDs (most notably, those connected with the well-publicized collapse of some brokerage houses in recent years), *every single one of the losses could have been avoided, if only a few of the many protective measures described in this book had been employed.* Most other forms of investment are burdened with a variety of unknowns which preclude accurate assessment of their safety; calculation of the safety of most investments is a contradiction in logic — it's impossible to measure their risk when they bear hazards you don't even know exist. In TDs, the opposite prevails. The investment has received such microscopic scrutiny, so many times, that all the variables have been exposed, and chance therefore has little to do with the safety of TD investment.

YOU CAN LEVERAGE ECONOMIC CYCLES WITH TDS

Trust deeds, like other types of investment, have a profitability cycle. There are intervals, usually more than five years apart, during which interest rates are abnormally depressed, and there are other times when the reverse is true. In most other businesses, the investor is forced to ride the reduced profitability of the down portion of their cycle, or get out of the market entirely. Not so if you specialize in trust deeds. If you recognize your position in the cycle, you can actually multiply your profits by shifting your investment strategy. You can switch back and forth between short and long term TDs and employ a variety of other devices, such as points and prepayment penalties, to cause market changes to leverage your yield. If you are knowledgeable enough, you can also switch in and out of real estate as various elements of the interest rate cycle make it profitable for you to do so. The techniques used to make these strategies work are discussed in the Other Approaches Chapter. If you include them in your planning, you can make impressive increases in your rate of return.

BENEFITS GAINED FROM REAL ESTATE

Paradoxically, TDs are highly advantageous for people who think they would really prefer an investment in real estate. Many people properly hesitate to invest in real estate through fear that they don't know enough about the business. For such investors, the best way to ease into real estate is through trust deeds; there is no safer way to learn the details of the business. In the process of investigating various TDs, you pick up a wide knowledge of real properties. You also encounter many people active in real estate who can help you later on. Best of all, during your meanderings through the TD market you also tend to stumble across bargains in real property.

TDS ARE FUN

A large element in the popularity of trust deeds comes from the fact that, for many people, the investment is just plain fun. There is a certain amount of satisfaction in logging the payments as they arrive, and in toting up the amount earned each month. There is confidence that, if a problem arises, you can generally bargain from strength and thus maintain a measure of control over events. And many investors, especially retired people, also enjoy the relatively minor effort needed to tend the investment once their money is placed.

FORECLOSURES ARE NOT AN ADVANTAGE

Most investors go into trust deeds believing that, should they have to foreclose, they will be in position to pick up bargains in real estate. The belief is a fallacy, however. Except for certain limited situations described in the Foreclosure portion of this book, major windfall profits of this nature rarely happen in TDs. Those potentially profitable foreclosures that reach the auction point are generally so beset by sharpshooters that few lenders gain significantly by the process.

DISADVANTAGES IN TRUST DEED INVESTMENT

LIMITED TAX ADVANTAGES

Trust deeds have a poor, partly deserved, reputation among high tax-bracket investors; certain professional people, such as doctors, stay away from TDs entirely. This is because most trust deed income is considered "ordinary income" by the IRS and therefore is fully taxable. The investment potential of trust deeds is thereby limited for some people. But the tax obstacle is much overrated (even for doctors). Though few in number, some very effective devices can be used to defer or modify the tax impact on TDs (see the Income Tax Appendix for details). Still, belief in the poor tax condition of TDs is so widespread that those who invest in them tend to be retirees, middle income taxpayers, pension plans, or others not much concerned with income taxes.

THE LIMITED LIQUIDITY OF TDS

If you believe you might have to convert your investment into cash later, trust deeds are a poor way to go. This is not because TDs are difficult to sell, as is often claimed. (When priced realistically, they can be sold virtually overnight.) The main difficulty is the cost of selling something which will automatically pay off, say, a year from now. An investor who, for example, sells his one year, 10% TD, at a 6% commission, pays the equivalent of over 16% interest for the money he receives. The problem is compounded, in the case of small TDs, by the fact that the dollar costs of selling a TD remain fairly constant no matter what its size; the cost of selling a $10,000 TD is not much different from that of a $40,000 TD, though you collect only one fourth the cash. Therefore, most investors in need of money choose to liquidate other assets, instead of their TDs.

OTHER DEFECTS OF TD INVESTMENTS

As pointed out earlier, TDs are an exceptionally safe investment if appropriate protective measures (described later) are used. But, depending on the type of TD, employing all the necessary steps requires time and attention to detail — an inconvenience many people prefer to avoid.

TDs attract an inordinate number of human barracudas, which must also be reckoned a defect. Something about the business draws people who hope to gain by preying on the innocence or gullibility of others. The private party lender with large amounts of cash is their favorite bait. Even the most expert and tough-minded TD investor loses something to such predators, because so much time and energy must be spent fending them off.

A WORD OF CAUTION

Private lenders have been doing trust deeds for many years with great success. No small part of this is due to the fact that most trust deeds are created in good faith, and the borrower usually finds a way to keep up his payments. But because most borrowers perform as agreed, a great number of these lenders sail peacefully through a minefield of unknown hazards. As a consequence, they become overconfident and never learn to employ the investment's basic requirements for safety.

5

With trust deeds, safety requires investigation. Though the borrower's integrity will carry you through most errors, you can't rely on his character completely. If the borrower defaults, defects in your procedures will certainly rise to the surface; and if they are serious enough, your entire investment can be blown out of the water. To be uniformly successful in TDs, you must pay attention to what you're doing (or what your broker is doing) and employ the steps described in this book. If you do so, you'll be able to match the record of the best operators in the business — at gratifying profits.

CHAPTER 2

Trust Deed Fundamentals

In California, trust deeds are the common form of real estate loan because special provisions in the state's law have made them far more efficient than the usual "mortgage" type of loan. In fact, California's trust deed form of lending is considered so superior that it is believed to have been the cause of much of the state's explosive growth. Fueled by such a convenient means of financing real estate, California has, in years past, outstripped most other states in real property development. So much so, that more and more states have come to copy the California approach; today, almost half of them replicate California's procedure.

DEED OF TRUST

The words "trust deed" are usually applied to the investment as though it consists of a single instrument. In reality, a trust deed exists in two documents: a "note" representing the obligation to pay, and a "deed of trust," which transfers ownership of the security to a trustee. These two elements can be combined in a single document, but they usually appear on separate pieces of paper that come into existence at the same time. The two documents can each be created at separate times, however, and each can stand alone pending arrival of the other. When cross-referenced to each other, they become a loan secured by real estate — the "trust deed" of common parlance.

By creating a trust deed, one major advantage is gained over other forms of real estate lending: The loan's security is placed in the hands of a third party, a trustee, who takes limited title to the property, and who is charged with arbitrating the agreement between the parties. This creates a capability of foreclosure in a remarkably efficient manner, should the borrower default.

Because the loan's security is placed in trust by the "deed of trust," the participants' names are changed: in a deed of trust, the borrower is called a "trustor," and the lender becomes the "beneficiary" of the trust.

Every deed of trust must contain wording which deeds the security to a trustee. It must also grant the trustee "power of sale" over the security if the security is to be used to satisfy the terms of the obligation. (See also "Power of Sale" in the Clauses Appendix B.) These otherwise innocuous elements of the agreement magically transform what would be considered a mortgage into a useful deed of trust; they give the trustee the ability to process foreclosure by nonjudicial means.

Your claim to the property as security receives public recognition when you record the deed of trust in the county where the property is located. The recorded document bearing the borrower's notarized signature then remains an encumbrance on the property until the loan is paid. Release of the security is accomplished when you direct the trustee to issue a "reconveyance," which is also recorded.

The chronological order in which deeds of trust are recorded determines the priority of their claim over other instruments recorded against the property. Hence, we have 1st, 2nd, 3rd, etc., trust deeds. There are infrequent exceptions to the rule, however, and they are explained in the appendix on Security Limits.

THE TRUSTEE

The law says that anybody, except the borrower, can be the trustee — even the lender. Nevertheless, most deeds of trust name as trustee independent organizations set up to render such services for a fee.

Which trustee is selected usually depends on whose deed of trust form is used — to encourage appointment of themselves as trustee, many organizations give away blank deed of trust forms with their name already entered for the purpose.

Although the trustee named in a deed of trust receives title to the security, nobody bothers to tell him of the event until later, when his services are needed. This is because the trustee only performs his service toward the end, when a release of security is required or when foreclosure becomes necessary. Notification earlier is superfluous; until the trustee is needed, the trustor (borrower) and beneficiary (lender) pass payments and communicate directly with each other, as though the trustee were not there.

Sometimes the trustee named in a TD will decline to perform because he subsequently went out of business. He may also refuse to act because he questions the legitimacy of the services requested. And sometimes you may prefer a different, more competent trustee for purposes of foreclosure. The law provides a way around these problems by allowing you to substitute another trustee if you follow a statutorily prescribed procedure. (See Substitution in the Clauses Appendix.)

PURCHASE-MONEY TDS

Purchase-money TDs are those used to finance the purchase of real estate (as opposed to loans against property already owned by the borrower). They include sale financing provided by third parties, as well as financing by the seller of the property.

The purchase-money distinction is important to an understanding of the basics of TD investment. California law assigns separate rules to such TDs, rules which materially affect the investor's rights.

Chief among the differences affecting purchase-money TDs is their exemption from usury; certain varieties are completely free from the strictures of usury, and others can avoid usury indirectly (see the Usury Appendix). Some varieties of purchase-money TDs can claim special lien rights to the security (see the chapter on Investigation). The enforcement of certain others is expressly limited to the TD's security — the lender is prohibited pursuit of the borrower's other assets when there is a default (see the Security Limits Appendix).

MORTGAGES

Mortgages also affect the fundamentals of TD investment. They play an alternative role, filling in and sometimes providing support where the TD agreement leaves off.

DIFFERENCES FROM TDS

Technically, there is little meaningful difference between TDs and mortgages. To the boundless confusion of those unfamiliar with the business, TDs are therefore sometimes called "mortgages" in California. Conventional terminology treats the two instruments as completely different forms of lending, however.

The most important distinction given mortgages and trust deeds is probably the method by which the loan agreement is enforced. Trust deeds transfer the security to a trustee, who becomes the primary source of enforcement. In a mortgage, the borrower retains full ownership of the security, and the lender obtains enforcement of the agreement by lawsuit — a cumbersome process at best.

AVOIDANCE OF MORTGAGES

Any real estate loan which does not deed the security to a trustee, along with a power of sale, is considered a mortgage. But the burdens of the law on a mortgage lender are so onerous that mortgages exist only by accident — because someone slipped up and failed to meet the requirements necessary for a trust deed.

Mortgages are almost universally avoided because the borrower is then endowed with exceptional rights — so many, in fact, that he can often act as though there is no right of foreclosure. As explained later in the chapters on Foreclosure, it may not be practical to foreclose a mortgage; some lenders find it easier to "pay the borrower off" than undergo the trouble and expense of the process. Indeed, a property may become *more* valuable because it is encumbered by a mortgage — a savvy purchaser will sometimes pay more than a property is worth simply because of his ability to extract concessions from the property's mortgage lender.

THE MORTGAGE FORECLOSURE ALTERNATIVE

Though mortgages themselves are generally avoided, their method of foreclosure is available to TD lenders, and it is sometimes used despite the cost of the process. This is because use of the TD foreclosure procedure limits the lender to collection from the loan's security — the lender cannot subsequently collect from the borrower's other assets, should there be a deficiency in the security. (See One Action Rule, in the appendix on Security Limits.) A non purchase-money TD holder (see Purchase-Money, earlier) who wishes to collect from the borrower's other assets may then find a mortgage-style foreclosure more appropriate, even though more expensive.

CHAPTER 3

Investing Through a Loan Broker

ADVANTAGES OF USING A LOAN BROKER

Most private money TD investments are conducted through loan brokers, people licensed by California's Department of Real Estate who either arrange new real estate loans, or who broker the sale of existing loans. There is good reason for this. Consider: In addition to the effort of attracting suitable borrowers, the broker bends all his expertise and time toward filtering out a swarm of unsuitable applicants. He handles all the paperwork needed to satisfy "truth-in-lending" legislation. If truly expert in the business, he brings to bear a vast knowledge about the administration of problem loans. Some brokers will also repurchase a bad loan rather than let one of their investors suffer a loss.

Therefore, many investors earn a higher net profit from brokered loans, even though dealing direct with the borrower may otherwise bring a higher interest rate.

Loan broker commissions are paid by the borrower, and this too makes brokered loans more profitable — though not so much as some brokers would have you believe. (Inevitably the lender indirectly absorbs some of the cost, because the commission affects the amount of interest the borrower can pay.)

If you invest through a loan broker, you also may be able to increase your profit by extracting a piece of the broker's commission in the form of "percentage points." During active portions of their business cycle, brokers often rebate a portion of their commission to lenders at a rate of two percent or more of the loan amount; the greater the volume of business you can deliver to the broker, the more points he will be prepared to share with you. This is especially true when TDs in the $50,000 to $100,000 range are involved. Such TDs require no greater effort by the broker, though the dollar amount of his commission is higher; he accordingly can share more of it with you.

Brokers benefit their investors still further by providing certain tactical advantages:

If you do not hold a real estate license you may be restricted by California's usury law as to the amount of interest you may charge (for details, see the appendix on Usury). By operating through a loan broker, however, you are freed from the usury limitation. In California, any loan secured by real estate which is "made or arranged" by a licensed real estate broker escapes the usury law. This is a marvelous advantage and gives a wider range of TDs to choose from.

Because loan brokers encounter greater numbers of prospective borrowers, they are in a better position to sort out loans suited to your needs. And when the loan is paid off, the broker's volume of activity enables him to have a replacement loan ready, so your money does not remain idle. In fact, some of the best brokers initially fund the loans with their own money, just to be sure they will be able to give their investors immediate service. To sustain this kind of loan volume, the larger brokers advertise for borrowers at a staggering expense.

Some brokers make a practice of tying down the borrower so he cannot change his mind about a loan. This is a major advantage not generally available to a lender. Because (in theory, anyway) the broker puts forth his efforts in exchange for the borrower's promise to pay a commission, he binds the borrower with a written, exclusive agency agreement. Later failure of the borrower to go through with the deal, simply on whim, may or may not

14

obligate him to pay the broker's commission — but in most instances, the borrower is not sophisticated enough to know when he can escape the commission, and therefore will go through with the deal. A lender operating alone is not sheltered by such an agency agreement; until a loan is actually completed, all the lender's preparatory effort can be wasted if the borrower changes his mind.

ON FINDING THE BEST BROKER

One of the most important requirements for a broker is honesty. Nevertheless, there will always be a few completely unprincipled brokers whose aggressiveness is developed to such a degree that they recognize no truth, only gamesmanship — tell the sucker anything so long as it makes the deal. In trust deeds, the difficulties caused by such people are multiplied; negative information is easily hidden because the broker normally stands between you and the borrower, separating you from direct access to information about the loan. You can counter this kind of broker's behavior by conducting your own investigation, but you're better off immediately rejecting him and going on to someone easier to deal with.

Apart from indications of honesty, there is no best way to find a good broker. The loan broker's license requires no special endorsement which might distinguish him from those who are simply real estate salesmen. Evident knowledge of matters discussed in this book is probably an identifying characteristic of a broker's technical competence, but the representative he assigns to you may not be as expert — and may not have the brains to know it. The search for the best broker actually involves scrutiny of a number of additional — sometimes intangible — indicators, faith in your ability to read character, plus some healthy down-to-earth skepticism.

EARMARKS OF A GOOD (OR BAD) BROKER

PROFESSIONAL ASSOCIATIONS

One possible indicator of a good broker is his membership in a loan broker's professional association called the California Independent Mortgage Brokers Association (CIMBA), located in Sherman Oaks, California. Loan brokerage has become a complicated business, one which requires obedience to laws almost as complicated as those surrounding the trust deed itself. Membership in a professional association brings with it a vigorous educational program designed to keep the broker apprized of every nuance of the law. Members are virtually deluged with association bulletins about the law and they consequently soak up more information than the broker who stands alone.

15

BROKER SUCCESS

An active, growing business — by itself — is not necessarily an indicator of a good broker. The loan brokerage business operates under a sort of "Catch 22" conflict: the more successful the broker becomes, the less time and inclination he has to keep up with technical details. Because the bulk of the investing public is too ignorant of TDs to detect incompetence, this kind of broker continues to do a thriving business. The most successful brokers are therefore sometimes only good salesmen.

The fact that a loan broker has been successful enough to last awhile is one of the best recommendations of all. A business that has been prosperous enough for him to earn a continuous living from it indicates a large number of other people have already found him reliable.

The foregoing is especially true of brokers who were around prior to 1980. Because of the spectacular collapses of a few brokers before 1980, further government controls were imposed on the business; brokers now must file reports so complicated they have to attend a two-day seminar to learn how to complete just one of the several varieties of forms required. Due to a decline in real estate activity and the increased complications, more than 50 percent of the brokers went out of business between 1980 and 1983. Only the most stable and well-organized brokers were able to survive such a searing elimination.

BROKER GUARANTEES

On occasion, brokers advertise that they guarantee the loans they place. This is a privilege granted very few real estate licensees in California. These are brokers who have obtained a "Real Property Securities Dealer" endorsement to their real estate license. To get the endorsement, the loan broker must, among other things, meet exceptional levels of financial capacity. The paperwork necessary to obtain the endorsement is awesome, and only the most determined brokers are able to pursue it through the real estate commissioner's bureaucracy. Those who are able to exhibit the endorsement are probably financially able to back up their guarantees and will be sound enough to hold your collections for you. The endorsement provides no greater assurance of the broker's competence or honesty, however.

All other loan brokers are prohibited from guaranteeing a borrower's loan. Some brokers nevertheless try to accomplish the same result by unwritten representations of protection, and by announcing that no lender has ever suffered a loss on their loans.

BROKER APPRAISALS

Brokers like to proclaim their use of "independent appraisers" in their security valuations. This may or may not be of value in qualifying them. An independent appraisal may be an honest attempt at an unbiased opinion of the security's value. Also, many brokers don't know how to make an accurate appraisal, therefore their use of an independent appraiser may indicate more accurate property valuations. On the other hand, when the appraiser is selected by the broker, and his fee stems from the broker's effort, valuations are easily influenced and few brokers guard against this.

When the broker evaluates the security is probably a better indictor of reliability. If his appraisal is made *before* recommending a TD, chances are he is conscientious enough not to waste your time on a flakey deal. Such valuations should not be based on a mere "drive by" (sometimes called "windshield appraisal") of the property. His evaluation of the property should include examination of comparable sales in the neighborhood and consideration of the many other factors discussed in the chapter on Appraisal. Furthermore, according to law, his evaluation must be provided in writing if he calls it an "appraisal."

SLEAZY TACTICS

Avoid brokers who apply undue pressure toward completion of a transaction; cancel out immediately if you are supposed to feel obligated to go through with a deal. Overt pressure is evidence that you are dealing with a person whose sole interest is his commission.

Be extra cautious if a broker attempts to minimize the importance of your security by pointing out that "you are not buying the property, only lending on it." Such a person is either a fool, or trying to deceive you.

BROKER ESCROWS

Some loan brokers prefer to handle the loan escrow. If you refuse the service, but the broker insists on providing it, you have reason to question his integrity. A broker who acts without the authorization of the person paying his commission, and who makes his handling of the escrow a condition of the deal, violates regulations of California's Real Estate Commissioner. He can lose his license as a result.

Similarly, some brokers insist on servicing their loans under the guise of aiding the investor. The benefits of the arrangement are discussed in detail in the chapter covering Administration. But, by servicing the loan themselves, brokers are able to separate the borrower from the lender, and that can be risky for the lender. Any broker who attempts to make this a condition of your business with him should be avoided.

THE PREPAYMENT INCENTIVE PROBLEM

Beware of brokers who brag about the number of prepayment penalties collected by their investors.

There are brokers who "churn" their investor's portfolio by forcing prepayments of TDs. In this way, the lender profits on collection of a prepayment penalty, and that makes the broker look good — and the broker gains a commission when the payoff money is reinvested.

To promote premature payoffs, these brokers deliberately focus on borrowers who are already in trouble financially. They do so believing that the troubled borrower will be required to sell his property in order to avoid foreclosure, thus forcing early payoff of the loan. The whole scheme has been made a shambles, however, by the fact that more and more borrowers are using bankruptcy as a device to postpone, or even eliminate, portions of their obligations.

ADVANTAGES IN BYPASSING THE BROKER

The investor sharp enough to conduct his own affairs is handsomely rewarded if he bypasses the loan broker. A loan broker may charge a commission of 15 percentage points to the borrower for placing a three year loan. If you are able to make the same deal and avoid usury, you can keep the points for yourself — and boost your effective yield by five percent per annum.

Investors who handle their own loans also profit because they have more freedom than loan brokers. The real estate commissioner carefully regulates the terms of certain broker-arranged loans. This is done in the belief that the limitations will protect the borrower from his own lack of sophistication in such matters. However, the borrower is sometimes willing to pay a premium to avoid being forced into a mold. If you offer to tailor a loan to meet his special needs, you can pick up extra chips.

The State of California's paperwork requirements on loan brokers spell greater profits to the independent investor, too. The individual investor functioning without the aid of a broker is still relatively free of such regulation; he suffers little of the overhead brought about by the staggering number of reports brokers are now afflicted with. Investors can compete head-to-head with broker's prices, and keep a much bigger part of the TD's earnings than was ever possible before.

CHAPTER 4

How to Find Your Own TDs

The key to finding the best TDs is "volume;" to put yourself in the path of as many offerings as possible. To get the best yields, you must provide yourself with the widest possible selection of TDs. Those investors who learn how to do this generally end up with the highest profits.

NEWSPAPER "FOR SALE" ADS

NEWSPAPER CLASSIFIED ADS

The best source of TDs is the "Trust Deeds for Sale" columns in the classified section of local newspapers. Major metropolitan dailies offer an astonishing quantity of them. Even better, TD sellers' price expectations are forced down to a realistic level by the cummulative cost of prolonged advertising.

"Money Wanted — Real Estate" ads are found adjacent to the classified "For Sale" columns, and these are also worth investigation. Even though the ads are for new loans, you need not fear you will be restricted by the usury law as to the amount of interest you charge; many of these loans will be exempt because they are "purchase money." Any number of other exemptions may also apply. (See the appendix on Usury for more on this.)

The Wall Street Journal is an excellent source for trust deeds, especially on Fridays. Since the cost of advertising in the *Journal* is enormous compared to other newspapers, only large trust deeds ($40,000 or more) tend to be offered. The yield and quality of the TDs offered are also better than those appearing in local newspapers.

ON THE AVOIDANCE OF BROKERS

Both advertisers and investors use classified ads to avoid brokers and the broker's commission. Sometimes they also use the ads to avoid the broker's salesmanship. Their efforts in this regard are aided by the real estate commissioner, who requires that brokers announce themselves in their ads. The word "agent," the broker's company name, or simply "broker," are the usual means of identification.

Investors sometimes avoid answering broker ads because there are always a few of them meant only to attract callers so that other, less desirable TDs may be promoted (the old "bait and switch" tactic of the merchandising industry dressed up in lender's clothes). Nevertheless, broker ads should always be explored. The frequency of misleading ads is so small that you should not be deterred from inquiring. The ads do turn up bargains every once in a while, and take only a few moments to check out.

MAIL ORDER TD BROKERS

All loan brokers sell existing TDs in addition to arranging new loans. A few, however, specialize in selling nothing but existing TDs, and they are a valuable source of business. Some of the more reliable ones, such as The Hope

Company of Downey, California, do a volume of business equal to that of the largest new-loan brokers. Others can be found through their frequent appearance in the "Trust Deeds for Sale" columns of the classified section of your newspaper.

SELLING TDS BY MAIL

The larger brokers of existing TDs do a surprising volume of business by mail. If you get on their mailing list, you can expect at least a monthly, and sometimes a weekly, offering of trust deeds. The broker's mailings only give skeletal details of the TD offered. The asking price shown in the mailing includes the broker's commission, which is negotiable. An address or other location of the security is given along with a brief description of the type of security, and, if possible, the most recent sales price of the security. Beyond that, you are on your own, though sometimes the broker may be able to help with additional information not included because of lack of space.

One-on-one salesmanship is rare among these brokers. Unless the TD offered is a large one and the broker feels that he has enough of a grasp of your needs, he won't bother to draw your attention to a particular item.

ADVANTAGES IN MAIL ORDER TDS

Yields in mail order existing TDs can be imposing when compared with new-loan rates. The mail order broker's overhead is small compared to the typical loan broker. Therefore, commission requirements are more flexible and are used as a buffer in sales price negotiations. Yields in existing TDs are also higher because there is less competition for the investment. Higher discount points can also be extracted from the TD seller than when dealing directly with the borrower.

Perhaps the greatest advantage in the brokered existing TD, however, is that the seller has a difficult time backing out of the transaction if he changes his mind. The broker is able to tie the seller down very effectively with a listing agreement obligating a sale at an agreed price, if it occurs within a given period of time. Your appraisal of the property, and time spent examining other aspects of a TD, represent a hefty investment. This is always at risk when dealing directly with the seller because of his ability to withdraw at will. Furthermore, unless nailed down by the broker's listing agreement, the seller has complete freedom to twist your arm over the price by threatening withdrawal from the sale, leading to loss of all you have spent on investigation of the TD.

HOW TO RUN YOUR OWN TD ADS

If you handle your own investments, advertising in the "TDs wanted" section of the newspaper is by far the best source of profitable TDs. For this approach to be successful, however, you must be sure the magic words "private party" are used in the ad. Such advertising taps a huge reservoir of borrowers and TD sellers who wish to escape doing business through a broker. The broker's commission looms so large in the public eye that you will be swamped with calls from people trying to save the cost of a broker.

WHERE TO ADVERTISE

The classified sections of major metropolitan newspapers are the best place to advertise. The real estate lending classifications in these newspapers are the closest thing there is to a central market place for private money real estate loans. Every noninstitutional TD borrower, seller, broker, or investor ultimately checks this portion of the newspapers. In California, the principal newspaper for this purpose is the Los Angeles *Times*. The *Times* has such a gigantic circulation that it dominates its geographic area.

The Wall Street Journal's "Mortages" classification is the next best place to advertise, but only if you have enough money to invest to make the extra cost of advertising worthwhile — say, $100,000 or more; WSJ ads are the most expensive of all newspapers. In spite of the cost, advertising in the WSJ can be rewarding because of its sophisticated readership. People who respond to these ads tend to be far more knowledgeable about the business. The ads therefore draw a better, higher yielding, response.

HOW TO ADVERTISE

Advertising in the aforementioned newspapers is not cheap and costs can easily get out of hand. Therefore, rather than run amok and put yourself out of business before you get started, some plan of control is needed.

The best way to cut cost is to keep the size of the ad as small as possible. This does not mean advertising with so many abbreviations that the ad looks like code. It does mean advertising with as few words as possible. Fortunately, your telephone number, and the fact that you are a private party, are the only essential elements; you will never be able to include enough other information to satisfy the questions of your callers.

The smallest ad permitted by metropolitan newspapers is two lines, which does permit some wording beyond your minimum needs. *The Wall Street Journal* requires minimum one-half column-inch ads; more space, really, than you need. Here, the extra room is better invested in white space around the ad to make it stand out.

Sundays are the best days to advertise in a metropolitan newspaper. Though Sunday advertising may be more expensive, the added cost is worth it. People who read these ads don't usually have the time to check them daily; they do so only on those days with the largest volume of TD advertisement — and Sunday ads outnumber weekday ads more than 2 to 1.

Wall Street Journal ads are best placed on Mondays, since there is no weekend issue. The paper's advertising staff will try to sell you on advertising in their Friday "Real Estate Mart." To do so is a mistake. Their Real Estate Mart draws such a huge volume of ads from people trying to unload large pieces of overpriced real estate that your lonely TD ad will be buried from sight.

Some investors believe you should say "principals only" in your ads, in order to eliminate broker inquiries. They are in error. Some brokers will respond to your ad anyway (as a "principal"). Furthermore, excluding all brokers eliminates those very good, one-man offices which cannot afford to advertise because they have so few TDs available.

OTHER SOURCES OF TDS

COUNTY RECORDER

If you are naturally organized in your work habits, you might find it worthwhile to track down TDs for sale the way the professionals do — at the county recorder. Very little extra effort is required once your basic procedure is set up, and the grade of TDs uncovered in this manner is often top notch.

The key to use of the county recorder is the lender's return address shown on every recorded TD. The county recorder requires this address on every deed of trust accepted for recording. Most of the time, the address will be that of an institutional lender or an agent, such as a loan broker. Sometimes, however, the address will be that of an individual lender: a person who took back a TD to help promote the sale of his property. Such a person is often in a mood to convert to cash and is willing to sell his TD to do so.

Digging the return address out of the recorder in the more populated counties may be next to impossible due to over crowding of the facilities. Obtaining the information in outlying counties is not difficult, however, once you learn how they keep their records (see also the appendix on Sources of Information). The easiest way to do this is to hire someone accustomed to the work. In many instances, you'll find people called "readers" who station themselves at the recorder's office in order to pick up specified information for their employers. Most readers also freelance and, if you ask them, will be glad to spend a few extra hours a day collecting the information you need. Their cost is not excessive, since the principal skill needed is an ability to withstand the boredom of the job.

To make efficient use of these people, you should provide them with blank sheets of gummed mailing labels. Ask that lender names and addresses be copied directly on the labels from the recorded deed of trust. Ask that only private lenders be written down, since institutional lenders or agents would be useless for your purposes. Such a distinction is easily made once the person becomes accustomed to the pattern of the recordings. Addresses should also be limited to those from TDs a year or more old, because you are much more apt to be able to make a deal among seasoned TDs.

When a stack of labels are accumulated, they are peeled off and attached to envelopes or post cards containing an announcement of your interest in buying trust deeds. Be sure to include the magic words "private party" in your message. The percentage of responses will be small, less than three percent, as a rule. Investment yields found among those who do answer, however, will be worth your while, since your only competition will be from brokers whose commission rates always seem dismayingly high to TD sellers.

MAILING LISTS

Mailing lists of the above lender addresses are also available in counties with a lot of real estate activity. There are enterprising individuals who make a business of selling mailing lists of recorded data from such counties, lender addresses included. Public Records Information (in Paramount, California), for example, cover only five counties in Southern California, but their lists pick up TDs from precisely those areas most heavily involved in private lender activity. Organizations such as these can be found by their ads which appear in legal publications.

Lists of addresses also appear in "legal" newspapers published primarily for the benefit of lawyers. These newspapers devote themselves almost entirely to the publication of legal notices. Because lawyers and persons of allied interest scan these papers so closely, other information (such as lender recordings) is also included. The quality of the copy is not good, however. Depending on the newspaper, you may find so many faulty addresses in the list that the cost of using them for advertising will exceed their value.

TDS FROM BANK TRUST DEPARTMENTS

Major banks have trust departments which administer the estates of people who have died or are judged incompetent. It's the nature of this type of situation that a large percentage of those with enough of an estate to warrant the use of bank services also manage to accumulate one or more trust deeds. To raise cash, the estate sometimes also tries to sell one of the trust deeds. Such TDs are invariably well secured and sometimes require very little effort to check out.

Trust department sales have one major defect. The investor is required to bid competitively on the TD, and all bids may be rejected if they do not meet some privately held minimum standard. Furthermore, the successful bid may require court confirmation, at which time it can be subverted by overbids. This method is desirable from the seller's standpoint but impractical for you if you need to spend money qualifying the TD beforehand. Nevertheless, there are sometimes ways to get around the problem, and these are discussed in the Negotiation section of the next chapter.

CHAPTER 5

Filtering Out the Dogs

Every form of business has its peculiarities, its secrets, which experienced operators learn to give special attention. In trust deed investments, the secret to success lies in learning how to "filter out the dogs," in knowing how to eliminate unsuitable TDs as efficiently as possible.

Anybody who spends much time with TDs soon learns that an astounding number of bad ones are being peddled as sound investments. So many, in fact, that you can lose money simply from the time wasted trying to sort through them all. Even though your separate TD investments each show a profit, the cost of investigation to eliminate the bad ones can put you out of business.

If you do business through a conscientious loan broker, the job of filtering out the dogs will be taken care of for you. If you wish to invest in TDs on your own — and make a sensible profit — you must learn to get rid of the bad ones as early as possible. You must have a filtering system designed to ask, first, those questions most likely to reveal reasons for rejecting a TD. With such a system you can, 90 percent of the time, learn within the first five minutes whether a TD is suitable for your purposes. With experience, you also develop an intuition about such matters and are often able to spot a bad TD before the speaker has finished his first sentence.

THE LOAN RATIO TEST

The TD's loan-to-value ratio is, by far, the most frequent cause for rejection. Also called the "LTV ratio," this figure represents the relationship between the amount of your loan (plus all senior loans) and the total value of the security. In the case of TDs bought at a discount, the loan-to-value ratio is based on your actual purchase price of the TD and not the face amount due since your cash exposure is limited to the purchase price. For instance, if you pay only $9,000 for a TD which has an amount due of $10,000, you should use the $9,000 figure as the loan amount when calculating the loan-to-value ratio. If the security is worth $40,000, and if there is also a senior loan of $11,000, your loan ratio is calculated: $9,000 (cash paid for the TD) + $11,000 (the senior loan), divided by $40,000 (property value) = 50% LTV ratio.

The frequency with which you reject TDs under this standard is a function of how stringent you are about your safety requirements. Since this book is based on rejection of all risks in your investment, the ratios recommended here are more conservative than those most lenders use.

Individual recommended ratios, and the logic behind them, are discussed in detail in the chapter on Investigating the TD. The following represent the basic ratios recommended in that chapter:

70% on single family residences;
50% on unimproved acreage;
40% on vacant lots located in a second home or
recreational subdivision;
65% or more (depending on economic conditions) for
commercial or industrial buildings;

65% for apartment projects;

70% for apartment properties of four units or less.

All these ratios are subject to revision upwards, depending on a number of factors explained in the chapter on Investigation. Most of the time, however, if the TD fails to meet the above standards, the margin of failure will be so large that the TD will also fail to meet any of the possible exceptions to the guideline ratios.

PRICE ELIMINATION

Whenever you find yourself negotiating with a person who expects an interest rate or loan discount amount which is more than 10% outside the price you are prepared to pay, you should drop further consideration of the deal. The chances that you will be able to negotiate to common ground are so small, or the effort to do so will be so great, that your time will be better utilized elsewhere.

Generally, you won't be able to tell at the beginning what price the other party expects. The seller of a TD may not have the slightest idea what price to ask and will probably be afraid of making a fool of himself by selling too low. Most of your competitors will quote prices under such circumstances, so you might as well join the crowd. The trick, then, is to waste little time asking superfluous questions. Get only the bare numbers involved, make your quote based on these figures, and then qualify your offer by making it contingent upon verification of all information about the TD.

If an offer is made to a TD seller and he responds that it is way out of line, you then may be able to pry out of him some idea of what he thinks a fair price is. Though he may have earlier told you he was too inexperienced to quote a price, he will give you an inkling as to whether it's worth your while to pursue the matter.

If you are approached by a prospective borrower for a new loan, you will always have to make the first offer. Prospective borrowers rarely have a clear idea of what they want, and they always shop around first; the only kind of rate expectation you will get from such a person will be the prices your competitors have quoted. Since your best rates are dependent on a wide range of variables (see Highest Yields in the next chapter), it would be impossible to issue an exact quote without going into a lengthy examination of the conditions surrounding the proposed loan. Therefore, after first qualifying the borrower with some of your other filtering tests, your best strategy is to quote two different types of loans, each with different payment terms. In this manner you may be able to attract the borrower's attention enough that he will return to you after sampling the rest of the market—and wasting everybody else's time first.

PROPERTY VALUATION

One thing for certain about property values: Those who offer you a TD will never undervalue the security; they always overstate it. Your only unknown will be the degree of overstatement. Estimates of the value of land, especially rural acreage, are the most notorious for exaggeration; wishful thinking is the dominating force here. Homeowners do a surprisingly good job of estimating their property's value, because they tend to keep close track of their neighbor's sales — except that the figures they use will be their neighbor's asking prices and not the selling prices. (The typical homeowner seldom tells his neighbors the final sale price.) Real Estate licensee valuations are no more reliable than others if the licensee is the borrower. The licensee's knowledge of the highest priced sales and listings in the area, coupled with the breed's natural tendency to start out high in the expectation of negotiating down, usually results in overstatement of his property's value.

Though you will not, at your first contact, be able to pin down the security's value with certainty, you should be able to make a reasonable approximation of it — sufficient, at least, for your initial screening of the TD. Use of the other party's valuation, seasoned by a knowledge of the varieties of exaggeration, should permit you to bring your estimate of the security close enough to apply your loan ratios. In truth, it is sometimes startling how accurate your guess later proves to be, once you have some experience.

If the TD you have been offered is an existing trust deed, the problem of over-valuation is much smaller. This type of trust deed is usually the product of a previous sale of the security, and this gives the best insight of all into the property's true value — a valuation based on the opinion of someone who was willing to back his judgment by purchase of the property. Furthermore, if the existing trust deed is several years old, the property valuation will also have the benefit of a cushion of inflation, as well as past reductions in the loan balance.

But even a valuation based on a property's past sale price is not immune to overstatement. The sale price may have been inflated by "creative financing;" i.e., it was increased to compensate for favorable loan terms. And every TD seller will tell you there were special circumstances in the sale of the property which forced an abnormally low price. Moreover, if the property's sale was a tax-free exchange of real estate (see the chapter on Appraisal), the sale price is certain to be inflated because the dollar values used in the exchange are purely arbitrary; both parties in a trade can give free rein to their imagination, so long as they each inflate their property's stated value equally.

REJECTIONS BASED ON TYPE OF SECURITY

COMPLICATED FORMS OF SECURITY SPELL TROUBLE

Some loans will always be beyond your capability simply because of the type of security provided. You will never be smart enough to accurately assess the risks inherent in all types of security. Some properties, hotels for example, are so enormously complicated that only lenders who specialize in them can know their dangers.

The foregoing notwithstanding, many lenders believe that an expert appraisal of the security will make up for their lack of experience in the property. But they are wrong. Without some knowledge of the form of security, you never know whether you have an expert appraisal, nor are you able to competently review the appraisal. You aren't able to gauge the quality of the property's management. And if you end up with the property after foreclosure, you will neither be able to manage it yourself, nor know how to spot someone competent to do so. To the extent of your ignorance, you can't even be sure you've used a loan ratio conservative enough to compensate for your ignorance.

BEWARE OF STOCK CO-OPS

One of the weirdest forms of TDs currently being promoted is a type secured by ownership in a "stock cooperative." A stock cooperative consists of joint ownership of a piece of property, such as an apartment building. Each share of ownership is accompanied by the right to occupy a specific portion (an apartment unit) of the building. A co-op differs from a condominium in that co-op members obtain title to a share of the entire property. Condominium ownership, on the other hand, gives title to a specifically described *piece* of the entire property. In a stock co-op, the TD is secured by a form of long term lease on the portion of the property the shareholder is entitled to occupy. The TD is therefore useless without a pledge of the stock ownership.

Some of the finest apartments in the eastern United States are financed in this manner, and many banks loan against them. This type of TD is now increasingly being touted in California, and it brings exceptionally high rates of return. But the TDs carry high rates of return because few lenders are interested in this type of loan. The lack of competition results from the fact that this is, again, a specialist's game. The complications, the unexpected twists and turns in the various agreements, make these TDs too expensive for most lenders to bother with.

REJECTIONS BASED ON SECURITY LOCATION

STAY CLOSE TO HOME

Common sense says that you should place a limit on the distance you will travel to reach a TD's security. But this is a matter of judgement, and many lenders get carried away in their eagerness for loans. They accept TDs at distances so great that the efficiency of their investment suffers.

When the security is located too far away, the biggest problem is the cost of your appraisal, or, if the appraisal has already been made, your review of the appraised property. Moreover, since you can never be certain that the deal for a TD will be completed, you must expect waste of the cost of your travel a certain percentage of the time.

Greater distances also increase the difficulty of checking on the borrower's treatment of the property. Furthermore, if you eventually take the property by foreclosure, the difficulties of management escalate sharply when the property is more than a few hours away.

EXCEPTIONS TO THE RULE

On the other hand, distance is no longer a factor if you become expert in real estate at a location remote from your geographic base. A recreational area some distance away, where you already have an investment, is a typical example. If your knowledge of the area extends to acquaintance with local individuals to whom you can turn for information, advice, and assistance, the TD might be feasible. Indeed, such TDs tend to produce unusually high rates of return, and this may offset the residual defects of distance.

ON OUT OF STATE TDS

Political boundaries are also a factor to consider in the location of your security. Scarcely any form of investment is more sensitive to variations in state law than trust deeds. Therefore, you should never venture outside your own state without the guidance of clearly expert counsel.

SPECIAL DANGERS TO WATCH FOR

Two hazards in TD investment which are not widely known should cause immediate rejection of an offer. They both involve borrowers who enjoy such special protection under the law that the security can be made virtually worthless to a lender. Only if you have an exceptional knowledge of the TDs, and of the facts surrounding them, should you consider them as an investment.

If a borrower becomes a member of the military *after* signing his TD, he will be protected from foreclosure by federal law. Under these circumstances, you must have judicial consent before foreclosure, a procedure so burdensome that foreclosure becomes impractical in all but rare instances. Therefore, unpatriotic though it may sound, you should consider rejecting any existing TD where the borrower is a member of the military if he borrowed the money while a civilian. Unless you have some other motivation for lending, you should similarly consider rejecting the TD if it is a new loan and the applicant borrower is a civilian likely to be drafted into the military. In either instance, you could end up with a TD that is no better than an unsecured loan.

Farmers represent another unacceptable hazard in TDs. They have the unique opportunity of entering bankruptcy and remaining sheltered by the bankruptcy court for years longer than other debtors, making bankruptcy an even more dangerous condition than it normally is. How this is accomplished is explained fully in the Bankruptcy Appendix. Therefore, unless you plan to be a lender expert in farm loans, you should avoid all TDs secured by farm property.

A subordination clause was once considered reason for rejection of a TD. But, as explained later (in the Clauses Appendix), subordinations are bound by so many legal impediments that they have become virtually unenforceable. Nevertheless, the problems created by the amount of argument generated continue to make such TDs unsuitable. Furthermore, the judicial pendulum is beginning to swing the other way and this may also cause a subordination clause, once more, to be reason for rejecting a TD.

Variable interest rate TDs also should be avoided when secured by property containing four or fewer residential units. Variable interest rate, here, refers to TDs with an interest rate that fluctuates in tandem with a specified standard, such as the Consumer Price Index. The statutory restrictions on this type of loan are so complex that the cost of figuring out whether you've complied with the law makes these TDs unprofitable for private investors.

OTHER FILTERING QUESTIONS TO ASK

If you are asked to invest in a 2nd TD, always ask who the 1st TD lender is. This can reveal clues to several potential problems. For example, if the 1st TD is not held by an institutional lender, it is apt to have all sorts of peculiarities in its terms which make the 2nd TD risky. Furthermore, if the 1st is not an institutional lender, you may have a leading indicator that something is wrong with the borrower or the property, which causes regular lenders to turn the deal down. Also, if the 1st is a "Cal Vet" loan, it's not really a loan at all, even though that's the term used by real estate people. The "borrower" in a Cal Vet loan does not really own the property and therefore cannot borrow against it. The security is in fact owned by the State of California, and the "borrower" is simply making payments for the property under a "contract-of-sale."

If the party you are talking to sounds too eager, or appears to be desperate to close the deal, beware! Ask a lot of questions. If you are talking to an overeager applicant, he may be trying to borrow money to stave off his creditors. If so, there is a chance he will be forced into bankruptcy no matter how good his security is. Problems of this sort feed on themselves because, once signs of weakness show up, alarmed creditors panic and descend on the borrower like a plague of locusts. Alternatively, if the other party is an overly eager *seller* of an existing TD, he may be trying to unload the TD for fear of the borrower's bankruptcy. There is an old saying among lenders that the best borrowers are those who don't need the money. The fear of bankruptcy courts makes such cowards of lenders these days that the old guideline has become a basic feature of much loan strategy.

If you have been approached by a borrower for a new loan, mention that you will need a credit application and that a credit check will be made. Such a comment will immediately chill further discussion in a surprising number of cases. Many of your loan applicants will have a bad credit history; their hope is that you, as a private lender, will not check on them as thoroughly as a regular lender would.

Though banks make it a rule to ask prospective borrowers the purpose of a loan, the question is largely futile. That notwithstanding, you'll hear about the loan's purpose anyway, for borrowers love to talk about their plans. But you will seldom get the complete truth, or whatever the truth is at the time of telling may not be applicable five days later.

A more appropriate question in your filtering process, and one crucial to any investment in a new TD, is how the borrower is going to repay the loan. This is especially true if the loan is for a short term and calls for a balloon payment at the end of, for example, three years. Again, you probably will not receive the complete truth, but you have to ask the question anyway. This seemingly obvious aspect of the loan is almost universally ignored by borrowers, even though it is essential to their fulfillment of the agreement.

If you're contemplating purchase of an existing 2nd TD, check the loan balances the other party gives you by adding them up. Most of the time 2nd TDs derive from the sale of real estate. When you add the balances due on the 1st and 2nd TDs to the supposed down payment at the time of sale, the total should equal the property's sale price. More than 70 percent of the time, however, the seller of a TD will make an error in one of the figures he gives you — an error that inevitably shows the loan less secure than as originally presented.

USING A BROKER AS A FILTER

Almost any offer of an existing TD received through a broker is evidence that someone actually is trying to sell a TD and not simply trying to plumb the market. TD sellers who do business through a broker must be serious about selling or they subject themselves to payment of a sales commission if they back out.

Beware, however, of the broker who either does not have a written listing for a trust deed to be sold, or who has had only a telephone conversation with a prospective borrower. This happens most often in the inexperienced, one-man type of brokerage office. A broker offering a new loan should have invested enough of his own time investigating the deal to assure you that he thinks it will hold together; if he hasn't appraised the security himself, or had an appraiser do it for him, there is no reason for you to assume the task on the off chance that you will be able to make the deal. Also regard with caution brokers who offer existing TDs for sale, but have not obtained at least a copy of the note and deed of trust, as well as copies of other pertinent supporting documents, such as a title policy. This is a sure sign that he will be slipshod in his use of your time.

LOAN SEASONING

Most of the loans you'll be exposed to will be relatively new — less than a year old. But if you're in the business long enough, you'll occasionally be offered older TDs, TDs which have been "seasoned" with monthly payments for perhaps 10 years or more.

Conventional wisdom says well-seasoned loans are particularly desirable because they are safer: The borrower has shown himself to be a responsible person through a history of regular payments and normal forces during the passage of time have made the loan more secure. But because so many investors have repeatedly been told the importance of seasoning, you'll generally find the loan a waste of time. Completely ignoring the fact that a new, less reliable, borrower may buy the property and take over the loan payments, many TD investors will bid far more for the loan than common sense would indicate. Unless some special circumstances exist which might reduce the competition for the loan, you're better off avoiding the crowd and concentrating on something more profitable.

CHAPTER 6

Strategies for Maximum Profit

THE HIGHEST YIELDING TDS

The most direct way of getting the greatest profit from your TD investment is to dare to be different. A herd instinct among lenders forces them to seek out only TDs generally acknowledged to be good investments. Consequently, the rate of return for less popular, but still safe, TDs is elevated to much higher levels than would otherwise seem reasonable.

Also, surprising ignorance is found among TD investors, and among some brokers, as to what "yield" is and how it is calculated. Unusual payment terms therefore tend to produce higher yields. (To understand this most important subject, refer to the appendix on Yield Calculations.)

Given the opportunity, you should aim for the following types of TDs:

- LARGE TDs, in the $50,000 - $100,000 range, command a substantially higher rate of return than others. They occupy a sort of no-man's land, avoided by big lenders because the investment is too small to bother with, and which the little fellow can't invade because he doesn't have the cash. TDs of this size are also more efficient than small ones; the time needed to investigate and administer a $100,000 TD is no more than that of a $3000 TD.

- TYPE OF SECURITY plays an important part in the size of your yield. The lenders' herd instinct causes them to mass around specific types of security, such as houses, making yields on other types of TDs rise accordingly. TDs secured by land can produce extraordinary yields because of the speculative character of most land borrowers. Condominiums are shunned by many institutional lenders because they don't want the bother of investigating the condominium association for possible defects. Apartments are avoided for fear of rent control. Commercial and industrial properties are regarded with distrust by many lenders because of the difficulty of appraisal. Any of these securities, and many even less favored, can nevertheless be acceptable so long as you use a conservative loan ratio, have an adequate appraisal, and develop a thorough knowledge of the property.

- RECREATIONAL SUBDIVISION TDs can produce rates of return beyond the wildest imagination if you play your cards right. These TDs are usually secured by vacant lots which have been sold by high-pressure salesmen to people who were captivated by their dreams more than by the property. The concept of this type of sale is so repugnant to most lenders that few who pride themselves on their common sense will touch these TDs. But a strange thing happens to this type of TD: Even though the borrower may have paid many times too much for the lot — and knows it — he will still hold on to it and continue to make payments under all sorts of adversities, rather than recognize that he has made a mistake. Though the default rate in these TDs is higher than normal, the staggering discounts at which they are sold more than offset the losses you must write off.

- MINORITY AREA TDs should give rates of return 50% or more higher than comparable TDs secured at other locations. And there is no real reason this should be so. Though the area may look like Berlin at the end of World War II, the market value of the property adjusts itself to its appearances, and a loan based on a realistic appraisal is as secure as any other. Furthermore, as long as there is an economic motive to hold on to the property, the borrower will be as solid as one from any other ethnic group. Your real risk in this type of TD is the consequences of social unrest. But so long as the borrower is able to obtain fire insurance, you are protected from even this hazard.

- SEMI-ANNUAL, or less frequent, payment intervals also mean higher rates of return for the investor. Most TD investors prefer regular monthly payments and, if the TD does not meet that requirement, the competition for it drops off sharply. The exception to the rule is the TD which provides for no installment payments, but only a final payment (including accrued interest) when the loan matures. This type of TD has tax deferment benefits (see the appendix on Income Taxes) and is popular among high tax bracket investors.

- COMPLICATED PAYMENT TERMS in a TD bought at a discount sometimes lead to unexpectedly high returns because the competition simply does not know how to calculate the yield; they lose track of what they are doing and every once in a while underestimate the rate of return. This is especially true of "all inclusive trust deeds" (see AITDs in the appendix on Clauses), TDs which incorporate a midstream change in the interest rate, or TDs which call for installment payments that decline in size as time progresses.

- A LOW INTEREST RATE shown on the face of the note should not have much bearing on the TD's acceptable yield, but it does. For no logical reason, a trust deed with little or no face-amount interest will not sell well, and it will require a disproportionately high discount to produce a yield good enough to entice buyers.

- PREPAYMENT prospects should play a part in your investment decision. Most TDs are paid off before their maturity unless they are of very short term or have exceptionally low interest rates. This almost always brings a higher yield. The increased yield may stem from the bonus received as a result of a prepayment penalty if such a clause is contained in the TD. If the TD has been bought at a discount, premature payment will raise your yield by shortening the period over which the discount is amortized. Although you won't always be able to predict the prepayment date exactly, surprisingly good estimates are possible. Ask the right questions of the borrower, and you will be able to foresee the payoff date of the TD with enough accuracy to base your investment on it.

• DUE ON SALE CLAUSES in 1st TDs elevate their prospect for profit well beyond the TD's face interest rate. If the borrower tries to sell his property, he must obtain your consent to the property buyer's assumption of your loan, or pay the entire loan amount off. If he chooses to pay the loan off, you may gain by its prepayment, as explained above. If he wishes to negotiate an assumption of the loan, you'll be able to charge him for your consent. And if the borrower loses the property through foreclosure by a junior TD, the new owner of the security will similarly be forced to comply with your requirements. (For more on this, see the Due On Sale section of the Clauses Appendix.)

• EXISTING TDs, sold at a discount, provide inherently higher rates of return than comparable new loans. The competition for these TDs is not as keen because their already established payment terms always eliminate a certain number of potential investors. Indeed, most institutional lenders are taken completely out of the 2nd trust deed portion of the market for this very reason, and because this type of loan does not meet their procedural requirements.

• 3RD TDs are a source of higher yields, especially if secured by a large piece of property. At one time there was practically no market at all for these TDs because of their speculative reputation. Today, however, they are relatively common and there is active interest in them. But, again, institutional lenders are generally excluded from this part of the business by the regulations under which they operate. Yields, therefore, trend higher in this type of TD. If the TD is a small one, perched on top of a large 1st and 2nd TD, it also bears with it the opportunity to acquire a large piece of property for a small down payment, should foreclosure become necessary.

OPPORTUNITIES FROM DIVORCE

Some of the most remarkable and profitable trust deeds on the market are those which arise from divorces. The typical divorce requires division of the couple's property, including any equity in their home. But sale of the home and division of the proceeds is a time-consuming and expensive process. Also, the wife often needs to remain in possession of the house because she has children to raise, and they must be insured a stable environment. The divorce attorney's solution to the problem is creation of a 2nd TD in favor of the husband for his share of the property.

Divorce TDs are customarily written with no interest, or at interest rates well below existing market rates; they also have no requirement for installment payments during their existence. The debt invariably becomes due in its entirety, including any accrued interest, when the youngest child reaches maturity, the wife remarries or dies, or when the house is sold.

More often than you might expect the husband later goes broke, and either he or a trustee in bankruptcy then must sell the TD at a discount in order to generate cash for the creditors.

The trust deed sometimes brings a good price. The peculiar nature of the instrument, the fact that it is usually well secured, and the excitement of gambling on the payoff, may attract a higher price from bidders than common sense would indicate. The wife may also be an active bidder (at a discount) if she foresees an event which will soon force her to pay off the TD anyway.

But normally the TD sells at a huge discount as a result of the unpredictability of the TD's payoff date. The investor must reckon not only with the wife's remarriage prospects, but also with the effect of the husband's absence on the care of the security, however feeble his efforts at maintenance may have been. And if the wife does remarry, you may never learn of the fact if the marriage occurs at some remote location.

Altogether, the inherent defects in this type of TD violate almost every objective of the typical TD investor. If, however, you can convince yourself that the TD will always be well secured, there is little risk in such a venture. The only risk lies in the size of your profit; as a crap-shoot, the divorce-TD is probably the most profitable one you will ever come across.

ABOUT THE TD MARKET

Perhaps the most striking feature about private money trust deeds is the fact that you never know for sure what the correct price is. No central bargaining place exists for TDs, as in the stock market. There is no uniformity between trust deeds (as between individual shares of stock) by which you can identify the market's perception of the TD's value. Very little cross communication takes place between investors as to their price goals; any two equally knowledgeable investors can look at the same TD and come up with radically different opinions of its value. In any TD, you never know whether you have invested your money at the best obtainable price.

Complicating the situation further is the fact that most borrowers and lenders are in the market only occasionally and have no repository of experience to draw upon. Many transactions are entered in ignorance, without a clear picture of how complicated TDs can be, which further distorts market rates. Many investors are unable to calculate accurately the TD's true yield, and this leads to still more irrational decisions. Some investors don't even bother to try and calculate yield; they base their investment decision on the percentage discount in the purchase of a TD without regard to its payment terms or the time the TD has to run — a 50% discount for a TD secured by land; 30% for apartments, etc.

Experienced investors adjust to this condition by resigning themselves to being outbid most of the time. They accept the fact that much of their competition will come from infrequent investors who gleefully outsmart everybody by snapping up TDs at rates scarcely better than those obtainable on government bonds. Getting the highest yield means making a lot of offers in the expectation of only a few acceptances. It also means that when you are successful, you immediately begin to wonder what's wrong and start looking for mistakes.

HOW TO NEGOTIATE THE BEST PRICES

Every TD investment requires some negotiation. Even if you invest through a loan broker, negotiation will be necessary, though perhaps not to the extent shown in this chapter. No one is going to offer you the best deal in the beginning; no one is going to accept your offer without checking it among the competition. A straightforward offer and immediate acceptance is rare. And when it does occur, one of the parties has a valid reason to wonder whether he might have done better.

COURTESY COUNTS

In TD negotiations, courtesy counts more than elsewhere. Some theories of negotiation suggest that success rests on exaggeration, rudeness and brutal behavior. And perhaps they are right, so often are these tactics used.

But trust deed negotiations are different. The wise trust deed investor is courteous. Not because he wants to be liked; it's because the business attracts more than its share of insensitive people. Courtesy therefore becomes more memorable as an exception. If you are dealing directly with a principal and not through a broker, the person you are talking to will probably be under some stress. Borrowing tends to batter the ego, and the borrower will therefore appreciate decent treatment more than at other times. And if a TD is being offered for sale, the seller is probably doing so because he needs cash badly and is receiving unkind treatment from his creditors.

42

Ego is a powerful and exceptionally quirky force in negotation; its influence overrides all but the most extreme differences in price. Treatment with dignity caters to this force. Even when it seems that courtesy is not appreciated, be assured its absence can chill negotiations beyond repair.

THE ADVANTAGES OF SPEED

The advantage of quick action has been pointed out several times in this book in different contexts. The rule applies equally to negotiations for trust deeds. Quick responses capture the other party's attention and tend to reduce the chance that he will shop the TD further among your competitors. If you couple your offer with a time limit for its acceptance, and can convince the other party that you mean it, you can restrict the search among your competitors still more. If you draw out your negotiation and sound too cagey or devious in coming up with your offer, the chances are that the other party will decide that better prices may be found elsewhere; he will probably conclude that you're too much of a bargain hunter.

An offer of speedy completion of the transaction may also help to bring about an agreement. It may sound contradictory, in view of all the precautionary steps recommended throughout this book, but at times it's best to offer to skip some seemingly important protective steps, such as an escrow or a beneficiary statement, if you can verify your safety by alternative means. Sellers of existing trust deeds in particular are often desperate for money, and if you can find ways to bypass time-consuming procedures you may be able to arrange a better deal than your competitors.

LOW BALLING

Unless a significant change in the facts of a situation occurs, do not alter your offer after is has been accepted. When used as a bargaining device, changing your original offer is called "low balling." It can easily kill the rest of your negotiations. A great number of publications have come out in recent years attempting to instruct the reader in negotiating tactics. Most of them recommend this ploy in one form or another. Used car salesmen regularly use the tactic when they deliberately quote a low price, only to raise it later when the prospective buyer returns and accepts the offer. But the strategy simply does not work, at least with trust deeds. Such sleazy behavior has become so well known that any hint of it is apt to cause resentment and will destroy the atmosphere of mutual confidence necessary for any successful negotiation.

APPRAISAL STRATEGIES

Clever negotiators will try to maneuver you into accepting a TD by encouraging you to look at the property before making up your mind. This is especially true among those who make a business of selling existing TDs. If you dislike something about the TD, they tell you that there are ways around the problem, and that you should first see the property ("You'll love it; it has a magnificent view"). The real purpose of this maneuver, however, is to get you to invest so much time in the TD that you cannot afford to walk away from the deal. For this reason, you should refuse to spend any of your own time on appraisal of the security until you have struck an agreement regarding price and until you feel that you have answers to all important questions about the offering.

BIDDING STRATEGIES

Some organizations, such as bank trust departments, offer trust deeds for sale on a bid basis only. In this manner they are able to represent to a court or other supervising agency that they have exposed the TD to the marketplace, received a number of offers, and picked the best of the lot.

Such trust deed sources can be valuable, but they often operate in a manner so careless of your time that they should be ignored no matter how attractive the trust deed appears. To find out if you are dealing with this sort of seller, you should ask if he is committed to a sale by bid, or will abandon it if the price does not satisfy the heirs or whomever may be directing the sale activities. If the seller requires such overseer approval, the probability that you are wasting your time is so great that the TD will ordinarily not be worth bothering with. The seller is probably hiding the minimum price because he knows it will discourage bidders; or he does not even intend to sell the TD and is simply trying to attract enough bids to establish the TD's distribution value among the heirs.

One way to get around this ploy is to make your bid contingent on verification, within a few days after its acceptance, of the value of the security and any other matters of concern. Another way to avoid the problem is to flush out insincere sellers by asking whether they will announce the successful bid amount. If the seller will not reveal the bid results, you can assume that the request for a bid is a formality, and you should spend no more time on the offer. If the seller is willing to announce all the bids, fine; even an unsuccessful bid will then be valuable because you then learn the prices your competitors are offering.

When bidding for purchase of an existing trust deed, your primary competition will come from other investors represented by brokers. You, as a private investor dealing directly with the seller, have an advantage here because any price the broker bids must necessarily include an allowance for his commission. A trust deed normally selling at 85% of its face amount may, for example, net the seller only 75% of face after the broker has taken his cut. If, in this example, you lower your bid to 79% of the face amount, you will be able to increase your profit yet overbid the competition.

The following broker commission schedule is an approximation of the amount of additional discount you may be able to extract from your bid.

$ Amount of Transaction	Broker's Commission Requirement
$ 1,000	9 to 15%
3,000	6 to 10%
5,000	5.4 to 9%
10,000	4.7 to 7%
20,000	3 to 5%
50,000	2.4 to 4%
100,000	1.8 to 3%

The above commission schedule may be assumed to be only the bare minimum needed by the broker to sustain interest in the transaction. If the broker expects to sell the trust deed to a large, repetitive buyer (such as a pension fund), he will settle for the lower rates shown in the table. But if he anticipates difficulty completing the sale, he may increase his commission requirement to the schedule's upper ranges, or even more. And if he thinks there will be little competition for the TD, he will increase his commission to whatever the market will bear.

It costs a broker as much to sell a $10,000 TD with a one year maturity as it does to sell a $10,000 TD with a 10 year maturity. His commission requirements therefore make no distinction as to the length of time a TD must run. Instances such as these create an opportunity for phenomenal profits for the private investor bidding on short term trust deeds. The 10 year trust deed may, for example, yield only 25% when your discount (including an allowance for some of the broker's commission) is amortized over 10 years. But if the TD has only a one year life, the portion of the discount allocable to the broker's commission is amortized over only one year and may elevate your rate of return to 40% on your invested capital.

COMPROMISES WHICH CAN SAVE A DEAL

The cornerstone of any negotiation is the necessity of satisfying the needs of both parties; without satisfaction there is no purpose to the transaction.

"Price" can be many things. Frequently, the other party cannot accept the reality of the current market rate. Never theless, by judicious compromise you may be able to satisfy the other party's price need in a slightly different way.

COMPROMISES ON THE PURCHASE OF DISCOUNTED TDS

- If the seller has difficulty adjusting to the size of discount you require, perhaps an offer to buy only the payments due on the TD over the next one or two years will be successful. In long term TDs, the largest part of the discount results from the postponed collection of later years' payments — the farther off the collection, the greater the discount must be to meet your yield requirements. If you purchase the right to the first few years' collections only, leaving later collections to the seller, your discount requirement shrinks. In this way, you may be able to salvage a deal and reap a slightly higher rate of return as a reward.

- The size of discount needed to sell a TD may be due to the TD's weak, or questionable, security. If this is so, the TD seller may be willing to bolster the security by pledging some of his own property as additional security (see the Deed of Trust portion of the appendix on Clauses for details). Or perhaps somebody else, such as a guarantor, can be induced to pledge the additional security.

- If the number of years required to pay off the TD necessitates an unacceptably high discount, you can some times reach an agreement by going to the borrower and offering to modify the TD to a shorter life (and a smaller discount). Offering to pay him a few percentage points of the loan amount may be a necessary lubricant in this case.

- If the seller feels his cash needs are only temporary, purchase of his TD can often be accomplished by offering him an option to repurchase the TD later. Such an option may or may not have an expiration date. If the option does have an expiration, however, you can almost be certain that the other party will never exercise it in time.

COMPROMISES ON NEW LOAN NEGOTIATIONS

- You can sometimes make a loan more palatable by arranging the payment terms so that the borrower need make only low (or no) payments during the first years, when his cash needs are greatest. In this situation, the loan is written so that payment amounts increase in later years, when he can better handle them.

- Remember, borrowers are hypnotized by interest rates. They will always go for the low interest rate — and higher points — even though the effective, long term cost remains the same. (This is especially true if you are willing to increase the loan amount enough to cover the cost of the points.)

- Sometimes you can achieve your profit goal by arranging the terms so that the interest is contingent upon the occurrence of some future event beneficial to the borrower. For instance, tying interest increases to retail sales above a certain figure, or tying the interest to the county assessor's valuation of a piece of property.

- You can also improve the chances for a deal by making two or three offers, each with a different combination of terms. This works wonders by grabbing the borrower's attention to the exclusion of the competition, and it also makes up for any deficiency in your assessment of the borrower's needs.

CHAPTER 7

Investigating the TD — What to Watch Out For

Experienced TD investors often claim that the best approach to the investigation of any TD is to assume the other fellow is a crook, and then work backward from there. Depressing as it may sound, there is considerable justification for this attitude. Truth is not a matter of black and white; it's a matter of degree. Truth exists only in the eye of the beholder, and anybody can rationalize his behavior. More important, however, is the way the approach can keep your antenna tuned for trouble. Such sensitivity is valuable, because you can never be certain that someone out there hasn't figured out a new way to outsmart you.

When investigating a TD, it's important that you let the other fellow do as much of your leg work as possible. Previous chapters have stressed the efficient use of your time while initially filtering out unsuitable TDs. So too should efficiency be kept in mind while investigating a TD. If the other party makes an assertion, make him back it up with a document, such as a title policy, appraisal, or copy of a TD. Don't waste your time skittering around collecting the information yourself. At this stage the other person will be trying to prove himself, and you might as well take advantage of it. Remember: The less time you have invested in the TD the easier it will be to back out if you want to. And the more time you can get the other person to invest in the deal, the more committed he will be to satisfying your requirements.

The best TDs, for reasons not always clear, are frequently those in which the deal is consummated quickly. Experienced TD investors regularly notice this phenomenon and tend to regard it as one of the fundamentals of the business. Therefore, once the deal passes your tests for filtering out the dogs, be prepared to move fast. Start your investigation as soon as possible. There is a natural tendency to procrastinate, to put the matter aside in order to think about it, to worry that if the TD is so good there must be something wrong with it. But if you wait, you will lose some of your best opportunities. The better the trust deed, the sooner someone else is likely to snap it up.

*   *   *

If you prefer to use a loan broker and restrict your investments to new loans, you may wish to skip this chapter entirely. When you invest in new loans through a loan broker, he should conduct your investigation for you. If, on the other hand, you do not have full confidence in your broker, or if you plan to purchase an existing TD, the investigative procedures discussed here will be useful. To simplify access to the information, the rest of this chapter has been divided into two parts. Part I covers only questions that must be asked about placement of a new loan. Part II is devoted to questions that should be asked before purchasing an existing TD.

Part I — What to Watch Out For in New Loans

INVESTIGATING THE BORROWER

Many people in trust deed lending tend to underrate the importance of their investigation of the borrower. They try to save time and simply rely on their judgement of the applicant's character after a brief interview; they believe that the quality of the security is more important. Much of the time they can get by with such an approach. But if you learn one thing in this business, it is how faulty your judgements of character really are; and experience soon teaches that total reliance on the security, alone, can lead to losses. Smart investors always investigate the borrower when they have the opportunity.

THE BORROWER'S CREDIT APPLICATION

A credit application, signed by the prospective borrower, is the first step in any investigation of an applicant's background. Without such a document, credit reporting agencies are prohibited by law from releasing information about the applicant. With a credit application, you have a launch point for questions that lead to information which will flesh out your picture of the borrower.

You can save yourself much time and trouble if you ask the prospective borrower to fill out an application at the credit agency's office. Arrange for the agency to collect the cost of the credit report from the applicant when he turns in the form. In this way, a borrower will become committed to the deal and be less likely to back out.

THE APPLICANT'S FINANCIAL STATEMENT

Most credit applications ask for a rudementary form of financial statement. If the statement shows significant assets other than the applicant's home, ask for details. Ask for a list of all the applicant's real property ownerships, as well as each note payable.

A listing of assets is valuable because it gives clues to the applicant's potential for bankruptcy (see the Bankruptcy Section, later in this chapter). It also provides a basis for negotiation later on if your loan runs into trouble (see the chapter on Administration). The listing of the applicant's liabilities also helps, because it may show real property loans which, by their nature, are not ordinarily picked up by credit reporting agencies.

CREDIT REPORTS AND HOW TO USE THEM

The principal value of a credit report lies in the information it reveals about applicants who tend to be late in their payments. If a pattern of delinquency shows up, you can be sure that the problem will some day leak over into your loan, no matter how persuasive the excuses given for past behavior.

Bad payment practices produce problems regardless of a borrower's wealth. No matter how much property a borrower owns, your ability to enforce the terms of your loan will generally be limited to the TD's security. The borrower's other properties won't help you at all. California's one-action rule (see the Security Limits Appendix) effectively insulates a TD borrower's other assets from your collection efforts.

You should also look for indications of a recent, sharp increase in the amount of borrowing by the applicant — especially borrowing for the purchase of consumer goods. As explained later in the Bankruptcy section of this chapter, this may be a warning of the applicant's preparation for bankruptcy.

Judgement liens handed down by a court sometimes appear in credit reports, but are not necessarily a problem; you have to examine such liens separately on their own merits. Sometimes a lien comes to life under circumstances so aggravating to the applicant (such as a lawsuit) that payment of the claim is resisted simply on principle. At other times, however, the lien appears because the applicant thinks it will not show up in his credit report. He may not realize that judgement liens can be recorded at the county recorder and are good for 10 years. Also, debtors often believe they can escape a judgement lien by moving to a different county; they don't realize that creditors routinely record a lien in several different counties when the debtor turns up missing from his usual residence.

If you decide to accept an applicant with a judgement lien against him, you must make sure your loan is conditioned on payoff of the lien. This is because a lien recorded ahead of your TD in the county in which your security is located, is senior to your TD; it functions like a 1st TD. It can be foreclosed against your TD's security and can cut you off and leave you with only an unsecured loan. The single exception to this rule occurs when your TD qualifies as a "purchase money" TD (that is, a TD taken by the seller of a property to finance its sale). *Judgement liens are never superior to a purchase money TD, no matter when the judgement is recorded.*

BORROWER POTENTIAL FOR BANKRUPTCY

A borrower's bankruptcy can be an impossibly expensive proposition for a trust deed investor. It can turn your investment into a loss, no matter how well-secured it is. Bankruptcy represents the single greatest potential risk in trust deed investment, because its occurrence is sometimes difficult to predict and therefore difficult to eliminate. Some lenders don't even try to detect the probability of an applicant's bankruptcy; they accept bankruptcy as an unavoidable cost of doing business and assume that a certain percentage of their profits will always be lost to it.

Yet, bankruptcy is predictable, albeit not as accurately as other risks in TD investment. For this purpose, the following guidelines should be kept in mind when investigating loan applicants:

An adequate cash flow is the first thing to look for in an applicant's background, because it eliminates the need for bankruptcy. Cash flow is not a clue to long term safety from bankruptcy, however. There is a risk that the borrower's cash condition will change during the years your TD is in effect; you never know whether an adverse lawsuit or other calamity will wipe out a borrower's cash supply.

A borrower's low equity in a property lessens the chance that bankruptcy will be filed simply to avoid your foreclosure. This is especially true if the borrower has other properties which would also be dragged into bankruptcy. Theoretically, the value of the property to the borrower, in excess of the amount he owes his trust deed lenders, can be so small that it's not worth fighting for. You can't always count on a borrower conducting himself in a rational manner, however. Indeed, a distorted view of his financial condition is the hallmark of a hard-pressed debtor. He will always place greater value on his property than is reasonable and therefore may try to save his nonexistent equity. His outlook will probably also be distorted by a mistaken belief that you will try to attach his other property to recover the money due; he will likely be ignorant of the "one action rule" and the way it limits you solely to the TD's security. If so, you may find yourself chasing him into bankruptcy simply on a misunderstanding.

Friends and relatives as creditors of the applicant are evidence of safety from bankruptcy. Their presence should dampen the borrower's enthusiasm for bankruptcy, because they too would be dragged down by such a move.

A profligate lifestyle may indicate the probability of bankruptcy; it may be evidence of the applicant's inability to be realistic about the standard of living he can afford. If so, that particular pigeon will someday come home to roost. When this happens, the borrower will be forced to either file bankruptcy, or to cut his expenses to the bone in order to stave off his creditors. Usually this type of person chooses the former.

Honesty, as defined by some people, requires them to regard bankruptcy as a form of theft. Though these people are less likely to file bankruptcy, such a characteristic is a slender reed to lean on. The sheer pressure of a few creditors' demands often forces a borrower to file bankruptcy simply to salvage some money for other, less clamorous, creditors.

An unsecured guarantee of the TD may provide unexpected safety from bankruptcy. In a practical sense, such guarantees are unenforceable for reasons explained in the appendix on Clauses. In terms of bankruptcy, however, the guarantee may protect you indirectly as a result of ignorance. Most of the time the guarantor will be a friend or relative who, on hearing of the borrower's imminent bankruptcy, will speak out loud and clear. Even though he has no property pledged as security on the loan, he will want no part of the entanglement of bankruptcy — especially when he was only trying to do the borrower a favor. Chances are, your warning that you expect the guarantor to make good on the loan will be just the fuse needed to ignite an explosion. The guarantor may berate the borrower so much that further thought of bankruptcy is discarded.

A secured guarantee backed by separately pledged property is, on the other hand, a reliable shield against the effects of bankruptcy. As is pointed out in the appendix on Clauses, you can have several deeds of trust, each signed by different property owners, all of them securing a single loan on which only one of them is the borrower. Then, if the borrower files bankruptcy, you can still foreclose on the guarantor's separately pledged property. To prevent your doing so, the guarantor must step in and cover the bankrupt borrower's obligation.

A prior bankrupt is a greater risk than a borrower who has no past record of bankruptcy. Bankrupts theoretically cannot refile for seven years after coming out of bankruptcy. Some lenders consider loans during that seven year period safe against a recurrence of bankruptcy. But the rule against refiling doesn't hold true in every case (see the appendix on Bankruptcy). Also, the borrower can still protect his property via bankruptcy, no matter how often he has filed in the past, by selling a fractional interest in the property to another person who then goes into bankruptcy himself. Be assured a recent bankrupt will have picked up this and other smarts during his ordeal; his knowledge of bankruptcy and attorneys (as well as other portions of the law) make him a greater risk to lenders than other borrowers. Be assured too that, if the former bankrupt's problem was poor money management, his past bankruptcy will not have cured him of the ailment. He will continue to be erratic in his future payments.

A sharp increase in borrowing is an indicator of a potential bankrupt. Many bankruptcies are planned a month or so in advance. Borrowers are counseled to load up with as much debt as possible when bankruptcy appears inevitable. This usually takes the form of credit purchases of cars, boats and various other grown-up toys. The theory behind this action is that subsequent bankruptcy will provide a shelter from creditors, and the debts will ultimately be cancelled. Although new law has muted the effectiveness of this stragegy, enough people believe in it that such activities may be a clear sign of imminent bankruptcy.

LOAN RATIOS TO LOOK FOR

A TD's loan ratio is the amount of your loan expressed as a percentage of the value of its security. It's method of calculation is explained in the chapter on Filtering Out the Dogs. It is a convenient way of measuring the safety of a TD in terms of the security.

LOAN RATIOS FOR HOUSES

Loans on houses are usually considered safe when you loan less than 70% of the market value of the house. But if the house costs more than $500,000, the loan ratio should be smaller, perhaps as low as 40%; the more expensive the house, the longer it takes to sell, and therefore you need a greater security margin. There also are many other exceptions to the 70% rule. These are discussed later in this chapter.

Contrary to popular belief, the potential for physical damage to a house under foreclosure should not be the major factor in your choice of a loan ratio. The borrower usually does not wake up to the fact that he will lose the house until too late to do much damage, even if he is so inclined. It is true that sometimes the borrower tries to trash the property by kicking holes in the walls, stripping it of light fixtures, and splashing paint and what-not on the walls. But the dollar cost of vandalism, as a percentage of the total value of the property, tends to be surprisingly small. Even in the unlikely event that the borrower removes toilet fixtures, and the furnace, and the air conditioning equipment, the repair cost seldom runs more than 10 percent of the total value of the property. Only when the structure of the building is damaged do the costs begin to soar. With fire insurance you can virtually eliminate that risk.

A far more significant erosion of your security margin results from the cost of time and aggravation during foreclosure. Consider: It can take two months after the borrower makes his last payment to get a foreclosure started (the month it takes to reach the next payment due date, and an additional month as a sort of grace period before starting foreclosure). Then, if everything is done perfectly, and promptly, another four months is needed to complete the foreclosure. Nothing in foreclosure is ever done perfectly or promptly, however, and seven months in foreclosure is a more realistic allowance. If you have to evict the owner, figure at least another two months. But usually you don't have an eviction; you have a repair job, instead — which takes two months (if you are well-connected with people who do that kind of work). And then, assuming you don't ask too high a price when you put the house up for sale, you must allow at least four months to sell the place. Altogether, you must allow a minimum of 1¼ years to the actual sale date of the property — if you don't have to contend with bankruptcy; if you allow for bankruptcy, you may need to add at least another year.

During all this time your money stands idle, earning nothing. And none of this reckons the cost of your own time running hither and yon trying to orchestrate the affair, a cost so awful that experienced lenders try not to think about it.

Dismaying though the foregoing may be, your out-of-pocket expenses from foreclosure are even higher. You must allow for trustee foreclosure fees, a broker's commission for resale of the property, taxes and insurance while the property stands idle, possible protection of the house while vacant, discount points paid to induce a lender to finance resale of the property, attorney's fees (especially if the foreclosure is contested), title insurance for both the foreclosure and resale of the property, escrow costs related to the resale, and, worst of all, advances you might have to pay senior lien holders to keep them from foreclosing also.

Fortunately, not all these costs occur in every defaulted loan. And it is possible to screen out most of the worst risks with the judicious use of loan applications and credit reports. If all the foregoing costs were to occur in the same TD, even a 70% loan would be too high. Most lenders settle for 75%; some accept even 80% as being safe. And, if certain guarantees are provided, 90% is sometimes considered acceptable. But whatever other lenders do, tread lightly if you feel impelled to go above 70%. Too often the higher ratios are based on self-delusions caused by the lender's never-ending need to get his money out and to work as fast as possible.

OTHER RECOMMENDED LOAN RATIOS

Almost all the factors used in reckoning the proper loan ratio for a house also apply to other properties. Other types of security have at least two additional variables, however, and these alter the margin you need if you have to force recapture of your investment.

Condominium units can take a 75% loan ratio — if the development as a whole is well-designed and constructed, is run by a good management company, has a sensible set of CC&Rs (see Covenants, Conditions, and Restrictions in the appendix on Appraisal), and is governed by a conscientious homeowner's association. Such developments are a joy to behold, and even an 80% loan ratio may be conservative in some cases. Most, however, are defective in one or more ways and this can cause the safe loan ratio to fluctuate wildly. Therefore, you need to consider each condominium development separately before reaching any conclusions about the appropriate loan ratio.

Apartment buildings merit loans of up to 65% of their market value with comparative safety, assuming there is no immediate prospect of rent control. If the units are duplexes or fourplexes, 70% is adequate. Ratios at higher levels should be undertaken only when you can be sure the development will receive quality management (management is everything when reckoning the value of the apartment units); it's easy for an owner to milk a property by packing the units with too many tenants in exchange for higher rental income; maintenance can also be deferred for long periods without obvious external signs of neglect.

Industrial and commercial building loan ratios are dictated more by economic conditions than are other properties. No matter what direction the economy takes, well-located properties of this sort are safe if you loan no more than 65% of their value. You can increase the ratio for a healthy business climate, present or anticipated. This type of property is one of the most sensitive of all to market forces, so watch your step if the economy looks like it's going to fall out of bed.

Land is traditionally considered safe at a loan ratio of 50%, for no apparent reason other than the figure is a nice round number. But where land is concerned, the major cost of default comes from the points you have to pay in order to finance resale of the property, and this can vary widely. In fact, you may have to finance the sale yourself by carrying back a TD for part of the purchase price. Then, if you need to convert the TD to cash, you will have to sell it at a discount. If the land is remote desert acreage, the discount on the TD will probably be so great that even a 30% loan ratio will be too high. On the other hand, if the land consists of a buildable city lot, it may resell quickly, require no financing on your part, and be safe at a 70% loan ratio. Therefore, you must examine each land TD on its own merits and be guided not at all by formula when deciding on a loan ratio.

Recreational or second-home lots recently sold in a pressure atmosphere usually cannot be assigned a loan ratio because you cannot determine their true market value. But, if the subdivision is an old one, its lots will probably have developed a resale price pattern. You may then be able to loan up to 50% of current market value with safety. In this case, your loan ratio should depend upon the amount of building activity in the area: the more building, the faster the lots will resell; the faster the resales, the less allowance necessary for foreclosure expense.

EXCEPTIONS TO THE LOAN RATIO RULES

A safe loan ratio, in conventional use, is supposed to be the maximum amount you can loan against a property and still recover your investment upon foreclosure. This has been the basis for the previously recommended ratios. But many factors extraneous to the security can enter into the decision. Factors which indirectly alter your risks and therefore create exceptions to the rule. If you are able to make these adjustments, you may be able to command higher TD rates than your competitors.

Short term loans with a balloon payment at the end often warrant a higher loan ratio, when there is evidence of the borrower's ability to meet the final payment on its due date. The shorter the loan period, the less opportunity for the borrower to work himself into bankruptcy, waste the property, or collect other bad habits harmful to the security.

Small TDs justify higher loan ratios if they are more than a year old and the payments are small in comparison to the borrower's income. This is true despite the fact that small-TD foreclosure costs warrant a disproportionately high security margin. In addition to the relative ease of making smaller payments, small-TD borrowers try harder to hold onto their property; they are much more likely than other borrowers to keep up their payments in times of stress.

A fast amortizing TD merits a higher than ordinary loan ratio. The faster the TD amortizes, the sooner the loan ratio is brought to a safe level. A provision in the TD's terms requiring extra payments against loan principal a few months down the line may help accomplish this. The key to this strategy is, again, the borrower's evident ability to sustain the higher debt service. Such a loan will then generally be safe if its loan ratio is brought to a reasonable level within the first six months.

A borrower's credit history influences the loan ratio, too. Not all credit reports are completely bad or exceptionally good. Most fall in between, and the ratios previously recommended are a reflection of that reality. An adjustment of as much as five points (up or down) in the loan ratio is justified for clear deviations from the norm in a credit report.

PROBLEMS TO WATCH OUT FOR IF THERE ARE SENIOR TDS

When placing a loan, it's important that you investigate the nature of any senior TDs present. Your junior position compels you to assume responsibility for them just as much as the borrower does. Indeed, their privilege of foreclosing your access to the security forces you to do so.

Investigation of earlier recorded (senior) TDs is best made before you open escrow for investment in your TD. To do this, you should have in hand a copy of the senior TD's note and deed of trust. If you are making a new loan on a property, the borrower should be able to provide you with these documents. If he has lost his copies of the senior TD, he should be able to get new ones from the lender.

When you receive the senior TD copies, you should ask about — or look for — the following:

Blanket encumbrance. If the senior TD encumbers other property in addition to your security, there may or may not be a problem. In this case, you may need a release clause in the senior so that you can separate your security from the other properties. (For clues on how to deal with this type of problem, see the appendix on Clauses.) Incidentally, blanket encumbrances are looked on with disfavor by most investors, though they are not uniformly bad. Therefore, if you find a blanket encumbrance in the senior TD, you should be able to command a higher rate of return on the 2nd TD.

Due-on-sale clause. (See also the appendix for the impact of this clause when found in a senior TD.) If this clause is present in a TD and turns out to be enforceable, it can force payoff of the TD when the security is sold. This has both good and bad aspects for junior TD lenders. If the borrower sells the property voluntarily, forced payoff of the 1st TD will usually result in a complete refinancing, and any 2nd TDs in the picture will be caught up in the payoff. This being the case, your 2nd TD probably will profit much more than anticipated because prepayments, as explained elsewhere, usually result in bonus profits to the lender. On the other hand, the clause often gives the senior lender the right to call the entire loan due upon changes in junior TD interests in the security. Your foreclosure on a 2nd TD, or even recording a new 2nd TD against the security, may trigger acceleration of the full amount due on a 1st TD — and wipe you out by foreclosure unless you pay up.

Release clause. (Again, see the appendix on Clauses for a detailed evaluation of the various forms of release clause.) The existence, or lack, of an effective release clause in the senior TD is worth noting when the TD's security consists of large acreage. If a senior TD has no release clause, the entire TD will have to be paid off if the borrower wants to sell any part of the acreage. This, then, may make your junior TD more valuable, since such a move would elevate it to 1st trust deed status. On the other hand, a large-acreage senior TD without a release clause decreases the value of the security because of inability to subdivide the property without paying the senior off.

Prepayment penalty. The presence of this clause in the senior TD diminishes the chance that the property will be resold, or that the senior will be paid off. Your chances of profiting from an early payoff are thereby reduced. The market value of the property is also reduced, since sale of the property is inhibited by the clause.

Prepayment privilege. This is a sneaker. The privilege to prepay any TD must appear on the note. In some circumstances (see the Clauses Appendix), its absence in a senior TD can prevent a borrower from early payoff of the senior. Such a restriction has a profound effect on the market value of the security because it makes sale or financing the property more difficult. Unless you make a point of looking for the defect, you may not discover it until too late. You can't expect either an appraiser or a title company to uncover the problem, because examination of the details of the property's financing is not among their duties.

Balance due on the senior TD. You should make a point of comparing the balance owed the senior lender with the balance that should be due if amortized according to the terms of the note. Any significant discrepancy may indicate a defaulting borrower. Worse, it may mean the senior TD holder is lax in his collections and therefore will also be slow to inform you of a default in his TD.

Senior TD payment terms. Unusual interest rates or payment requirements in a 1st TD have a deep influence on its 2nd TD. The value of all real estate is tied to the available financing. The presence of exceptional differences in the 1st TD's terms can therefore do much to either raise or lower the quality of your security. Your prospects of collecting a profit from a prepayment are also affected by the terms of the 1st TD; a complete refinancing and payoff of the 2nd may become necessary to escape the burden of a senior loan with an oppressive interest rate or payment requirements.

Senior TD payment history. The senior TD is a top notch source of information about a borrower's payment habits. If you get a chance, you should always try to examine this part of the borrower's life. If the senior reports a pattern of erratic payments, even though the borrower is now current you can probably anticipate the same treatment.

Part II

WHAT TO WATCH OUT FOR WHEN BUYING AN EXISTING TD

Virtually all the concerns mentioned in Part I of this chapter, on investigating new loans, also apply to investigating the purchase of existing TDs. As a purchaser, however, your investigation is complicated by your inability to command the cooperation of the borrower. Because the borrower's loan is already in place, he has no incentive to help you; he couldn't care less whether you buy the TD.

WHY DOESN'T THE BORROWER BUY THE TD?

A curious phenomenon surrounds the sale of existing TDs: seldom does an inexperienced TD seller consider offering the TD to the borrower. Still, you never know whether the borrower fails to buy the TD because something is wrong with him financially. Ordinarily you would want to ask why, if the discount is so good and the borrower has so much money, you should be so favored as a buyer of the TD. But you can't ask the question because, if you do, it may remind the seller of the borrower and thereby kill your chances of a deal. And even if you do ask the question, you can't count on an honest answer, nor will the answer be verifiable. Therefore, your best strategy in this situation is to simply shut up and rely on other investigative procedures for your protection.

ASK FOR THE SELLER'S TITLE POLICY

The TD seller should have received a title policy insuring his interest in the security at the time his TD was created. It simplifies things for everyone if you collect a copy of the policy at the initial stages of your investigation. Among other things, the policy will include an accurate description of the security's location — important information, because errors in the seller's description of the location are common. If other TDs are secured by the property, they too will show up in the title policy. You will also learn if any easements are recorded against the security, information usually omitted by sellers because they think it unimportant.

With a title policy in hand, your subsequent procedures will also be expedited. Appraisers prefer to work from a title policy's description of the property; they too want to be spared the vagaries of other people's property descriptions. And when the deal goes to escrow, the title policy can be passed on to the escrow officer; escrow officers are delighted to receive the title policy, since they trust participants' descriptions even less.

A WARNING ABOUT 1ST TDS BACKED BY A 2ND TD

Normally, a 1st TD backed by a 2nd TD is considered an exceptionally safe investment. The 2nd acts as a form of guarantor to the 1st, since the 2nd can be cut off by foreclosure if he does not cover the 1st's payments for a defaulting borrower. If the payments pose no problem for the 2nd, human nature will take hold and the 2nd will usually cover the borrower's payments, even though the 2nd may ultimately lose by doing so.

But the presence of a 2nd can signal danger also. If the 2nd is financially unsound and appears likely to file bankruptcy, your access to the security may be impaired. If the 2nd files bankruptcy, the 1st will be stayed from foreclosing simply to protect the 2nd's security interest. The stay, in this instance, applies even though the borrower himself is not in bankruptcy and is resigned to loss of the property by your foreclosure. (For more on this subject, see the appendix on Bankruptcy.)

ASK FOR COPIES OF THE NOTE AND DEED OF TRUST

As part of your investigation, you should ask the seller for copies of his original note and deed of trust so that you may examine them for potential problems. Copies of these documents must ultimately be provided the escrow anyway, so you might as well call for them now. If they have any defects, now is the time to find them, since it's much easier to cancel the deal at this stage.

HOW TO EXAMINE THE NOTE AND DEED OF TRUST

On receipt of copies of the note and deed of trust, set aside time for an uninterrupted examination of their details. You will want to be able to look at each document with microscopic care in order to spot the least inconsistency in these papers. Inconsistency is the flag you look for in this sort of examination. It may be your first clue to a deeply buried problem which could rise to haunt you later on.

Compare all signatures found in both the deed of trust and the note. The signatures must correspond with the way the names appear in the documents. Compare all signatures in the note and deed of trust with those that appear in other documents; discrepancies could indicate a forgery.

Most investors rely solely on title insurance for protection from defects in signatures, and that's a mistake. The kind of examination described above costs little in time, while no form of title insurance will ever fully compensate you for the problems created by a fraudulent TD.

Compare the stated current balance of the note with the balance when amortized according to its terms. A significant difference may mean the borrower has defective payment habits; or it may mean there has been an undisclosed amendment to the note which could create endless problems related to its seniority (see Modification Trap in the chapter on Administration). If there has been an honest error in calculation of the loan balance, discovery at this stage may also save you from overpaying for the TD.

WHAT TO LOOK FOR IN SECOND HAND TDS

If you are buying a TD from someone who bought it from the original lender, you will need copies of documentation evidencing his ownership of the TD. The evidence of ownership comes in three parts:

(1) a copy of a title policy insuring the second owner's interest in the TD;

(2) the original lender's endorsement on the back of the note transferring ownership to the second owner; and

(3) a recorded assignment of the deed of trust transferring the beneficial ownership of the TD to the second owner.

To protect yourself, you must subject the documents to the same close scrutiny previously given the note and deed of trust. Watch especially for the wording used in the transfer. The chances are high that something will have been done in the endorsement which weakens the TD. As explained in the chapter on Escrow, there are various forms of transfer, and the least effective form is often used. Whatever form is used, you will inherit its limitations when the seller passes the TD on to you.

WHAT TO LOOK FOR IF THERE IS A "POWER OF ATTORNEY"

If any of the documents you have seen have been signed by an "attorney-in-fact," you should ask for a copy of the "power of attorney." A power of attorney is a written authority to sign documents and perform other acts on behalf of someone else. To serve your requirements, the power of attorney should have been recorded in the county in which the TD's security is located.

You should ask for a copy of the power of attorney because your title insuror will need it before insuring your ownership in the TD. You will also want to examine it to see if you can detect a problem which will kill the deal later on. If the seller does not have a copy, he should be able to get one from the county recorder.

A recorded power of attorney is supposed to be rescinded by also recording a revocation with the county recorder. Nevertheless, title insurors routinely ask for an affirmation of the power if it is more than a year old, even when a revocation has not been recorded. So should you.

The usual defect found in a power of attorney stems from an inability of the attorney-in-fact to do all the things he thinks he can: the power of attorney may have expired; the document may give authority only over a different piece of property; it may not permit the attorney-in-fact to transfer ownership in the TD; or it may not allow him to pledge property as security on a loan. Only those acts named on the form are allowed, and it's all too easy to omit something through oversight.

CHAPTER 8

Appraisal of the Security

The important point to remember about appraisals is that you should never trust the opinion of experts. You always run the risk that an expert's valuation of a property will be distorted by self-interest, misunderstanding of your objectives, or simple ignorance. Therefore, you must always be prepared to check the accuracy of an appraisal and follow your own instincts about the property, no matter how impressive an appraiser's credentials, no matter how well reasoned his valuation of the property.

Instinct plays a part in all intelligent property valuations, whether by a professional or a layman. The appraisal numbers, by themselves, can otherwise be too misleading. A professional appraiser, truly expert about a property, develops an immediate "feel" about its real value when looking at it. If the property valuation is complicated, he may make a few calculations on the back of an envelope, but that's all. The rest of his appraisal is a process of "backing into" a decision sometimes already unconsciously made. He accumulates additional data only to prove the accuracy of the valuation to himself, and to convince his client that he has done enough work to justify his fee.

In trust deed investment, most of the time you will only have to engage in what is called "review appraisal:" somebody tells you what he thinks the property is worth, and you check around to verify the accuracy of his valuation. Usually this involves little more than visiting the property and checking with a few local real estate brokers to determine how much similar properties in the area have sold for. Once you have information sufficient for a decision, you need waste no further time gathering additional data; it's the quality of information that counts, not the quantity.

You should never fail to go out and look at the property yourself before accepting it as security. This rule applies even when investing through a loan broker who, presumably, has done your investigation for you. In looking at property yourself, you often pick up unexpected details which will help you in management of the TD later on. More important, you gain a more accurate picture of the property. Oral or written descriptions — and even photographs — are never sufficient for property valuation; they only provide a mind's-eye image of the security that is invariably altered by an actual visit.

Your review of an appraisal should include a search for pitfalls in the property's valuation, traps which are easily detected once you know what to look for, but are often ignored through lack of attention. This chapter shows you what to watch for to uncover problems of this kind.

ABOUT LENDER PROPERTY VALUATIONS

Lenders value real estate differently than other people. Lenders must look at a property in terms of its forced liquidation value and forced liquidations seldom approach full market value, especially when the property is vacant land or income property. Most people determine a property's value by comparison with the highest recent sales prices of similar local properties.

Lenders must value a property at its lowest sales price — and go back a year or more to find it — and then sometimes discount the price still more to eliminate distortions caused by creative financing.

APPRAISAL PRELIMINARIES

As pointed out before, one of the secrets of profitable trust deed investment is the early elimination of unsuitable trust deeds. Since inflated representations of property values are one of the most common causes for rejecting TD offerings, it pays to develop a system of reviewing as much of the property value as possible from your desk — before committing yourself to the time and expense of a visit to the property.

Use a telephone as much as possible at this stage. For this purpose, a library of telephone directories comes in handy. By telephone you can call brokers local to the property and possibly get a preliminary reading of its value. Local government agencies, title companies, nearby property owners, appraisers, and many other sources of information are at your fingertips through a local telephone directory.

If the property is acreage with a rural location, look it up on a geological survey map (see the Sources of Information Appendix); if the map shows that the property is an inaccessible mountain top, you will be saved a drive to the property to discover the same thing. These maps also may reveal whether the property is located in the middle of a natural watercourse, on a flood plain, or on an unbuildable slope.

At this stage, you may be provided with a copy of an assessor's map of the property. Such a map can also tell you much about the property's real value. Public roads and utility easements are generally shown on assessor's maps. Verification of property lines and parcel size is also made easier when you have one of these maps.

If the property is described by "metes and bounds," you should ask for a map of its boundaries so that you can find its exact location when you visit the property. If a map is not provided, you will need to plot the property's boundaries yourself, or have someone do it for you. "Metes and bounds" is a method of describing the direction of a property's boundaries in terms of their degree of angle found on a compass. It is a form of description increasingly rare in California as the law forces more and more property locations to be described by subdivision map (see the Legal Descriptions portion of Appendix A). Whenever a metes and bounds description is used, you can assume the property has erratic boundaries, and that the boundaries will be difficult to find unless you have a map on hand when you visit the site.

LOCAL BROKERS — THE SECRET TO REAL ESTATE APPRAISAL

One of the best kept secrets about appraisal is the extraordinary value of local real estate brokers as a source of information. No one will have as much information about a property as a nearby real estate broker. He will have an amazingly detailed picture of its history, covering the circumstances of each of its prior sales, as well as its past sales prices:

"So and so died and his widow sold the house to XYZ, who ran the place down something terrible before he sold it to ABC, who has been doing a pretty good job fixing it up since then. ABC paid $X for the place, but he got it at a bargain since it was so run down, and the market was depressed at that time anyway. Right now the place should sell for $XX if you get the right kind of financing."

Though professional appraisers don't usually like to admit it, even they make a practice of visiting one or more local brokers and rely heavily on broker information.

Best of all, the local broker's information is free. All real estate sales people like to talk to lenders. They are flattered when someone asks them for information. If you mention that you are a private lender, they will be even more interested in talking to you. Financing is the principal lubricant in every real estate sale, and brokers always have a sale in a state of near collapse because "the right kind of financing" is unavailable; they all live in hope of finding someone who will loan at below market interest rates and thus save a sale.

Extracting the information does require patience, however. The conversation tends to follow a pattern: If you ask the broker his opinion of the property's current market value, you will learn that the property "is worth no more than someone will pay for it," and you will have a deuce of a time distracting him from contemplation of the wisdom of that homily. A better approach is to ask him what price he would pay for the property if he intended to turn around and resell it at a profit. Better yet, restrict your questions to only the sales history of the subject property and its neighbors.

A word of caution about broker valuations. If the property is bare land, the local broker's information can be misleading. His office may be a front for, or otherwise economically tied to, the success of the area's principal developer. If so, the information he provides will always carry an element of "hype" brought on by a need to promote profitable sales.

VIEWING THE PROPERTY — WHAT TO LOOK FOR

When you visit the property, carry a camera with you so that you can take pictures of it. Professional appraisers routinely take pictures as an aid in describing a property to their clients. Your purpose is different, however; you want evidence of the "before" condition of the property in the event the owner later ruins it through neglect. If the owner starts to "waste" your TD's security through deferred maintenance (see Waste, in Appendix B on Clauses), you will have evidence of the fact. With pictures as evidence of waste, you then have enough ammunition to foreclose and thereby stop further loss of your security. With pictures, you also have enough tangible evidence to go to court and enjoin the owner from further damaging the property.

HOW TO AVOID APPRAISING THE NEIGHBOR'S PROPERTY

It's easy to appraise the wrong property; even experienced appraisers do it every once in a while. The address you have been given may be wrong, or you may write it down wrong. Sometimes a borrower will deliberately give you the location of a more valuable neighboring property, to dupe you into lending more than his property is worth. And sometimes you will appraise the wrong property without any assistance, simply because you become confused about which direction you are pointed.

Most errors in property location occur when the security is a single lot within a large tract of similar lots of a subdivision. If you are not certain where the property is located, your best protection is identification of the lot by means of an assessor's map. On arrival at the property, count the number of lots from the nearest street corner to the property address, and then compare the location with that shown on the map. If you do not have an assessor's map in hand, make a memorandum of your count of the intervening lots, and then compare the count with a copy of the map received later on.

HOW TO FIND PROPERTY LINES

Most of the time you do not have to search out the property's boundary lines; the boundary will be evident from the fencing, or the boundaries will be unimportant because the property is bare land, no different from its neighbors. Sometimes, however, you will have to make a special effort to find the boundaries, to verify that there are no encroachments or unusual features that might detract from the property value.

The traditional way of finding a property's boundary is by pacing the distance from a known point (such as a street corner) to the edge of the property. Then you pace the property's boundary for a visual grasp of the character of the property. This is easy to do because each person has a natural length of stride which can be used as a means of measurement. While conventional wisdom says that the stride should be three feet long, most people cannot reach that distance without stretching; and when they stretch, their accuracy falls off. The best measurement is a comfortable pace where the length is determined by experimentation. Count the number of steps needed to walk a known distance in your normal manner, and then divide the distance by the number of steps to find your average pace length. With only a little practice, you soon will be able to pace distances of 100 feet or more with an accuracy of plus or minus five percent, even when your path is obstructed by rocks and bushes.

More exact measurements of property lines are sometimes necessary in order to be sure there are no encroachments on the property (see Special Problems in Appendix A). For this purpose, appraisers use a wheeled device which they push along the ground. The mechanism's wheel is coupled with a counter which translates the wheel's rotations into feet and inches. The type used by professional appraisers customarily has a wheel diameter of 12 inches or more. This variety can be expensive, but it also is very accurate. Cheaper versions, made out of plastic and with a much smaller wheel diameter, also are available. They too are capable of doing the job so long as the wheel is rolled on a smooth surface.

LOOK AT THE LAY OF THE LAND

When you look at the land:

- Ask yourself whether the property appears to have the remnants of a natural water course through any part of it. If it does, even if the water course is now a dry, shallow ditch, that part of the property may be unbuildable because of limits imposed by the municipal building department.

- Look at the slope of the land to see whether it is a continuation of a gentle slope from neighboring properties. If so, the building department will probably claim it subject to "sheet overflow" of water (even in the middle of the desert), and prohibit any building unless its floor level is 18 or more inches above the surrounding terrain.

- Look also for an unbuildable slope on any part of the land. Unbuildable, in this case, does not mean that you cannot build; it means only that construction on that part of the property is impractical.

- Look for heavy brush, or even thick grass, near those boundaries of the property close to neighboring structures. If the brush or grass can be construed to be a fire hazard (even though it is native growth) the local fire department will probably demand an expensive weed abatement project if you foreclose on your loan. (They wait until after a foreclosure because they figure a lender can better afford the cost of the abatement work.)

- Look for signs of a regularly used pathway across the property. This could be considered a "prescriptive easement" (see Special Problems, Appendix A), which gives users of the path the right of its continued use, despite your protestations.

- If the property does not front on a public roadway, look for the legal route of access to the property (you may need an assessor's map for this). If the only right of access to the property requires climbing a steep slope, legal entry may be impractical, and the property will be landlocked and un-buildable. (See also Access, in Appendix A.)

- Look for signs of encroachment or intrusion by neighboring property owners in the form of construction which overlaps the property lines. (The problem this creates is also discussed in Appendix A.)

WHAT TO LOOK FOR IN THE PROPERTY'S BUILDINGS

When you visit the property, you should especially watch for the following because they are commonly missed in appraisal:

- The condition of the building, its landscaping, and that of its neighbors, is all important. No matter how expensive the building may be, if it is declining for lack of care, or if the neighborhood is declining, the trend will probably accelerate and the property will be worth less in the future.

- Look for signs that the building was put up in an exceptionally slap-dash manner. All buildings seem to show some signs of sloppy work, but some are so bad that you can be sure that, with the inferior materials probably used, their decline in value will be much more rapid than normal. (They also will be much more difficult to insure.)

- An often overlooked concern is whether the building is serviced from the same utility meter as the building on an adjoining parcel. Not many people realize that this can be done, but common metering does some-times happen when a property is divided but the division goes unre-ported. When it does happen, you can be sure the cost of arranging separate utility services after a foreclosure will be staggering. That's the reason separate metering was not installed in the first place.

- Look for signs of recent construction in the building. This may tell you that the property is subject to a "mechanic's lien" (see Special Problems, Appendix A), which has a higher security claim to the property than your TD.

HOW TO MEASURE A BUILDING

Most of the time, you will not have to measure the size of the building because it will have been done for you, or other steps in your review will eliminate the need to do so. If you do have to measure the building, you can make the task easy. All you have to do is measure the exterior dimensions of the building, excluding less valuable appendages such as porches, garages, carports, etc. The square foot size of a building is not measured on a room-by-room basis, as many people think; the only time you must measure individual room dimensions is when it is necessary to segregate portions of the building because of their radically different construction costs (such as offices located within a warehouse).

Large buildings can be measured with sufficient accuracy by stepping their dimensions off, using the pacing procedure described earlier. With smaller buildings, you will probably need to make direct measurements, and this can be done with the "wheel" described earlier; simply run the wheel on the outside walls of the building to find its dimensions.

In some cases, the building's walls may not have to be measured in order to know its size. An experienced appraiser or real estate sales person can accurately estimate the square footage of a tract home simply by looking at it — and so can you after you have measured a few such properties.

WHEN YOU VISIT AN APARTMENT OR COMMERCIAL BUILDING

If the property is an apartment or commercial building, you should consider talking to some of the tenants during your visit. Verification of the rental rate in this manner is always a good idea because owners tend to exaggerate these figures. You also may want to talk to the tenants to find out whether they have any offset claims against the owner (offset claims, and the problems they represent, are discussed in the Escrow chapter, which follows). A brief chat with some of the tenants will also be profitable because it gives a far more vivid picture of the condition of the building, its maintenance, and the character of the prospective borrower, than you could ever gain from behind a desk.

WHAT TO LOOK FOR IN AN INDUSTRIAL BUILDING

When you visit an industrial property, look for features which make it useful to the largest variety of prospective buyers. Many industrial buildings are constructed only to the needs of the building's original occupant; to build for wider use would be a waste of money, in the developer's view. But this tends to limit the number of businesses that can use the building. The market value is thereby reduced, sometimes far below the cost of its construction, a fact not always taken into account in property valuations.

Among the features needed for a marketable industrial building is sufficient ceiling height in its non-office portion. A height of 14 feet or more is desirable, for it satisfies the needs of almost all businesses. A 12-foot height is almost as good. If the building does not have enough ceiling height, there is little chance that it can be altered later on.

An industrial building's electrical service never seems to be enough to satisfy its occupants; they always seem to be tinkering with the system at mind-boggling expense. To find out how heavy the electrical service is, ask the present occupant; you will learn more about the adequacy of the building's service than you would ever want to know, for it's a favorite topic among these people.

Look also for loading docks, the more the better. This is another item which must be incorporated into the building when first constructed. Even though loading docks may be superfluous to the building's present occupant, they give the building an exceptional premium in the resale market because they are not all that common.

WHAT TO LOOK FOR IN AGRICULTURAL PROPERTY

Agricultural property requires the attention of an appraiser specializing in the specific type of farming underway. Even then, agricultural lending is such a chancy business you can never be sure about one expert's opinion of the property's value. Therefore, it pays to check an agricultural appraisal with local brokers, farmers and suppliers to the business. Even though you know nothing about farming, it will also pay to visit the property yourself and form your own opinion about its operation.

When you look at the property, don't fail to observe the condition of the crop. Does the crop appear healthy, or does it look stunted? How does it compare with neighboring crops? If the crop is less than that of its neighbors, is it because of inferior soil or water or terrain? If there are no neighbors with a similar crop, is it possible the land is devoted to the wrong crop?

If the property is served by well water, is the well located on the portion pledged as your security? (If it isn't, you will be without a well after foreclosure.) And if there is a well, how much is it worth? How old is it? (Wells have a limited lifespan which depends on local soil conditions.) Has the well been tested recently as to the volume of water pumped? How stable is the water table the pump draws upon?

FURTHER REVIEW

Much of the time, the person you are dealing with will hand you supplemental documents to support his representation of the property value. These should always be reviewed if only because they cost so little in time to do so. If you know what to look for, they may offer crucial information about the property's value.

TITLE REPORTS

If the property owner hands you a copy of his title insurance, look at the dollar amount of insurance shown on the policy. A title policy issued to a property owner insures him in an amount equal to his purchase price; if it differs from prior information you have received about the sale price, someone may be trying to deceive you. Check the title policy's description of the property location; though by now you may be sick of the property's legal description, the slight additional effort is worth while, because an error here is catastrophic. Check the title policy also for mention of additional encumbrances, or easements, that you have not been told of; half the time you will learn something new because owners skip this sort of information thinking it "unimportant."

ASK FOR COMPARABLE SALES DATA

The very best proof of a property's market value is the price other people have paid for similar properties. These are called "comps." If you have not gathered enough "comps" already, you may be able to collect more by calling the local brokers, title companies, and the owners of adjacent properties. If you don't have the time for such an effort, ask the person you are dealing with to make the search for you. For a nominal sum, you also may be able to obtain a professional appraiser's oral report of the comps contained in his files.

No property is perfectly comparable to another in real estate. Each is unique in one manner or another. To make comparisons between properties, you must make estimated dollar adjustments for the differences between them. Adjustments are necessary for such matters as different features in the buildings, differences in location, and for the length of time since the comparable sale took place.

Comparable sales can be misleading due to the circumstances of the sale. Sale prices on bare land are especially unreliable in this regard; people who buy this kind of property usually do so by mistake, not knowing the property's defects until long after the sale is consummated. Watch out, too, for evidence that the sale price of the property is inflated because the seller financed the sale at easy terms; when people buy real estate, they buy the financing right along with the property and an attractive loan package can inflate a sale price as much as 50 percent.

APPRAISALS BY THE COUNTY ASSESSOR

Each county in California has a tax assessor who, for purposes of taxation, fixes a value on each parcel of real estate in the county. If you use the right approach (see the Information Sources appendix), you may be able to pry loose important background information used by the assessor in reaching his valuations. The valuations themselves are otherwise a matter of public record but are of negligible use in the appraisal of property.

Assessor's values are often represented as being uniformly low and therefore considered a floor in any valuation of a property. The fact is, the assessor's valuations are sometimes too high, especially when his staff is unable to keep up with a rapid decline in property values in any given area.

HOW TO USE A DEED AS A PROOF OF VALUE

A copy of a deed on an adjacent property, obtained from the county recorder, may tell you how much the property sold for. Each sales transaction in real property is taxed at a rate based on the transaction price. This tax amount is shown on the face of the deed (it may also be shown on the unrecorded back of the deed instead, to hide the sales price, but this is a trick not often used). The tax rate is 55 cents for each $500 (or fraction thereof) of the property's sales price. If there is an existing loan on the property, and the buyer takes over the loan, the loan amount is deducted from the taxable sales price. Therefore, in those transactions where there is no existing financing, or where you can estimate the amount of the existing financing, you can calculate the property's sales price from the amount of tax. Beware, however, of the all-too-common ploy of creating a false property value by paying extra taxes; borrowers sometimes use this stunt to obtain a larger loan.

ABOUT PHONY ESCROWS

Investors in existing trust deeds are often shown escrow documents as proof of the property's escrow sales price. This kind of information requires investigation before it is accepted as evidence of property value.

In the past, fraudulent or misleading entries on escrow statements have been made to encourage investors to purchase TDs created during the escrow. The fact that such entries are illegal protects you but little once your money is invested and the people you have been talking to disappear.

One way the fraud is perpetrated is to show an escrow statement with a buyer's substantial down payment against an inflated purchase price for the property (most TD investors believe that the more cash the buyer puts into a property, the more valid the sales price). But to create the down payment, the seller and buyer separately agree that the buyer is to later receive reimbursement for charges such as a "referral fee" which rebates part or all of the down payment. The TD is then sold at a deep discount when it comes out of the escrow, but still at a price more than the property is worth. The borrower on the TD (buyer of the property) then defaults, lets the property go by foreclosure, and he and the seller disappear with the TD investor's money.

To detect this kind of fraud, the escrow company should be scrutinized as to its independence. Though the deception can be carried on without the connivance of the escrow, it requires a level of affability found only in people with closely related business interests. Ask yourself if the escrow company is owned by, or connected in some way with, the broker making the sale? Is the escrow company still in business? How long has it been in business?

The details of the escrow agreement should also be examined. Does it show that part of the property's purchase price was exchanged real estate? If so, how do you know the valuation of the exchanged property was reasonable? Real estate exchanges are a common feature these days, largely as a result of their tax advantages. But when an exchange escrow is involved, the exchange values are purely arbitrary. Both the buyer and seller can (and usually do) overvalue their exchanged property by equal amounts, thereby inflating the transaction price.

THE USE OF FEE APPRAISALS

On occasion, you will be provided a copy of an appraisal made by a professional in the business. The appraisal usually appears in a "narrative" form. That is, the appraisal details the data gathered by the appraiser and explains the way he reaches his opinion of the property's value. This kind of appraisal is always a valuable document to have. It contains a wealth of information about the property that you probably would never have the opportunity to dig out by yourself.

The appraiser's *opinion* of the property value may not, however, be so useful. The quality of his opinion is subject to his degree of expertise in the type of property under consideration. The appraiser may also be influenced by his perception of the needs of the person who hires him. If he has been hired by a lender, he may be too conservative in his appraisal (he thinks he can never be faulted as long as his valuation is too low). On the other hand, if the borrower hires him, his opinion could be tilted toward the high side, because the borrower shops the appraisal around until he finds an appraiser who will give the highest valuation. In fact, the tendency to be influenced is so common that it has become a source of a trite joke, even among appraisers: One of their most prestigious professional organizations identifies its members with the designation "Master Appraisal Institute," or by the initials "MAI." Members take pride in the label, for it requires extensive evidence of professional competence, and is not lightly bestowed. Nevertheless, it's become an overworn observation among real estate people that the letters stand for "made as instructed," so often are the member's value judgments affected.

Appraisers can also be wrong because they are too sterile in their approach. There are three classical methods of valuing a piece of property:

(1) Comparison of the subject property with past sales prices of comparable properties (i.e., "comps").

(2) The cost of replacement of the subject property.

(3) The price at which an (income) property becomes economically feasible for investment purposes.

Each of these approaches is statistical. They each are based on verifiable historical data. And an appraiser is undeniably correct when using any one or more of them in arriving at the value of a property. Yet the value of a property can also be affected by the public's current perception of the property's future market trend (called speculation) in a way never shown by historical data. Furthermore, none of the statistical approaches mandates an appraiser's adjustment for the quality of construction; two office buildings of equal size, located next door to each other, can have exactly the same valuation—even though one is built with such shabby materials it would need an investment of an additional $100,000 to bring it to the level of the other.

THE PERFECT APPRAISAL

The perfect appraisal never existed. An approximation can sometimes be obtained, however, if the property is encumbered by a 1st TD. If the 1st TD lender is a mortgage banker, he likely will have an exceptionally high grade appraisal on file, primarily because he knows how to choose an appraiser who is both competent and independent of the borrower. If so, the mortgage banker may be willing to let you look at the appraisal, especially if you can convince him that your entry as a junior lender will help him. If permission to read the appraisal is refused, you can accomplish virtually the same result by asking him what his loan ratio requirements are. Borrowers invariably try for the highest loan amount a lender will tolerate. You therefore can calculate the 1st TD lender's appraisal by dividing the original amount of the loan (say, $70,000) by the loan ratio (say, 70 percent), to arrive at the property value (in this case, $100,000).

GOVERNMENTAL LIMITS ON VALUE

In California, the use of every piece of privately owned property is controlled in some way by state, county, or city regulation, and sometimes by federal regulation also. Any appraisal of California real estate is therefore incomplete without allowance for the regulatory impact on market value.

Most of the time, the effect of government regulation is automatically reckoned when you base your valuation on comparable sales in the area. For instance, prior sales of essentially similar houses within the same tract will all reflect the same influence of government on market value. If the properties differ in any material way, however, the disparity in government regulation prevents measurement by comparison.

In this regard, a few high risk situations stand out. Watch out especially when the security you have been offered is:

- Unimproved acreage.

- An unimproved lot within a recreational subdivision.

- Commercial or industrial property within an area undergoing transition from one type of use to another.

- Property with buildings that have been changed structurally.

In each of these situations you may need to protect yourself by checking with various governmental agencies to make sure there are no hidden traps.

THE MUNICIPAL PLANNING DEPARTMENT

All private property in California is "zoned." "Zoning" is the attempt to classify land by limiting its use to specified activities. Use of the land in a manner outside this classification can bring administrative, and even criminal, sanctions down on the property owner. The local municipality's "planning department" is the agency charged with administering this part of the law. The planning department therefore is one of the most important reference points you have as to a property's value.

The effect of a property's zoning goes far beyond the surface objectives of the law. Bureaucracies don't function well in a vacuum; they require specific rules to be able to operate effectively. Planning departments therefore tend to require ever more detailed zoning classifications. Standards are often set in such matters as the size of the parcel of land to be used, the maximum number of occupants, the shape of the parcel, the amount of parking to be provided, the distance buildings must be set back from property lines, and even the size of rooms in the buildings. Failure to meet these requirements causes the property to be branded "substandard," and further construction or use of the property can be prohibited.

Changes in zoning laws can wipe out the value of your security with frightening rapidity, especially when "down zoning" occurs. Down zoning is the reduction in intensity of those uses of a property permitted under a community's zoning laws. For example, land which is zoned to permit apartment construction is suddenly rezoned to a much less valuable classification such as single family residential; or land zoned for heavy industrial use is reclassified to light industrial; and land zoned for single family residential is sometimes even reclassified to open space (no construction at all).

Down zoning seldom occurs if the property has structural improvements on it which are being actively used. The greatest risk of down zoning occurs when a community undergoes a fit of tidying up its growth patterns. When that happens, the municipal government usually takes a swipe at inoculating itself against intensive use of the land. Unimproved property located in areas undergoing transition then becomes particularly susceptible to reclassification.

WHEN TO CHECK WITH THE BUILDING DEPARTMENT

Whenever you see a building which shows signs of haphazard or abnormal construction, you may be looking at work that has been done without the approval of the municipal building department. Every work of improvement on every piece of privately held land in California requires a building permit from a government building department. To obtain a permit, the work must be done in conformance with certain minimum standards of quality. Many people try to save money by circumventing the process, and construct to a cheaper, less stringent, standard. If the unauthorized work is discovered, the municipality can fine the property owner, demand that the building be torn down, or require that the work be rebuilt to meet the minimum standards. In any event, cure of "substandard" construction can be a monumentally expensive process, and the part of the property so afflicted must be reckoned nearly valueless.

If the proposed security consists of unimproved land located in a community with a recent sharp increase in population, a brief call to the local building department may then also be in order. You may find the land completely unbuildable, in this instance. If increased population puts an intolerable strain on municipal services, one or more local governmental agencies will step in and issue a moratorium on further construction until the problem is corrected. This commonly happens when a community relies on individual septic tanks as a means of sewage disposal; too many septic tanks can then trigger a moratorium when it is feared that the water they throw off will pollute the underground water supply. Inadequate water systems are also a cause for building moratoriums; construction is stopped in this case because the community suspects the water supply may be stretched too thin to serve the needs of its residents.

SPECIAL PROBLEMS IN APPRAISAL

This chapter has been devoted to routinely encountered pitfalls in the valuation of real estate, problems you should be aware of if you are to review the valuation of any piece of real estate. There are also other, less frequent, pitfalls which you need to know about, but only when reviewing the specialized types of real estate in which they are found. Special traps of this sort have been relegated to the back of this book, in Appendix A, for reference when the occasion arises.

The following types of property are those most likely to carry the sort of specialized risks described in Appendix A:

- Condominium units.

- Restaurants and other types of commercial property that require special equipment.

- Raw land with a location described by something other than a subdivision parcel number (see the "Legal Description" and "Legal Subdivision" subsections of the appendix).

- Raw land which is reached only by crossing a neighbor's property (see the Legal Access and Easements subsection).

- Any kind of property with a neighboring structure which protrudes over intervening property lines (see the Encroachments and Property Lines subsection of Appendix A).

- Any kind of building which shows signs of recent construction (see the Mechanic's Liens subsection).

CHAPTER 9

Escrow

The most important thing to know about escrows is that the escrow company will inevitably foul up the job somewhere along the line. Escrow fees are simply too small, considering the complexity of the job, to warrant the attention necessary for perfect performance.

Fortunately, most escrow errors are minor or can be offset by other procedures. If you chance upon a poor escrow officer, however, major damaging errors will occur with such unsettling frequency that even the most expert observer will be unable to catch them all. And if the errors are not discovered before the escrow closes, repair of the damage may not be possible.

Know also that almost all escrows are biased to some degree, despite the profession's representations to the contrary. No matter how much escrow officers try to maintain their independence, their operations are always influenced — in sometimes subtle, unconscious ways.

Occasionally, you can bypass the complications of escrow by skipping the entire process; you and the other party may simply exchange money and documents across a table instead of passing them through an intermediary. But situations where you can do this are rare. Most of the time you need someone who stands between the parties and acts as a sort of stakesholder — an escrow officer who collects the money and documents, and then dispenses them when the transaction is completed. This way, you can also unload all the mind-numbing detail of the paperwork on the person who handles the escrow.

ESCROW BASICS

An escrow is given substance when the principals in the transaction (buyer/seller, lender/borrower) draw up "escrow instructions," which are addressed to a third party who has agreed to be a stakes holder. When the principals sign the escrow instructions, the document becomes a contract binding them to perform their share of the transaction as described. The instructions are therefore often also called an "escrow agreement."

To provide the escrow with cash necessary for its performance, an opening deposit from the TD investor is generally given the escrow holder along with the signed escrow instructions. The balance of the money due from the investor is paid shortly before close of the escrow upon notice from the escrow officer of the exact amount due. In order to avoid delaying the escrow's close for clearance of the investor's personal check, final payment is usually made by cashier's check.

When all the participants to the escrow have finished their respective tasks in the instructions, the escrow holder sends the insuring title company those documents which need to be recorded. The title company then "brings down the title;" that is, verifies that there have been no intervening claims recorded since the escrow was opened. Recording usually occurs the next day, whereupon the escrow holder completes the transaction by distributing the remaining documents and cash in the manner directed.

Depending on the documents required and their availability, an escrow may take anywhere from a couple of hours to several weeks.

PREPARATIONS FOR ESCROW

For the TD investor, the most important part of an escrow occurs before it starts. The decisions made and actions you take at this stage determine the strength of your position, and therefore the success of your objectives during escrow.

THE OPENING DEPOSIT DECISION

One of your key objectives in the escrow should be limitation of your cash commitment until the very end of the process. Ideally, your opening escrow deposit should be barely enough to keep the deal alive.

Many layman investors are lured into opening the escrow with a hefty initial payment because escrows usually contain phrasing which provide for the automatic return of their money if the terms of the agreement are not met. But as a practical matter, you must assume that any money you deposit in escrow will be locked in until the other party releases it. Even though the escrow may stipulate the return of funds on the failure of some contingency, the other party may otherwise find some way to dispute the refund and allege that the escrow company's return of the money was in violation of the terms of the agreement. Unless you have an escrow officer willing to take a chance on your behalf, the signed consent of both parties to the transaction will be required before refunding any part of the deposit.

If the parties to the escrow cancel and cannot agree on terms for dispersal of funds previously deposited, the money simply remains in the escrow's bank account until it "escheats" to the state (that is, becomes property of the state), or until the escrow files "an action in interpleader." The latter procedure is a petition for judicial determination of the dispersal and is done at the expense of the principals to the transaction. To avoid such a confrontation, the investor usually must buy the other party's signed release of the escrow in order to retrieve the remainder of his deposit.

Given a sufficiently miserly opening payment, you can expect much anguish and lamentation among others interested in the transaction, depending on their degree of experience. In hopes you will feel more committed to the deal, a savvy broker or TD seller will try to talk you into opening the escrow with a maximum amount of money "in order to show your earnest intent." But the more money you deposit, the more you'll be inclined to accept negative information which shows up during escrow; rather than fight for return of the deposit, you're apt to minimize the importance of the information. If you give too much attention to cries of protest and deposit the full amount demanded, you may end up with a TD you wouldn't otherwise consider acceptable.

THE PROS AND CONS OF BROKER-DIRECTED ESCROWS

Most TD investors place their money with the aid of a broker and let the broker act as escrow holder for the transaction. There are important advantages in this kind of arrangement. Brokers usually are able to perform the service without charge since it involves only negligible additional effort on their part. The broker's escrow is also inherently more efficient because he already has possession of all the documents and is acquainted with the details of the transaction.

Nevertheless, broker escrows are rarely the best approach. Since the broker's commission is dependent on completion of the transaction, his handling of the escrow's paperwork may be influenced by his need to close the deal. Furthermore, such bias may not be evident; every escrow can, to some degree, be jiggered one way or another and still remain within the realm of acceptable conduct. Therefore, unless you're convinced the broker is completely reliable, an outside escrow, selected and supervised by yourself (perhaps with the aid of the broker), is the best arrangement.

All rules have exceptions: Whatever his weaknesses, the broker's escrow may be the best choice if he plainly will perform better than anybody else known to you. Short of outright fraud, almost any experienced TD broker's escrow can be made acceptable if you insist on use of your own paperwork procedures, as described in this chapter. On the other hand, an inept outside escrow officer, ignorant of TDs, may be virtually impossible to control; such people can slip errors past your defenses in ways that seem to approach genius in their imagination.

CHOOSE YOUR OWN ESCROW OFFICER

The escrow holder is supposed to be chosen by both parties to the transaction, acting in unison. In actuality, you alone can specify the escrow holder. You have the money, and if you insist on your choice strongly enough, making it a deal breaker, the other side will almost always back down.

If you're dealing with an experienced trust deed seller or broker, you'll run into strong resistance to your efforts to choose the escrow officer. The other party will demand choice of his preferred escrow officer because he "knows" the person is competent, the officer has handled many escrows for him in the past, all his escrows are processed through that particular officer. But the other party's close relationship with the escrow officer is your strongest reason for avoiding such a person; if there's going to be any bias in the escrow, you might as well make sure it's tilted toward you instead of the other person.

FINDING THE BEST ESCROW

When searching for the best escrow holder, concentrate on choosing the escrow officer and not the escrow company. The escrow officer manages all the transaction's paperwork for the company and is the focal point of all the activity. If you have an incompetent escrow officer, no amount of company procedure can fully protect you.

The distance from an escrow company's offices should not be a factor in your choice of an escrow officer. It's possible to deal with an officer for years by mail and telephone, without meeting the person face to face, and still get good service.

Escrows conducted by title companies are commonly thought to be more reliable. There is some tendency in that direction, but it is only minor.

Bank connected escrows are a poor place to look for a TD escrow officer. Something about the banking business reduces the odds that a competent TD escrow will be conducted.

Escrow officers who are experienced in completing the Truth-In-Lending paperwork (see the Escrow Appendix) required for some types of new loans are especially valuable. Real competence among escrow officers in this part of TD investment is so precious that many defects normally considered important can be overlooked.

An escrow office's use of preprinted escrow forms for TD transactions indicates valuable experience in TDs someplace in the organization; at least somebody in the office has been busy enough with TDs to try to save time with already-typed TD escrow forms.

An escrow officer's experience in other than TD transactions is worth little. In fact, lack of TD experience by such people sometimes poses a greater danger than an error-prone escrow officer; they often try to bluff their way through the job, and that can be dangerous unless you are experienced enough to call them on it.

Avoid escrow officers with a crowded or cluttered office. All escrow officers have to handle numerous escrows at the same time. In order to juggle the astonishing detail of all the escrows simultaneously, the escrow officer's operation must be organized far beyond that of a normal business person. If the officer's work area is disorganized, there is increased chance that something will be misplaced or forgotten. Scattered paperwork may also indicate the escrow officer is buried under too heavy a work load and is dashing frantically from one task to another, unable to complete any.

OPENING THE ESCROW

PREPARATION OF THE ESCROW INSTRUCTIONS

The appendix contains a separate section describing various escrow instructions you should ask for. Review of these instructions is best made when you have an actual transaction at hand. Drafting appropriate escrow instructions is the most technically demanding part of the TD investment process. Your most efficient employment of information on the subject will therefore occur when you can put it to immediate use.

Unless you are represented by a reliable broker, you should attempt to open the escrow yourself rather than leave it to the other parties in the transaction. Many "sharks" try to dictate last minute changes in the deal in order to take advantage of the normal tendency to be less vigilant after negotiations are completed. They sometimes falsely claim the changes are "customary." Such conduct is unethical, sometimes illegal, and not very smart — and very easily stopped by dictating the escrow yourself.

Communication of your requirements may be aided by providing photocopied excerpts of those portions of the Instructions Appendix you wish included in the escrow. In most cases, the escrow officer or your broker will then be able to draft one or two sentence instructions which comply with your wishes.

You may encounter opposition to some of the escrow instructions called for in the appendix. Few escrows for TD investment are ever drawn with the investor's interests in mind. Most are dictated by others whose basic purpose is to avoid complications which might hinder completion of the transaction. The protective measures suggested in the appendix therefore may be something of a jolt to those accustomed to doing business with passive investors who trust to everybody's good will.

TIME LIMITS ON THE ESCROW'S FORMATION

The longer the other party to the escrow delays its signing, the greater the chance someone else will turn up with an offer which will make it worth his while to back out of the deal. Therefore it's a good idea to put a time limit on the other party's return of the signed escrow instructions; better yet, hand carry the instructions for the party's signature, as brokers do.

Escrows for sale of an existing TD are especially vulnerable to collapse if delayed too long. Indeed, some TD sellers deliberately stall their signature to gain time to find a higher price. Excuses for the delay then tend to follow a pattern: My wife is out of town, in the hospital, has not yet agreed to sign; I want my lawyer (broker, brother-in-law) to check it over first; I don't like this part of the escrow instructions — a (minor) amendment is needed; our mail service is terrible. In the interim, the seller scurries around offering to sell the TD to anybody willing to beat your price. Moreover, he has a good chance of success if the price you have negotiated is anywhere near or below the market.

PROTECTIVE MEASURES DURING ESCROW

ALWAYS BE READY TO CANCEL

You always will receive additional information about your prospective investment during escrow. Some of the information may be negative, and you should be prepared to ask yourself whether you would have opened the escrow had you known about it beforehand. If not, you should cancel.

It's hard to bring yourself to cancel an escrow. It's a universal weakness to diminish the importance of negative information once the escrow has been opened. Only a very sturdy soul is able to pull the plug when everything otherwise appears satisfactory. TD sellers and borrowers regularly take advantage of this characteristic by hiding negative information until later, claiming ignorance of its importance.

CONFIRMATION STATEMENTS

Later, among the Escrow Appendix requirements, detailed descriptions are provided of some very special documents which are essential to your protection. These are the "(property) owner's offset statement" and the "beneficiary statement." The offset statement is used when you are purchasing an existing TD and you wish to obtain the borrower's signed confirmation of such matters as the balance due, etc. The beneficiary statement is employed when there is another (1st) TD senior to your (2nd TD) investment — and you need verification of the current status of the senior loan.

You should never permit a broker of unknown character, or borrower, or any trust deed seller, to hand carry these documents for signature. If you do, there is a risk that negative information in the documents will be muted in some way to lessen its impact, or that additional comments of an adverse nature will be omitted. If you're unable to handle the confirmation requirement yourself, the escrow officer will be able to do it for you by mail.

If time is short and the documents must be hand carried, however, delivery for signature should be made only by yourself or a trusted representative.

Obtaining the borrower's signature on an existing TD's offset statement occasionally is a problem. In fact, it's surprising the problem doesn't occur more often. It surpasses this writer's understanding why any borrower would ever sign any form of offset statement, much less one including the various waivers suggested in the Escrow Instruction Appendix. The law imposes no obligation on the borrower to sign or even recognize receipt of your request for an offset statement. Furthermore, the borrower may be compromising his rights in a manner completely unforeseen if he signs the offset statement. Nevertheless, most borrowers do sign the statement, though with no great alacrity.

If it appears that the borrower will be reluctant to sign an offset statement, your personal handling of the matter may solve the problem. Sometimes borrowers refuse to sign the statement because they want to sabotage the sale of their loan so they can buy the TD themselves at a lower price; or they may object to signing the statement because of concern over waiver of some minor aspect of their rights of offset; or they are just cantankerous. Your personal delivery of the offset statement gives you a chance to discover the true reason for refusal to sign in these instances, and to assess its importance.

Your personal handling of the offset statement has other advantages also. It's remarkable how a much better picture of the borrower's character and other aspects of the investment can be gained by a personal visit. And the requirement for the borrower's signature on the offset statement provides a perfect excuse to do so.

LOOK FOR BLANKET ENCUMBRANCES

At some point prior to the close of escrow, you should receive a title report on your prospective security (see Title Insurance in the Escrow Instruction Appendix). If your escrow is for a junior TD, be sure to check the title report for evidence of a "blanket encumbrance" by the senior TD. A blanket encumbrance is a lien against real estate which encompasses other properties in addition to your TD's security. It's usually discovered during examination of the TD's title report.

Senior TD blanket encumbrances can create all sorts of problems for junior lien holders. These are described in detail in the AITD portion of the appendix on Clauses. (AITDs are the most common hiding place for this type of situation.) Under certain circumstances, a blanket senior encumbrance may even cause the junior lien holder to be stripped of his security in ways beyond the junior's control. If you stumble onto a 2nd TD with such a condition, you should decline the opportunity to lose your money, whatever gyrations the other party offers to go through to offset the problem.

A WARNING ABOUT PAST DUE TAXES

The appearance of delinquent taxes on any title report received during escrow indicates a weak borrower. Past due real property taxes and their penalties are reported on title insurance as "sold to the state." This can scare the bejesus out of those who have not previously seen it, although the phrase means little. Taxes actually can go unpaid for up to five years before the state may foreclose on the property. For this reason, some owners use delayed tax payments for additional financing. The state has hiked the dollar penalties so high for such shenanigans, however, that an owner who does delay his tax payments is bound to be a bad risk.

LOOK FOR HOMESTEAD WARNINGS

If information received during escrow reveals that the borrower has filed a "homestead" on his property, be especially cautious about the loan. According to state law, a homestead filed before the deed of trust is recorded exempts up to $55,000 (and sometimes more) of the property from foreclosure by the TD lender. Although the remaining value of the property may appear sufficient to secure a subsequently recorded TD, its usefulness as security is effectively destroyed, and the TD should be rejected out of hand. Even if the TD was recorded before the homestead was filed and is presumably unaffected by the exemption, the homestead's filing tells something about the borrower's attitiude toward his debts; its appearance may be the first sign of a bad credit risk.

INSURANCE DANGER SIGNS

If your prospective TD's security includes property with building improvements on it, your escrow instructions should require that you be insured against fire and other damage to the property (see the Instructions Appendix). If you receive a request for close of the escrow ahead of completion of this requirement, immediately stop and investigate the reasons for the request. When delivery of the insurance policy is delayed because the insurance agent is slow (a common occurance), you may be able to accept, instead, a temporary single-sheet promise of coverage from the agent called a "binder." (There is some controversy about the effectiveness of binders, however, and they should only be accepted with caution.) If, on the other hand, the delay has been brought about by the borrower's slipshod attitude toward his insurance, or worse, because he is past due on his premiums, you'd better take another look at the deal. Experience shows that such conduct is a certain omen of a shift-less borrower and obtaining his future compliance with other TD terms will be a constant struggle. You may be better off cancelling the deal in such instances.

NOTE ENDORSEMENTS

Transfer of ownership in an existing TD involves (in part) affixing words of "endorsement" on the back of the note. Because the form of endorsement has such subtle and far-reaching effects on the quality of investment, the escrow instructions contained in the appendix are very exact as to the wording to be used. But if the escrow follows the usual pattern, obtaining compliance with your endorsement instructions will probably require reemphasis. Just about everybody in the business, brokers and escrow officers alike, love to add words such as "transfer and assign" to the endorsement — apparently in the belief that the more ways the transfer is described, the more certain it will stick. But inclusion of superfluous wording can have disasterous consequences if the loan later goes sour. Unless you are very clear as to the exact wording to be used, you may end up classified an "assignee" and will be subject to the borrower's "personal defenses" in payment of the note: If the person who sold you the note obtained the borrower's signature through misrepresentation, or if there was a failure of the consideration in the note's origin, the borrower will be able to refuse payment and you will be unable to foreclose.

CHAPTER 10

TD Administration and Collection Tactics

The administration and collection of a TD is generally the easiest part of the business. Once all the variables and uncertainties involved in making the original investment are dealt with, most trust deeds settle down to a simple process of accounting for collections.

But even at this stage in TD investment, a few traps occasionally show up, and steps must be taken to avoid them. Measures can also be taken which will help enforcement of details of the TD such as the insurance clause. And if the loan turns sour, there are ways of working around the problem to eliminate potential losses. This chapter describes ways to go about such tasks; it tells how to keep small problems from becoming big ones.

FIRST STEPS AFTER ESCROW

DOCUMENT REVIEW / TAKE YOUR TIME

Time should be set aside for a detailed, unhurried inspection of all the documents received from escrow. The high risk of escrow error has already been commented on, and it is at this stage that errors will most likely become evident. When examining the note, check especially the date on which interest starts to accrue. Most escrow procedure is thin on this point, and more errors are found in the beginning interest date than in any other element of the note. Early review is essential because errors are more easily corrected while everybody is still around and the details are fresh in mind.

If you have purchased an existing TD, check the adequacy of the note's endorsement from the previous lender. Also make sure the endorsement is securely attached to the note. Most escrows paper clip or lightly staple the endorsement to the note, risking horrendous problems from its loss.

PRESERVATION OF THE NOTE

Extra precautions against loss of the note itself are necessary. Other documents are important, but they don't need as careful safekeeping. Deeds of trust, assignments, and other recorded papers can all be duplicated from records maintained by the county recorder, and the copies will be considered admissible as evidence in court when certified by the county recorder. Replacement title policies and escrow papers can be obtained from their places of origin; missing insurance policies and appraisals are major inconveniences when lost, but their absence is seldom fatal. A missing or lost note, however, can be more than an inconvenience. Possession of the original of the note carries with it a presumption of ownership, regardless of whether the bearer is the note's named owner. Without the original note, your position in any nonjudicial foreclosure or litigation will be made more difficult. For that reason, the original of the note should be kept in a safe deposit box or similarly secure location.

Before safekeeping the original note, make a photocopy, front and back, for your current files. The photocopy will save digging out the original note should a question arise (as almost invariably it does) concerning its exact wording. And if the original is somehow destroyed or misplaced, a photocopy showing all the original note's signatures will save you much inconvenience later, should foreclosure be necessary. (See Missing Documents in the Foreclosure Appendix for more on this.)

SENIOR TRUST DEED NOTIFICATION

If you are a junior lien holder, a letter should be written to the senior lender advising him of your address and telephone number and that you are also a lender on the property. Assure him that you recognize your responsibility to protect senior lenders, and state your willingness to step in to cover any defaults. Such a letter, coupled with a request that you be notified of any default, often goes a long way toward encouraging the senior's goodwill.

Attaining the senior's goodwill can be valuable if the borrower defaults in his obligations: Unless the senior is agreeable to some other arrangement, the borrower's failure to keep up his payments will ordinarily compel you to step in and cover senior defaults. Furthermore, unless you've given the senior appropriate notice (see Request For Notice in the Escrow Appendix), an uncooperative senior may not bother informing you of a default in his loan until he gets around to commencing foreclosure — after as much as a year's past due payments have accumulated. And unless the senior is obliging enough to coordinate his efforts with you, the borrower's filing bankruptcy will trigger independent legal action by the senior, the cost of which may be deducted from your security.

LOAN BROKER COLLECTIONS

Perhaps 99 percent of the loans negotiated by loan brokers are also administered by them on behalf of their investors. And this is too bad, because lenders then miss out on the most satisfying part of their investment.

FOR YOUR PROTECTION

If you delegate your TD's collection to a broker, you should always retain possession of the original note. Give the broker only a photocopy; in the remote possibility that the broker files bankruptcy, the bankruptcy court may otherwise consider the broker's possession of the note as evidence that it's part of his property. Until you can prove the note is yours, your loan will be considered an unsecured obligation of the broker, and you will have to take your chances collecting solely from the broker's assets, along with all his other creditors. Without the note in your possession, you may not even be able to commence foreclosure if the TD borrower quits making his payments.

Also watch whether you are automatically provided with a written agreement of your collection arrangements with the broker. California's Department of Real Estate requires this of all loan brokers. Failure to provide you with a signed copy of the agreement signals clear disregard of the law and should be immediate cause for separating yourself as far as possible from the broker.

ADVANTAGES OF LOAN BROKER COLLECTIONS

Borrowers gain from loan broker collections by being shielded from private lender's sometimes clumsy or incorrect loan administration. Private lenders also gain by the broker's timely and expert administration of loans during the collection period. Lenders who are in retirement particularly enjoy this latter feature because they want to avoid the distraction of loan management.

But loan brokers gain most of all from a collection arrangement. It enables them to isolate you from outsiders, including the borrower, thereby reserving your funds as a source of future commissions: When the loan comes due, the borrower goes to the broker, rather than to you, for new money to pay off the existing loan. When a loan is to be paid off, the loan broker knows about it in advance and is able to have another TD ready to take up your cash from the final payment; and with a new loan immediately available, the broker knows you will be less inclined to shop other brokers for a better deal.

Furthermore, you'll probably have to pay for the broker's collection service. Broker collection agreements generally provide for the lender's payment of a monthly service charge and (especially when there is a surplus of lenders around) may even call for payment of a "setup fee" to cover the cost of the initial paperwork. Also, virtually all collection agreements provide for deposit of collections in the broker's trust account, resulting in delay in use of the money until it reaches the investor's hands.

ADVANCING

"Advancing" was once a popular feature in the loan broker's array of services. It involved making regular payments to the lender, whether or not the broker had collected from the borrower. Many investors considered this a great convenience since they could count on payments arriving on a specific day each month, and thus not be dependent on the vagaries of a borrower's payment habits.

But advancing has also been used by brokers as a means of disguising borrower defaults, in order to encourage the lender's continued investment through the broker. Some of the most spectacular collapses of loan brokers in recent years have resulted from brokers advancing payments to one investor

94

from money collected on behalf of another investor. As a result, brokers are now prohibited by state regulation from advancement to investors unless their license bears an "Article 6" (sometimes called "real property securities dealer") endorsement — a rare arrangement because of difficulties in qualification imposed by the real estate commissioner (see also Broker Guarantees in the Loan Broker Chapter).

BANK COLLECTION SERVICES

Financial institutions, such as banks and savings and loans, volunteer their "note collection services" to private lenders who also are their depositors. The service is sometimes free, or offered at negligible cost, because it brings additional deposits to the institution.

Bank collection services occasionally make sense when a lender changes addresses frequently and needs a regular location for payment. Otherwise, the service saves only the necessity of calculating the amount of interest in each payment (and even that savings is lost when you use a preprinted amortization schedule). On the minus side, collections handled by such institutions can be harmful. The bank provides no follow-up of past due payments. Nor do you learn that a payment is past due until three or four days later when you fail to receive the bank's notice of collection in the mail. Some savings and loans also have exceptionally fussy collection rules (considering the advantages they gain). Worst of all, the borrower may be unable to communicate with you because he has only a savings and loan collection address.

HOW TO SET UP YOUR OWN COLLECTIONS

PAYMENT BOOKS ARE A WASTE

Private money lenders commonly employ a payment book, passed back and forth with the borrower, as a means by which the parties keep track of a loan. The practice is so universal that, if the escrow office has not been told otherwise, it will probably send you a payment book as a courtesy.

Conventional wisdom says your sending the payment book to the borrower acts as a reminder of the payment due. Perhaps in some cases that is true. But if a borrower is sloppy in his payment habits, a lot more than a payment book will be required to change him. Furthermore, use of a payment book sometimes will lead the borrower to believe that he can claim payment was not due because you failed to return the book.

AMORTIZATION SCHEDULES; THE SIMPLE SOLUTION

Transmittal of an amortization schedule to the borrower, with a letter explaining that its use is aimed at saving needless shuffling of a payment book, is the best of all collection arrangements. To sharpen the borrower's attention to his obligation, you might also accompany the schedule's transmittal with an admonition that "because the payment schedule is expected to be sufficient reminder of the promise to pay, it is our practice to commence default procedures immediately when payments are not promptly made."

Amortization schedules, printed by computer exactly to the terms of your TD, are obtainable through data processing companies which specialize in that kind of work. Their ads are found in the real estate section of every major newspaper. The larger ones, such as Delphi Systems in Santa Monica, are also well-known to most people in real estate. The cost of the service is negligible.

PROPERTY INSURANCE ENFORCEMENT

According to the terms of the deed of trust, the borrower must provide fire insurance protecting the security in a manner "satisfactory to the beneficiary." This clause appears on the reverse (the fine print) of the deed of trust and is explained in more detail in the Clauses Appendix.

Failure of the borrower to provide you with adequate insurance constitutes a default and technically is a basis for foreclosure. Nevertheless, many private lenders find the provision extremely difficult to enforce. Major lenders guard against the problem by purchasing blanket insurance protecting all their security in such instances. But private lenders can only purchase replacement insurance as the occasion arises. One way to protect yourself from the problem is to pay the borrower's past due insurance premium, and then tack the premium onto the amount of the loan. Another way is to order separate coverage from your own insurance carrier, at the borrower's expense, each time a borrower defaults on the insurance portion of his obligation. To use the latter approach, you must be on good terms with your carrier because the insurance premium he is permitted to charge comes nowhere near compensating him for the paperwork involved.

If you try to purchase your own insurance, most agents will initially refuse to write the coverage because you're not supposed to be able to obtain insurance on property you do not own. They don't realize that, as beneficiary under a deed of trust, you have an equitable interest in the property and therefore an insurable interest. In such cases, you may have to prove your insurability. In California this is usually done by referring to the case Alexander v Security-First National Bank 7C2d 718, 62 P2d 735.

The borrower's insurance policy should specify whether you are 1st, 2nd, 3rd, etc., loss payee. That is, as 1st trust deed holder you should be named 1st loss payee, as 2nd TD you should be 2nd loss payee, and so on until finally the property owner is named. If you are the 1st TD holder on a property, you should consider demanding that you be given the original copy of the insurance policy. The requirement may not be enforceable, but institutional lenders routinely insist on it because of its tactical value: If the 1st TD lender has the original policy in his possession, the insuror will be unable to cancel the coverage unless he gains the lender's consent, either by retrieval of the original policy, or by obtaining a receipted notice of cancellation.

LATE CHARGE RULES

The late charge sections of California law receive more than their share of attention by the legislature because amending them is an easy way to demonstrate legislative compassion. As a consequence, restrictions on the application of late charges have become so severe that most private lenders find it impractical to enforce the provision. In spite of this, an allowance for late charges is still a desirable feature in your TD; it may supply an incentive for more prompt payments among borrowers unsophisticated enough to believe in living up to their promises embodied in the note.

If you wish to collect late charges, you first must have permission to do so in the note portion of your TD. (See Late Charges in the Clauses Appendix.) Without an allowance for late charges in the note, the cost of late payments can otherwise be recovered only by suing the borrower in court for damages.

RESTRICTIONS ON THE SIZE OF LATE CHARGE

All late charges must reasonably reflect the "actual cost" of a past due payment. The lender's administrative costs, loss of interest, and extra bookkeeping are considered "actual costs" within the meaning of the law. If a late charge exceeds actual damages, the excess is considered a "penalty" and is uncollectable.

All loans made by unregulated lenders after Jan. 1, 1976, are restricted to a maximum late charge of 6% of the combined principal and interest portion of the installment payment due, or $5, whichever is greater — when the loan is secured by single family, owner-occupied real estate.

Any loan negotiated by a licensed real estate broker (regulated lender) who does so in the expectation of collecting a fee for the service, can carry a charge of up to 10% of the installment due, or $5, whichever is greater — if the loan is a 1st TD of less than $20,000, or a junior TD of less than $10,000.

All lenders are prohibited from making more than one late charge per installment. All lenders are also prohibited late charges on past due balloon payments. Except for the actual damages test, there are no other limits on the amount of late charge in either private party or brokered loans.

ADVANCE NOTICE REQUIRED

With the exception of lenders subject to special regulation, loans made after Jan. 1, 1976, may not assess a late charge unless the installment is 10 or more days past due. The borrower must also be given notice 10 days in advance of each enforcement of a late charge provision, and if he covers his past due installment during the notice period, the late charge cannot be assessed. Lenders who make a practice of sending monthly payment notices which contain a warning of the late charge satisfy the 10-day notice requirement.

ANNUAL ACCOUNTING OF TD ACTIVITY

If the borrower provides you with a written request for an annual accounting of his payments, you must provide one per year free of charge. If your loan is secured by property containing four or fewer residential units, and the loan is purchase money, or a refinance of purchase money, you are required to automatically provide an annual accounting before 60 days after the end of the calendar year. In both cases, if there is an impound account connected with the loan, payments to and from the impound account must also be reported. All annual accountings must contain a 10-point size notice that the borrower may request additional accountings (for which you may charge a statutory fee so minuscule that it's scarcely worth the bother). Willful or repeated failure to comply with any qaulified request for an accounting can result in your payment of a fine of $50 to $200. If you have given the borrower a monthly statement or a passbook, the requirements of the law are considered satisfied.

BENEFICIARY STATEMENTS

Any borrower, junior lien holder, or escrow holder can also request a report from the lender on the current condition of the loan. The report is commonly called a "beneficiary statement" unless it's used preparatory to payoff of the loan; if it reports only the calculation necessary for payoff of the loan, it's called a "beneficiary demand."

THE LENDER'S OBLIGATION

When requested, the lender's beneficiary statement must show the TD's interest rate, balance due, payment requirements, delinquencies, advances, late charges, and due date(s), and whether it is transferable. If the loan has an impound account, a report may be required showing payments from the account for taxes, insurance, assessments, or any other charges, as well as the account's current balance. As of Jan. 1, 1983, any person entitled to request a statement can also call for a copy of the note and deed of trust. As lender, you can require proof that the person requesting the statement is an entitled party. In the event of nonjudicial foreclosure, the privilege of requesting a beneficiary statement expires two months after the recording of a notice of default. Right to a demand expires on first publication of the notice of sale.

If you do not meet a request for a beneficiary statement within 21 days after its receipt, you are liable for any actual damages the requesting person might suffer as a result of the delay. The person who requests the statement can also collect a statutory penalty of $300 each time you fail to respond as required by law.

You are currently entitled to charge a maximum of $50 for providing a beneficiary statement, but only if the TD expressly allows the charge. Not many standard forms of TD contain such a clause.

BENEFICIARY STATEMENT TRAPS

Most requests for a beneficiary statement arrive from an escrow company. The request is usually accompanied by a beneficiary statement form to be filled out. The form may require editing to avoid compromising your position. Perhaps in hope of gaining an unguarded response, the escrow's form sometimes includes requests for information or acknowledgements which go beyond the requirements of the law. Also, no escrow form will suggest that you can charge a fee for the statement; if you expect to be paid, you must add a demand for the fee's "payment even though the escrow is cancelled." Many escrow forms also call for your return of "the beneficiary's copy of the fire insurance" — a burdensome task outmoded long ago.

Inattention to the code requirements for a beneficiary statement is not uncommon and can be expensive. This portion of the law is especially dangerous to those lenders who attempt to discourage a property buyer's assumption of the loan by being uncooperative about escrow requests for information. The law is also dangerous to those large lenders who become too bogged down in administration to provide the report within the prescribed time period. Private lenders, too, are exposed to the penalty when they go on vacation or are incapacitated at the time a request for a beneficiary statement arrives. Despite the foregoing, not many penalties are assessed, chiefly because of borrower ignorance and because of a sense of fair play among escrow personnel.

BALLOON PAYMENT NOTICES

California law requires that borrowers under certain types of trust deeds must be given 90 to 150 days advance notice of balloon payment obligations. The notice must show the payment due date, the amount of payment due including accrued interest and other charges, name and address for payment, and (if the TD carries such a provision) the borrower's right to refinance the final payment. Transmittal of the notice need only be by first class mail. The law applies only to TDs originated after 1983. Other exceptions to the requirement are provided by the law, but because the notice makes such good sense, it's wise to provide one whether you need to or not.

The note portion of your TD may sometimes contain a conflicting provision allowing a more lenient 60- to 150-day timespan for balloon payment notices. Such provisions are a product of another portion of California law which once required "arrangers of credit" (real estate licensees, usually) to include the wording in certain purchase money TDs originated after June 30, 1983. The law has since been changed to require all balloon notices follow the 90- to 150-day rule.

Failure to comply with either balloon payment notice section of the law does not invalidate the borrower's obligation nor your right to receive payment. Your right to enforce collection (by foreclosure) is only postponed until the notice period has been complied with.

PROBLEM COLLECTIONS

A CURE FOR DEADBEATS

Every lender who spends much time in the business ultimately encounters a borrower who, for no rational reason, is regularly late in his payments. The type is usually able to pay but simply does not assign a very high priority to the payment due date. Thirty or more days late is prompt by this person's standards, and no amount of pestering by letter, telephone, or other means makes much of a dent in his timetable. Moreover, as time passes, his delinquency periods tend to expand unless he is brought into line.

Borrowers such as these can ruin your investment if you let them continue in their habits. Late charges, even if you are able to collect them, are seldom enough to cover the cost of following up past due payments. And if the TD amount is low enough, the cost of follow-up can wipe out all the interest earned; it can turn an otherwise profitable small TD into a loser unless you cure the problem.

Your ultimate weapon with this kind of borrower is a declaration of default. The cost to the borrower of your recording a notice of default is so high that the need for current payment then becomes indelibly etched on his mind.

Since you are dealing with a borrower who, in this case, is only shiftless, you should give him advance warning that you intend to use default procedures as a means of enforcing the loan. The most effective way to do this is to

100

send the borrower a carbon copy of the transmittal letter to the trustee which initiates foreclosure; the letter should direct the recording of the default if payment is not forthcoming by a certain date.

Normal prudence requires a wait of 10 days past the payment due date before recording a notice of default (see the Foreclosure - First Three Months chapter). But technically, default occurs one day past the due date; you can send the trustee your letter and papers declaring default on the next business day after the due date, along with instructions not to record the NOD for 10 days. If the borrower comes through with his payment before the default is recorded, the trustee will probably try to charge him with a relatively minor cancellation fee. If the borrower fails to move fast enough, however, the trustee will extract the full amount allowed by law. Either way, your action is certain to provoke much pious indignation, but you can be sure that the payments will never become past due again.

LOAN SALVAGE OPERATIONS

If you have a poorly secured loan, threats of foreclosure such as described above tend to be less effective: The closer the debt amount approaches the value of the security, the less incentive for the borrower to keep the property. In this case, a borrower's default in his payments will require different tactics; you may have to employ one of the following compromises in order to salvage the most from your investment:

- If you are a junior lien holder, you might offer a moratorium in your payments in exchange for the borrower's assurance that he will keep the senior TD current (and thereby continue to reduce the total debt).

- An offer to ease off on your payment requirements in exchange for a pledge of more security is often an attractive alternative. The additional security doesn't have to be real property; it can also be personal property such as furniture, cars, or boats pledged under a chattel mortgage. And if the borrower himself can't provide the extra security, perhaps he has a relative who will.

- You may be able to encourage the borrower to keep active in his payments by offering to lower their size in exchange for a higher interest rate. This approach works best when the borrower has an exaggerated idea of the value of the property, a fairly common condition.

- If the borrower has other property of value, real or personal, he may be willing to swap some of it for a reduction in the amount of his obligation, especially if he had planned to sell it anyway. You may have to also offer the added inducement of reduction in the size of the monthly payments in this case — an unimportant sacrifice if reduction in the loan amount gives you the ability to foreclose without loss.

- Offering a moratorium on payments in exchange for the addition of an unsecured cosignor to the borrower's obligation may help (see also Guarantors in the Clauses Appendix). This becomes a particularly canny move if the borrower later becomes charmed with the thought of bankruptcy; he might think twice about that approach if he believes bankruptcy would permit you to chase the cosignor's assets instead.

- Sometimes you must recognize that carrying the borrower any further is futile. If so, you can often reduce damage to your investment by paying the high points necessary to attract another lender who will refinance the loan; in effect, pushing the problem off onto someone else.

- Borrowers in difficulty frequently reach that state because they are financial bunglers; nothing they do has any practicality, in a business sense. If you can help this type of person straighten things out, you're ahead. One way you can do this is to find a buyer for the property, and then finance part of the sale. Another alternative is to ease the borrower's burden by negotiating an easier payment schedule for him with the senior lender.

- If you acquired your TD by purchase from another lender, you may be able to bypass all the foregoing and collect directly from the TD's former owner. Depending on the form of transfer and type of loan (see Endorsements in the Escrow Chapter), the person who sold you the TD can be held secondarily liable for the borrower's obligation. Many lenders with a troubled loan neglect consideration of this approach because enforcement involves a tedious judicial process. But if the former lender has assets vulnerable to your collection, and understands you are determined to pursue your rights, you may not have to go to court to collect. A stiff letter from your attorney outlining the realities of the situation — and offering the other party an opportunity to repurchase the TD in lieu of paying for court ordered reimbursement — may be all that's necessary to recoup your investment.

- Trouble shooters are available who specialize in loan salvage operations such as those described above. If the loan is large enough, you might consider bringing in such a person to do the work for you. The high price charged for the service may be cheap compared with the gain an expert can extract from the situation.

THE MODIFICATION TRAP

Whatever compromises you work out with the borrower, be careful not to disturb the seniority of your lien. Many of the devices previously described could conceivably cause a 1st TD to drop to 2nd TD position if the change in the 1st TD interferes with the safety of the 2nd. Even if there is no 2nd TD around at the time you modify your TD, you have to be careful because a later recorded 2nd TD can squeeze in ahead of you if you fail to give public notice showing the date of your change. Therefore, to protect your seniority you should give public notice of the date of modification by recording the agreement at the county recorder, as well as by obtaining written consent to the change from any existing junior TD holder. Forms for this purpose can be obtained from any competent real estate attorney, or from one of the other sources of advice described in the appendix on Information Sources.

Modifications also backfire because they lead to conflict between the parties. Negotiations can become heated, and so convert a passive borrower into an aggressive combatant. Even when an agreement is finally reached and reduced to writing, your problems may still not be over because it will be only a memorandum of *some* of the thoughts of the participants. Moreover, it will always be flawed at its inception because, no matter how expert its draftsmanship, it can never be completely prescient of all the variables that might arise. In truth, the only effective modification is one so profitable to both parties that they have a mutual incentive to make it work, in spite of its defects.

PAYOFF PROCEDURES AND STRATEGIES

When the borrower prepares to payoff your TD, you enter a critical period in a TD's administration. If the borrower simply pays the balance due, all you have to do is execute some paperwork acknowledging the payoff, and that's the end of it. But many payoffs aren't that simple. Unless you make the right moves, the borrower can inadvertently extract much more than he is entitled to from the situation — at your expense.

THE LENDER'S STATUTORY OBLIGATION TO RELEASE

Full payment of a TD requires release of its encumbrance of the security. That is done by the trustee under a procedure called "reconveyance." Upon direction from the lender, the trustee executes a reconveyance document, gives public notice by recording it, and then usually passes it on to the borrower.

When a note secured by a deed of trust is paid off, Civil Code Sec. 2941 requires the lender to initiate the first steps toward cancellation of debt. To do so, the lender executes a "request for reconveyance" which is sent directly to the trustee — unless the borrower requests in writing that it be sent elsewhere (such as to an escrow office). The lender is obligated to start the paperwork for release and cancellation whether the borrower requests it or not. If the lender fails to perform as required by law, the borrower may collect a statutory penalty of $300, and demand reimbursement for damages caused by the failure.

Strangely, the statutes do not set a time limit for issuance of the reconveyance; though the code once required the lender's action within 30 days, the legislature managed to lose the time limit in a change of wording intended to tighten the law's effectiveness. Most authorities continue to refer to the old 30-day limit as the rule, however.

The lender is permitted to release the security only when fully paid in accordance with the terms of the deed of trust, or when the borrower separately agrees to the release. Release on the lender's separate decision to do so is prohibited. Without such a condition, the lender could otherwise convert the obligation to an unsecured debt by release of the security, and thereby gain access to the borrower's other assets as a source of collection (see also Security Limits, in the appendix).

The law also provides a means by which the *borrower* can release his property of a TD's encumbrance without the assistance of the lender. In lieu of reconveyance, the borrower may clear his property of the encumbrance if he is able to post a surety bond and meet certain other procedural requirements evidencing his right to the release. The procedure is most often used when a release of the security is discovered defective many years later, and the lender can no longer be found.

PAPERS REQUIRED FOR RECONVEYANCE

To issue a reconveyance, the trustee will require the original note, deed of trust, your request for reconveyance, and payment for the effort. You should also provide the name and address of the security's current owner if different from that shown on the TD. If you purchased the TD from someone else, you should also enclose the original of the assignment by which you took ownership, as well as the originals of any previous assignments. Absent the assignment itself, its recording reference is acceptable — though the trustee may grumble about such a shortcut. It is not necessary, or even desirable, to mark the note "paid," or to enter any other words of cancellation on its face. To do so creates the risk that the note may not be reactivated if, for reasons explained later, you must reverse your authorization to reconvey.

Separate request-for-reconveyance forms are available from any title company, but they are not essential unless you intend to release only part of the security (see Partial Reconveyances). The back of the deed of trust already carries request for full reconveyance wording in an abbreviated and simplified form.

Your signature on the request for reconveyance must appear exactly the way you took ownership of the TD. If the lender is a partnership, trustees commonly require two general partner's signatures as a condition of reconveyance. If the lender is a corporation, the corporate seal, plus one officer's signature, will usually suffice.

For protection of the documents and evidence of your compliance with the law, everything mailed to the trustee should be sent certified, return receipt requested. If you hand carry the documents, be sure to get a dated receipt listing the documents given the trustee.

YOU CAN CHARGE FOR YOUR TIME

Both the trustee and the lender are entitled to charge a fee for their separate efforts in regard to the reconveyance. The lender's portion of the fee is sometimes called a "forwarding fee," and the trustee's portion is called the "reconveyance fee." Despite the different fees, the law permits only a single charge for reconveyance. You therefore must include the trustee's fees with your own if you wish to charge for your work. Your fee need not be limited to out-of-pocket expenses, but must be reasonable within the context of the time spent. Trustees are by no means uniform in the rates they charge; you need to check ahead of time in order to figure their cost in a reconveyance.

Both the lender and the trustee are entitled to payment of their fee before commencing their respective part of the reconveyance.

FOR YOUR PROTECTION IF YOU ARE A BORROWER

If someday you find yourself in the borrower's position, and you have just completed *prepayment* of your note, you should consider demanding a copy of your note marked "paid in full." The precaution may be necessary to avoid the risk of having to pay your note off a second time. Instead of passing the note on to the trustee and requesting a reconveyance, an unscrupulous lender might peddle the TD to an innocent third party. The third party can then go to you, the borrower, and demand payment because he is a "holder-in-due-course" (see Endorsements in the chapter on Escrows). As holder-in-due-course, the third party is free from defenses based on a dispute between you and the original lender. Unless you can prove the payoff, the third party can demand payment and force you to go to the original lender for recovery of your money.

PARTIAL RECONVEYANCES

A partial reconveyance is required if a release is to be given on only part of your security. Partial reconveyance procedure is exactly the same as for full reconveyance, except that you should never relinquish the original note to anybody but the trustee. You may find yourself out on a limb — unable to initiate foreclosure or other action — if you were to surrender the note to an intermediary, such as an escrow, where the document could be tied up with the slightest dispute. The trustee will return the original documents upon completion of the partial reconveyance (or earlier, if you change your mind about reconveyance) so you may enforce the remainder of the obligation.

WHEN THE NOTE IS LOST

If you lose the note portion of your TD, the conventional practice is purchase of a "lost instrument bond" as a substitute for the original note required for reconveyance by the trustee. But there is an alternative solution, one much simpler than the customary treatment. As beneficiary, you can substitute anybody as trustee, including yourself (see Substitution, in the Clauses Appendix). If you substitute yourself as trustee for purposes of reconveyance, you not only save the cost of the bond but also place yourself in position to charge trustee's fees as well as the usual beneficiary costs, without having to supply the trustee with the note. (Many lenders, in fact, make a practice of substituting themselves — or their surrogates — as trustee, just for the additional reconveyance fees.)

The document by which this is accomplished is called a "substitution of trustee and full reconveyance" and is obtainable from most title companies. It combines the required phrasing of both substitution and reconveyance. It need be recorded only once to accomplish both tasks. You do have to pay two recording fees, however, since the county recorder charges for each of the combined instruments.

HOW TO HANDLE AN ESCROWED PAYOFF

Payoffs processed through an escrow require surprisingly finicky treatment if you are to avoid needless exposure to risk. Escrowed payoffs are initiated with the escrow's request for a "beneficiary demand" (see Beneficiary Statements, earlier). Most escrows accompany their request for a "demand" with their own form for you to fill out. The form used by the escrow should seek only to establish the figures necessary to accomplish the payoff and to coordinate the payoff's paperwork. But usually the escrow seeks to accomplish more, and usually the lender makes several strategic errors when dealing with the situation.

Borrowers use the time during escrowed payoffs as an excuse to avoid making their monthly payments. The demand should therefore include an admonishment to the borrower that: "To avoid default, payments must continue to be made when due during the time the property is in escrow. If change is then created in the amount demanded, an amendment will accordingly be forwarded."

Escrow form letters usually request the lender to send the note, deed of trust, assignments, etc., to the escrow along with the demand itself. But you are not obligated to, and should not, surrender control of these documents until cash payment has been received. Because you have too much at stake to take chances (see Phony Escrows, later) — and have no need to do so, however small the risk — your beneficiary demand should also carry an instruction that: "Documents evidencing the debt and its release will be forwarded upon receipt of the payment herein demanded. If payment is made by escrow check, or check other than a cashier's check, any action taken toward reconveyance will be delayed pending the beneficiary's confirmation that it has cleared the bank."

Make no mistake, there will be strong pressures to "simplify" things by releasing the documents according to the escrow's instructions. You will be told that the company responsible for the escrow is a statewide organization and is not about to jeopardize its reputation through improper handling of your (puny) transaction; that the escrow company will be liable for any errors it makes in its procedures or calculations; and that the escrow company's "trust account" check is sufficient payment. Insofar as trust account checks are concerned, the information will be correct; even the borrower's personal check may be tendered as payment. But escrow trust account checks are no better than the integrity of the escrow company itself — a matter almost impossible to determine with certainty. To protect yourself from potential defects in the escrow, you're entitled to withhold all reconveyance documents until the bank acknowledges (some two or three weeks later) that payment according to the demand has been converted to cash.

Suggestions that you can retrieve your documents later, if you don't like the way the escrow company handles the matter, should also be rejected. Once you surrender the documents to the escrow, you lose control of them. Very little of practical worth can be done to force their return if things don't work out as planned. If you relinquish your documents too early, your interest accrual calculations, prepayment penalties, and other charges demanded will suddenly lose significance and become subject to "interpretation."

COMPROMISE PAYOFFS

On the other hand, the other participants in a payoff have equal reason to mistrust your proper delivery of the documents after payment. They fear you may dally in your performance, and thus slow completion of the rest of the deal. Their position then may become nearly impossible if the timing of events following the transaction is crucial.

Such concerns can be alleviated by offering to trade your documents for cash, "across the table." Most lenders go a step further and compromise by agreeing to make the exchange through someone believed to be independent, such as a title company or a trustee. If you use the latter procedure, you should assure yourself of the intermediary's independence by choosing someone remote from the escrow company's area of operation; local title company offices, especially, are otherwise likely to relax their supervision of the exchange if they do business with the escrow company on a regular basis.

To initiate a compromise payoff, you issue the usual beneficiary's demand, except that the demand is addressed to the intermediary. Only a carbon copy is sent to the escrow. You append a letter to the escrow's copy which says that when payment is ready you will surrender the documents to the intermediary, who will release them upon completion according to your demand. In due course, the escrow informs you when the exchange of payment for documents is ready. You then send the intermediary the original copy of the demand along with the documents (certified, return receipt requested).

CANCELLATION OF RECONVEYANCE REQUEST

In spite of your precautions, you may discover you have been shortchanged in payment. If so, you have one card left to play.

Most trustees don't get around to recording reconveyances until at least several days after receipt of instructions to do so. If you act fast enough, your notification (first by telephone, and then by letter) to the trustee that something is wrong will bring things to an immediate halt. Because recording the reconveyance represents an impairment of your security interest, Civil Code Sec. 3412 says you are entitled to cancellation of the instrument in such instances. Even if the reconveyance has already been recorded, you may still be able to obtain its cancellation if there has been no other change in the title of the property.

108

PHONY ESCROW PAYOFFS

Sometimes borrowers set up a sham escrow to postpone the necessity of having to come up with a balloon or other lump sum payment. To this end, the borrower opens an escrow with a strawman, perhaps expecting later to substitute a real buyer or new lender who will provide money for the payoff. If this causes the existing lender to deposit the original note and deed of trust in escrow preparatory to the payoff, foreclosure will automatically be postponed until he can force their return. Even if the lender retains control of the documents, he will probably postpone the foreclosure proceeding anyway because he believes it might impede the supposed escrow transaction. With such tactics, a borrower can generally obtain an extension of six months to indefinitely, unless the lender is alert to the practice.

CHAPTER 11

Foreclosure — The First Three Months

To many people, foreclosure is an interesting process. Though largely procedural, it is interwoven with a variety of subroutine, which the tacticians among us find captivating. But some trust deed investors never experience a foreclosure; until circumstances force them to do so, they would consider learning its tactical details a needless exercise. In the latter case, this and the ensuing chapter on foreclosure can be bypassed; foreclosure will become interesting only when it appears you'll have to start default proceedings on your TD.

SPEED IS ESSENTIAL

Your most important concern in a foreclosure should be how efficiently the procedure is conducted. Though the trustee should handle all the details for you, not many do so in the most expeditious manner. If you want fast action, you may have to track every procedural stop along the way, and then prod, hand carry, mail special delivery, or do whatever is necessary to assure yourself that no time is lost — all at your own expense. Strictly speaking, the time required to complete a foreclosure can be as short as four months. Without your monitoring events and pushing things along, a foreclosure can take seven months or more to complete.

Not every foreclosure needs to be pushed to its conclusion. The smaller the TD, the less profitable it becomes to expedite. Foreclosures initiated simply to get the borrower to make up past due payments also don't require additional effort. In fact, most foreclosure efforts fall in this last category; many lenders never do experience a complete foreclosure.

The decision whether to push for prompt foreclosure is important because the longer a foreclosure takes the greater the opportunity for problems to arise: The borrower can file bankruptcy; he can milk or waste the property, leaving nothing but a shell; the property can be vandalized; natural catastrophies can occur; senior lien installment payments build up; insurance charges mount; market changes can make the security less valuable; unpaid real estate taxes accumulate. And worst of all, the borrower may begin to rearrange his thinking to blame you for his problems — and then take retaliatory action.

CHOOSING THE TRUSTEE

Also important to your foreclosure is choice of a suitable trustee. Trustees vary greatly in technical competence, and not all will be amenable to your efforts toward expediting the foreclosure. By law you are entitled to change trustees (see the appendix on Clauses), so you might as well convert to the one you think is best suited to the job.

In terms of technical ability, title company trustees and the larger independents rank among the best. The common denominator here is the volume of foreclosures handled. Generally, the greater the number of foreclosures the more experienced the trustee (and that's important because much of the job can't be learned from a book). Leaders in the business, such as 1st Independent Trust Deed Service, also maintain a battery of lawyers and others capable of solving virtually any problem in a foreclosure.

Lawyers often suggest themselves as trustee. In most cases this would be a mistake. Unless the lawyer handles foreclosures as trustee on a relatively frequent basis, he won't have enough experience to do a good job, no matter how well versed he is in the law. But if the lawyer is experienced in the practical aspects of real estate (usually through personal investments), as well as foreclosure, he may have greater than normal value as trustee. His presence may give the borrower advance notice of your preparation for a fight, and thus deflect a potential challenge of the foreclosure.

Another measure of competence is whether the trustee is a member of the California Trustees Association. This organization maintains an active educational program which keeps its members abreast of recent developments in the business. The members also pick up a lot of valuable information from the chitchat that goes on during their quarterly meetings.

The smaller, independent trustees are more likely to provide the flexibility needed for a prompt foreclosure. Your choice, here, is a function of whether you need a large trustee of widely known ability, more than one who is flexible. If you think the foreclosure might be contested (and some kinds always are), the known integrity and expert staff of a large trustee can be an advantage when you appear in court.

One last point. Care must be taken in all your actions during foreclosure. Because people are always prepared to ascribe the worst motives to a lender's foreclosure, virtually everything you do during the process will be regarded with suspicion. Fearful of becoming embroiled in a lawsuit, trustees try to subject their foreclosures to extraordinary standards of fairness — and demand that somebody else be substituted as trustee, if they feel you have not met those standards. For their own protection, title insurors in turn examine the trustee's procedure for signs of favoritism before agreeing to insure the property's new ownership after a foreclosure. And, after all is done, the foreclosure can still be set aside pending review in court if a judge can be convinced the sale price may have been "grossly inadequate" or there was even a remote possibility of unfairness by either the trustee or lender. Given such a climate, any move you make during a foreclosure — especially if the property is very valuable — should be made with great delicacy.

FORECLOSURE IS EASY (USUALLY)

Some lenders put off foreclosure because they think it is troublesome and complicated. And in some cases that may be true. But with the assistance of a competent trustee (or expert loan broker), the burdens of the job are lifted from your shoulders. In most types of foreclosure, your involvement need be only in getting the foreclosure started.

Even so, if you have a foreclosure you probably will want to familiarize yourself with the procedure anyway — if only to ensure that supervision of the foreclosure is at its best. The amount of time needed to do so is small; there are only two or three critical points in the entire process, and these are interspersed through four or more months. In order to adequately track the foreclosure, all you need to do is learn the basic steps and review their procedure as each rises in turn.

NONJUDICIAL FORECLOSURE PROCEDURES

Nonjudicial foreclosure simply means foreclosing without bringing the matter into court. California's Civil Code establishes the procedure by which this is done.

THE BASIC PROCEDURE

In a nonjudicial foreclosure, the lender customarily opens fire by delivering a "declaration of default and election to sell" to the trustee. Using the information provided in the declaration, the trustee then draws up and records a "notice of default" at the county recorder in the county where the property is located. Written notice of the event is also given all parties of interest in the property.

If the borrower does not cure his defaults in three months, notice of an impending foreclosure sale is published on one day in each of three successive weeks. The published notice is also recorded, posted at specified locations, and all parties with an interest in the property again receive a notice. If the borrower does not redeem his property by the sale date, a public auction is held in order to satisfy the claims of the lender.

The borrower has the first three months after the default is recorded to reinstate the loan. To reinstate the loan — that is, continue it as before — he must cure his defaults and reimburse the lender for the expenses of the foreclosure. After the three months expire, the borrower has only the right of redemption. During the redemption period (sometimes called the "publication period"), the lender can insist that the borrower pay the full amount due on the TD, plus costs, if the foreclosure is to be stopped.

Theoretically, the total time from beginning to end of the foreclosure can be 112 days, but it never works out that way. Delays in transmittal of documents, intervening weekends and holidays, problems in getting the publication started, and other factors all combine to make it rare that a foreclosure sale is held in less than four months.

PROSPECTIVE CHANGES

See Supplement at the Back of the Book.

THE ELEMENTS OF JUDICIAL FORECLOSURE

The alternative method of foreclosure is by judicial means. This involves filing an action in Superior Court for judicial determination of your right to be paid. If the borrower fails to deny your claim (that is, "defaults" by not answering your "complaint"), you receive a "judgement" which can be collected against his assets. Unlike a nonjudicial foreclosure, a redemption period of three months to a year follows the asset's foreclosure sale. During the redemption period, the borrower remains in possession of the property and it is unmarketable.

The period to completion of a judicial foreclosure can be shortened if you waive your right to a "deficiency judgement;" that is, if you waive any right you might have to attach the borrower's other assets in satisfaction of the debt. If you agree to limit your claim to the TD's security, the redemption period after the foreclosure sale disappears; but a 140-day waiting period *before* sale is required.

Neither approach is as fast or as inexpensive as the nonjudicial process. Moreover, the time and cost of judicial foreclosure can rise to impossible levels if the borrower protests your claim (that is, answers your "complaint"). In some courts you may then have to wait two years before trial. If you do go to trial, the amount you shovel out in attorney's fees will dwarf anything you could possibly imagine, and only part may be recoverable.

In spite of its defects, judicial foreclosure may be the only alternative in some instances. For more on this subject, especially as it relates to deficiency judgements and to the "one action rule," see the appendix on Security Limits.

COSTS RECOVERABLE FROM FORECLOSURE

The trustee's fees and expenses incurred during foreclosure are a direct obligation of the lender, and are added to the loan as part of the costs of the foreclosure. The amount the trustee can charge is rigidly limited by law. Calculation of the amount is fairly complex and is best obtained straight from the trustee, as the occasion arises.

There are other costs you can charge a borrower if he wants to redeem his property from foreclosure, but they are subject to wide interpretation. Most trust deeds are vague on the point. Ideally, the trust deed should provide for recovery of costs necessary to enforce the terms of the TD (see Costs of Enforcement in the Clauses Appendix). But standard title company forms do not make an express allowance for such charges; they only allow costs necessary to protect the security, and this can be pretty limited when subjected to judicial interpretation. In fear of a lawsuit, most trustees therefore require specific permission in the trust deed before allowing an item as a chargeable cost.

DECISIONS BEFORE FORECLOSING

SECURITY VALUE IS EVERYTHING

Preliminary to any decision to foreclose, you should have a fairly accurate idea of the value of the security. Just about every decision you will have to make (including whether to foreclose at all) hinges on the amount recoverable from the security. Furthermore, it's just as important not to undervalue the security as it is to avoid overvaluation.

ABNORMAL VALUATION FACTORS

In appraising the security for this purpose, keep in mind that foreclosure introduces factors abnormal to customary pricing. The amount bid for the property at the foreclosure sale will always tend to be low because of bidder expectations of a bargain. Also, you probably will have to finance part of the property's resale yourself, with a loan worth less (30% less, on average) than its face amount.

On the other hand, the presence of junior interests make the property worth more in a foreclosure than would otherwise make sense:

(1) Junior interests, such as easements on the property which were recorded after your trust deed, tend to improve the security value. Such easement holders will generally pay a premium for the property because foreclo-

sure will cut them off. And if your foreclosure *does* cut off the easement, the property may still be worth more because the restrictions imposed by the easement are removed.

(2) The same applies to lessees who rented the property subsequent to your TD's recording; they too can be cut off by foreclosure of the property, and therefore have an incentive to buy in order to protect their leasehold improvements.

(3) Junior trust deed holders are also usually willing to overbid; they know that any surplus from a sale must first come back to them as a reduction of their loan.

OTHER ELEMENTS IN THE FORECLOSURE DECISION

With a well-secured loan, you may not want to foreclose. You may not want the aggravation of doing so, or you may not want to foreclose out of simple humanity. Given these conditions, you can simply do nothing. You can let past due payments pile up until the borrower gets on his feet again. At present, this kind of postponement does not alter the priority of your loan, nor does it obligate you to continue the favor.

If there is insufficient security, it's worthwhile to carefully study the borrower's chances of recovery. If you conclude no, then the sooner you foreclose the better; accept the fact that you will have a loss and get on with the foreclosure before the loss increases. But if you decide the borrower does have a chance of making up his payments, you had best try to make a deal with him. Alternative approaches, in this case, are discussed in the Problem Collections portion of the chapter on Administration.

THE DEED IN LIEU OF FORECLOSURE OPTION

If the borrower has resigned himself to loss of his property, you may be able to make a deal with him for a "deed in lieu of foreclosure." That is, you buy the security for the amount due on the loan, plus enough to make it worth the borrower's while to sign it over to you. This way you are saved the cost of foreclosure, and the borrower gains some cash. The borrower also avoids having his name plastered throughout the public records by your foreclosure.

Caution: See the appendix on Special Problems in Foreclosure if you need to become involved in this type of transaction; it has some trouble spots which require special attention.

WHEN TO START FORECLOSURE

Technically, the borrower is in default after the end of the business day a payment is due. Because of strong judicial bias in favor of the borrower, most lenders allow an additional grace period of at least 10 days (especially when the TD bears a late charge provision susceptible to claim as extension of the due date). If delay beyond such precautionary period appears futile, the best approach is to declare default without further waste of time. To postpone longer can only lead to greater expense. (See also, the Cure for Deadbeats section of the chapter on Administration.)

RECORDING AHEAD OF SENIOR LIENS

If the property is encumbered by a TD senior to yours, you should try to get your foreclosure recorded as far ahead of the senior as possible. The further you are ahead of the senior, the more time you buy before being forced to meet the senior's payments.

If you do not have enough jump on the senior, you can buy more time by covering the senior defaults. By law, the senior must accept a junior's advances, and the junior is entitled to tack the advances onto his foreclosure amount. The junior is also allowed to charge interest (at a rate prescribed by the TD) on his advances; he loses nothing by the procedure.

RECORDING AHEAD OF BANKRUPTCY

If the borrower's bankruptcy seems imminent, you should record his default as soon as possible. Once bankruptcy is filed, all further legal action — including recording a default — is automatically halted (stayed). But if you manage to record the TD's default ahead of the bankruptcy, you may gain some advantage later on. (See the appendix on Bankruptcy for details on this strategy.)

If you're not sure whether bankruptcy has been filed, it's best to go ahead and record the default anyway, chancing you will beat the filing. At the same time, make sure the trustee understands that you are only trying to get on record, and that no large fees are to be incurred until it is determined whether bankruptcy has been filed. If bankruptcy has already been filed, your recorded default will otherwise automatically be void, and so will your claim for any expenses connected with it.

Be careful about this. If you record with knowledge of the bankruptcy, or even if it can be proved you had knowledge of the *intention* to file bankruptcy, you can be socked both civil and criminal penalties. Fortunately, such penalties are seldom applied except in the most gross cases.

THE DECLARATION OF DEFAULT

HOW TO START

If several individuals are named as beneficiary on your TD, any one of them should be able to sign the declaration of default; most trustees nevertheless refuse to act unless all the beneficiaries sign the declaration. The trustee will also require the originals of the note, deed of trust, and any assignments connected with the TD's ownership. (If you're not able to provide original documents, see Missing Documents in the Foreclosure Appendix.)

THE BASIS FOR DECLARATION OF DEFAULT

Declarations of default are usually based on a borrower's failure to pay according to the terms of his note. In theory, a declaration can also be initiated when the borrower neglects to perform any covenant in the deed of trust, failure to provide fire insurance, for instance. Except for due-on-sale clauses (see Clauses Appendix), foreclosures based on nonmonetary defaults generally are unenforceable because they are so difficult to prove. Trustees therefore try to have a default in a covenant reduced to a money damage before initiating foreclosure. That is, they require the lender to pay the fire insurance premium, past due real estate taxes, or whatever, before considering them forecloseable items. Some trustees are so fearful of being caught up in litigation over slander of title that they refuse to act unless there also is an accompanying default in the loan payments.

Large lenders with a number of loans outstanding have to take care that the claimed default is not based on mistake. Payments collected by these lenders are sometimes booked under another person's account. Sometimes borrowers also have more than one loan outstanding with the same lender, and the supposedly past due payment is applied against the wrong loan.

WORDING THE DEFAULT FOR THE MOST EFFECTIVE COVERAGE

A trustee can process foreclosure only for those defaults named in a declaration. The borrower need not cure defaults not named in the declaration if he wishes to stop the foreclosure. Hence, typical default wording is expanded to catch as many types of borrower failure as possible. Wording which picks up both current and future defaults is common: ". . . default in the installment payment due February xx, 19xx, plus all later installments to become due and all sums properly advanced under the terms of the deed of trust." Sometimes the prospective defaults are also specifically named, to the consternation of borrowers only contemplating the default.

THE NOTICE OF DEFAULT

The actual notice of default is drawn from the information and authority provided in the "declaration of default." Many trustees bypass the declaration altogether and simply have the beneficiary sign the notice of default itself — thus eliminating the separate paperwork created by the declaration. The latter procedure is more efficient but it increases the chance of delay if an error is discovered; the beneficiary must then be chased down for signature on a replacement NOD.

Notice of default wording may vary somewhat but, according to the Civil Code, certain minimum notice phrasing — in specified type size — must be included.

Only the original trustor (borrower) name is shown in the NOD. If the property was sold subsequent to creation of the TD, the buyer of the property — the person currently responsible for payment of the TD — is not named in the notice. This invariably distresses previous owners who discover their name has shown up in the newspapers and county recorder as a defaulted debtor.

RECORDING THE DEFAULT

A DANGEROUS BOTTLENECK

The period between the declaration of default and actual recording of the notice of default is critical in foreclosure. Until recording is accomplished and the clock starts running, the borrower may cure the default without charge. Costs incurred by both you and the trustee will then be wasted. Also, the longer the recording is delayed, the greater the opportunity for the borrower to work himself into bankruptcy, and thus stay foreclosure.

Unless you follow up and expedite the operation, the trustee may take four weeks or more to record the default. Trustees process their paperwork as it's received. If the trustees' staff is overburdened, a delay of several weeks may occur before they start on your foreclosure. You may have to insist on priority treatment and hand carry the paperwork if the default is to be recorded promptly.

Most defaults are recorded by the insuring title company on behalf of the trustee. Some title companies take it on themselves to search the title *before* recording the notice. This, by itself, can delay the recording a week or more.

Your letter instructing immediate recording, and accepting responsibility for the consequently clouded title, may unplug this bottleneck. If it doesn't, tell the trustee to use a different title company.

A SHORTCUT FOR FASTER FORECLOSURE

Technically, the beneficiary (lender) has the right to issue and record his own notice of default. (By law, either the trustee or beneficiary may sign the NOD.) Some lenders therefore arrange to sign and record the default by themselves and postpone bringing the trustee into the picture until near the end of the reinstatement period, several months later. This way the default can be recorded sooner, and the trustee's fee is saved if the default is cured promptly.

Most trustees are reluctant, or flat out refuse, to handle a foreclosure where the lender records the notice of default, however. Title companies take a similar attitude and may refuse to insure the foreclosure. They fear a procedural error, or that the lender may fake some of the notice requirements in his zeal to get the foreclosure going. Only when you can convince the title company and trustee of your reliability can you take advantage of this shortcut.

STEPS REQUIRED AFTER THE NOTICE IS RECORDED

DEFAULT NOTIFICATION REQUIREMENTS

The borrower and certain other parties must be given notice of the default by certified or registered mail postmarked within 10 days of its recording. All other parties entitled to notice must be informed by a copy of the notice postmarked within 30 days. Parties who must be notified within the 30 day period are those others who might reasonably be expected to have an equitable junior interest in the property. This would include other encumbrancers and suspected leaseholders.

If the borrower has sold the security to someone else, both the present and previous borrowers are usually given notice — even though the original borrower (owner) disappeared long ago, and his notice is expected to be returned unopened.

Technically, a notice of default need only be mailed to the person's last known address. If the addressee has moved and left no forwarding address, the notice should nevertheless be valid. If the postman returns a notice unopened because the addressee refuses to sign the return receipt, the service is still valid — but the trustee will then send a notice by ordinary mail anyway.

Despite the foregoing, caution sometimes dictates scattering the notice of default in the direction of every potential equitable interest in the property. If a party has several addresses, a copy of the notice is sent to each of them. If the borrower for some reason has dropped out of sight, a search is made for possible locations and notice is sent to all of them. If it's not clear whether a person is entitled to notice, he gets one anyway. This shotgun approach leads to extremely well-publicized foreclosures in some instances.

COMPLIANCE WITH REQUESTS FOR SPECIAL NOTICE

Anybody, including a complete stranger, can record a "request for special notice" against a TD. This entitles him to a copy of any notice of default thereafter recorded on the TD. Furthermore, the notice must be in the mail, certified or registered, within 10 days of the default's recording. A request for notice is commonly used by junior lien holders to assure themselves of notice of default within 10 days; juniors otherwise need not be notified for 30 days. The request for special notice is also used by people interested in purchasing real estate out of foreclosure. For instance, a neighbor or other person familiar with a property who thinks the ownership is likely to be foreclosed, may record a request for notice in hopes of getting a crack at buying the property at the foreclosure sale.

THE TRUSTEE SALE GUARANTEE QUESTION

As part of the foreclosure procedure, the trustee orders a "trustee's sale guarantee" from a title company. The guarantee or "TSG," as it's called, is a form of title report that details certain information necessary for the foreclosure. It lists the names and addresses of all those of record who are entitled to notice, gives the property's legal description, and also tells which newspapers can publish the foreclosure notices.

Trustees often insist on purchasing the TSG at the outset, explaining that the law requires them to do so. But the law does *not* require them to do so. It merely requires that notice be given to prescribed parties within a certain time period. The TSG is used initially only to find out which parties are entitled to notice. If you are able to identify those to be notified without the aid of the TSG, its purchase can be postponed.

Ordinarily, postponement of the TSG profits you little, since the borrower must pay the cost of the TSG when he cures the default. But when you use the foreclosure simply to force the borrower to pay more promptly, postponement of the TSG can be valuable. Its hefty cost is a severe blow to the borrower who tries to cure, it can destroy any chance of the borrower's cooperation in the future administration of the loan, and it makes cure of the default much more difficult for the borrower.

If you're not sure of those to be notified of the default, purchase of a "letter report" from the title company can be used as a temporary substitute for a TSG. You can ask for a report which reveals only those people entitled to notice of the default. Due to its abbreviated nature, it's much cheaper than a TSG. Best of all, a letter report's cost may be applied later against that of the TSG if one becomes necessary.

THE REINSTATEMENT PERIOD

JUNIOR LIENHOLDER RIGHTS

Junior lienholders have a right of reinstatement equal to the borrower's. By curing senior lien defaults within three months, the junior is able to stop the foreclosure and thereby protect his interest in the property. If the junior is a TD, he can tack the cost of curing the default onto the debt amount and go forward with his own foreclosure. If the junior is not backed by a TD — a judgement lien holder, for instance — he can only collect the cost of the default by court action.

A junior cannot force the senior to sell his position. Juniors often try this when a senior's foreclosure is well in advance and they would like to step into the senior's shoes. It's nice if the senior agrees, because then the junior can enjoy the fruits of the senior's greater diligence. But the senior has no obligation to sell. If the senior refuses to sell, the only way the junior can protect himself is by covering the senior default and tacking the amount advanced onto his own foreclosure.

THE PARTIAL PAYMENT TRAP

A slippery borrower may try to sabotage a foreclosure by tendering a monthly payment after a default is recorded. The payment may be proffered in the guise that it was in the mail before the recording, or that it is an effort to pay part of the obligation. More likely, the borrower hopes your greed will cloud your common sense and cause you to swallow his bait. Once he has you hooked, he may successfully argue that the payment discharged the default pursuant some oral agreement.

To protect yourself, you need to return any partial payment with an advice of the full amount due — and be sure the return is well documented.

Partial payments do have their place in foreclosure, when in accordance with a written agreement. This usually amounts to a lender's acceptance of a partial payment, given in exchange for an adjustment in the foreclosure timetable. In truth, the procedure is a sharp move if your loan exceeds the value of the security. Any time you can reduce the size of your investment in that type of situation, you should take advantage of it.

CANCELLATION OF DEFAULT

Upon full satisfaction of the default, the trustee must execute a "notice of recision." The notice is recorded at the borrower's expense, or it is sent to the borrower to record. The recording of the recision cancels the default at the county recorder.

This is an improvement on past practices. The law formerly did not require a written recision. The document was optional. Many lenders did not bother with it because they assumed the default died a natural death after it was cured. But without recognition of the cure at the county recorder, the default remained on the public records. Completion of a foreclosure has no time limit, and therefore the default would appear to be alive. Many would continue to show up years later, to the perplexity of title searchers trying to unravel a property's ownership.

NEGOTIATIONS DURING REINSTATEMENT

Negotiation is an inevitable part of some foreclosures, especially where the property appears valuable. When negotiations occur, they also tend to be stressful. They often are conducted in an atmosphere of emotion, insufficient time and incomplete information. To function most effectively in these circumstances takes courage. You may have to make judgements based on faith in your own common sense, and ignore what others say. Beware of market valuations based only on numbers; they usually end up being too conservative. More often than not, decisions must be made on only slight indications of changes in market value. Most important of all, don't lose sight of the fact that the value of the property is the controlling element in any decision.

BORROWER DELUSIONS

A strange condition of human nature is worth noting here. A surprisingly large number of borrowers slip into another world after a default is recorded. Time suddenly seems to have little significance. Reality is suspended, and what the borrower thinks "should be" prevails. Efforts by lenders to negotiate a plan which would benefit both parties are ignored. The borrower's valuation of his property is exaggerated. In his mind, the certain prospect of the property's sale at an imposing price is always just a few weeks away. Without doubt this phenomenon is a major cause of occasional foreclosures at bargain prices.

JUNIOR/SENIOR NEGOTIATIONS

Senior lien holders should also be included in your negotiation efforts. Senior lien holders generally do not want the property as a result of foreclosure — they foreclose because they want their money. This is particularly true of institutional lenders who, more than anything else, want to see the regular monthly loan payments continue. The senior lien holder is therefore often inclined to help out a foreclosing junior. Sometimes an offer of something more than the senior had before is necessary to encourage his assistance. An increase in the senior's interest rate, restoration of monthly payments, or the payment of points, are all effective in such cases. In return, you should be able to gain a reduction in monthly payment amounts, postponement of a due date in the senior's loan, or even an agreement to increase the senior loan amount after you have foreclosed.

EVIDENCING THE NEGOTIATIONS

All communication with the borrower during foreclosure should be documented. Every discussion can lead to misunderstanding, sometimes deliberate, which can be a source of argument used in court. Letters or witnesses to conversations make good evidence, but may be impractical. Taped telephone conversations may be convenient, but are illegal unless the recording has the consent of the borrower. (An illegal tape is also inadmissable as evidence in court.) To obtain a consented recording, explain that you are taping the conversation to save writing a letter; most borrowers will give their approval in such circumstances.

WHEN THE BORROWER "WASTES" THE SECURITY

"Waste" is decreasing the security through action or lack of action; it's the throwing away of value through neglect of the property. Though expressly prohibited by the deed of trust, waste can be expected whenever the borrower gives up hope of retaining the property. The worst kinds of waste occur in agricultural and various kinds of rental property. Other forms of waste, and the counter measures you can employ in case you have this problem, are described in the appendix on Special Strategies.

THE MILITARY EXEMPTION FROM FORECLOSURE

BASIC RULES OF EXEMPTION

In 1940, the Soldiers and Sailors Civil Relief Act was passed to provide certain military personnel protection from foreclosure. The draft was active then and its dislocations brought financial pressures on those in the service of their country. Because no politician wants to be branded antiveteran, the act still exists; no property owned by a serviceman can be foreclosed without the consent of the court if: (1) the serviceman incurred the obligation *before* he entered the service *and* (2) foreclosure is attempted while he is in service or within three months after discharge. If the property is owned by a joint tenancy, tenancy in common, or partnership, of which any one member is an exempt serviceman, the foreclosure is stayed just as if the serviceman owns the entire property.

NONMILITARY AFFIDAVIT — MISLEADING FORMS

Foreclosures subject to the military exemption are rare. There are so few, in fact, that many trustees ignore the exemption entirely. Those trustees that do concern themselves with the exemption ask their beneficiaries to sign a "nonmilitary affidavit" before starting foreclosure; that is, a statement that the borrower is not in the military nor has been within the past three months.

The form of nonmilitary affidavit usually used is misleading. It doesn't distinguish whether the borrower incurred the obligation before or after going into the service. As a consequence, lenders who are asked to sign the form often misunderstand the extent of the exemption. They think it applies to all servicemen, and therefore give up trying to foreclose on any military borrower.

MILITARY STATUS SEARCH SERVICES

If you are not certain of the borrower's military status, the trustee can employ a search organization to determine the condition. This requires time and money. Furthermore, the cost of the search comes out of your pocket if the borrower is discovered exempt from foreclosure.

If a search is to be made, the sooner it is initiated the better. It may take weeks or even months and can cause an expensive delay in the foreclosure if not begun early enough.

CHAPTER 12

Foreclosure — The Redemption Period

Foreclosure redemption periods are by far the most dramatic part of the otherwise bland business of TD investment. Most of the action that occurs in foreclosure is compressed into the three or more weeks spanning the borrower's right to redeem. The prospective sale is published; people with an

127

interest in the property suddenly begin to take the foreclosure seriously; if the property is valuable, outside bidders start to become interested; and the borrower wakes up and tries to make a deal with everybody in sight. And depending on the play of events, you sometimes end up with a fat profit, without realizing you have done so until the very last minute.

Apart from its fascination, you may want to keep track of this part of foreclosure for the amount of strategy it involves. With knowledge of the trade-offs described in this and the previous chapter, you will be equipped to follow events and sometimes interject your views when it is profitable to do so.

REDEMPTION RIGHTS

During the first three months, foreclosure can be halted and the loan reinstated to its former condition by simply curing the default and paying certain related costs. (See Costs of Enforcement in the Clauses Appendix.) After the three months have expired, the foreclosing lender has a right (but not an obligation) to demand the full amount due under his TD, plus costs. The payment in this case is called redemption. Only those with an equitable (contractual) interest in the property, and others named by statute, have the right of redemption. Any one of the property's owners, or any junior lien holder, can redeem. Judgement lien holders and other encumbrancers also can redeem, but seldom do so because they must go to court and foreclose judicially in order to collect the redemption payment.

The redemption period begins automatically three months after the notice of default is recorded. No special notice or paperwork is required to signal its start.

The length of the redemption period is one of the most misunderstood aspects of nonjudicial foreclosure. The usual assumption is that the period is 21 days, because the law says that publication of notice of the sale must commence at least 20 days in advance. (It's therefore sometimes also called the "publication period.") In reality, the redemption period extends right up to the point the trustee opens the bidding at the foreclosure sale. And that seldom occurs in fewer than 30 days. A wait of 70 days for the foreclosure sale is more common. Even then, the period is sometimes extended still more by the sale's postponement.

Furthermore, the borrower may have a special right to redeem which continues past the start of the foreclosure's auction. Theoretically, once the sale starts the borrower's redemption right stops; if he wants to keep the property, the law requires that he enter the bidding, and pay cash for the purchase price just like any outside bidder. But, ostensibly out of confusion, and more likely out of compassion, most trustees will stop the auction if the borrower comes dashing up at the last minute with the redemption price. Claiming there is no clear authority other than case law prohibiting redemption at this stage, the trustee will stop the bidding and postpone the sale in order to consult an attorney. And when the sale is postponed the redemption period is automatically reopened, thus giving the borrower opportunity to pay the redemption price and retrieve his property without argument. In effect, the borrower's right to redeem therefore extends right up until the property is knocked down to the highest bidder.

Both the state of California and the U.S. also have limited rights of redemption of the property extending beyond the auction. In fact, unless appropriate steps are taken, their right of redemption can extend indefinitely. In both cases, the right applies only to certain recorded tax liens, and can be severed if a separate notice of the foreclosure sale is given the appropriate government agency 25 days ahead of time. The way you go about doing this — plus other information on how to cope with the problem — is provided in the Tax Lien section of the Special Strategies Appendix.

REDEMPTION PERIOD PROCEDURES

The law requires publication of advance notice of foreclosure sales. It says publication must commence at least 20 days before the sale date, but not before expiration of the three-month reinstatement period. Furthermore, the publication must be in a newspaper of general circulation within the city, judicial district, or county in which the property is located. And it must appear once a week for a total of three times.

At least 20 days before the sale date, copies of the notice of sale must also be sent in the same manner and to the same parties entitled to the notice of default. The notice must also be posted at designated locations and recorded at the county recorder. The notice's recording must occur at least 14 days prior to the scheduled sale date.

The sale itself must be conducted between the hours of 9 a.m. and 5 p.m. on a regular business day, Monday through Friday, at some publicly accessible place in any county where some part of the property is situated.

Unless the trustee happens to be especially active in the county where the property is located, a "posting and publishing service" is usually hired to perform some or all of the above tasks.

CHOICE OF THE SALE LOCATION AND TIME

The prospect of a TRO (temporary restraining order) hangs like a cloud over every foreclosure of consequence (see Court Ordered Delays, later in this chapter). If you suspect your foreclosure may be so affected, you should choose the prospective sale location and time yourself, rather than let the trustee do so. If you're allowed to insert your own views, you thereby may be able to substantially reduce the threat from a TRO: To become effective, the restraining order must be taken to a courthouse for signature by a judge and then served on the trustee or beneficiary. Because TROs are usually last minute affairs, service is customarily made on the trustee just before the auction. Therefore, by asking that the sale be scheduled at a place distant from a court house, at 9 a.m. of the first day of the work week, service of an effective TRO is made more difficult.

PUBLICATION TACTICS

START THE TRUSTEE AHEAD OF TIME

Early arrangement for publication can reduce delays in the redemption period enormously. The publication part of the period is highly susceptible to bottlenecks. If the right moves are not made at the right times, shocking delays can occur. To avoid undue procrastination, preparation must be made for publication while you're still in the three months reinstatement period.

Most trustees prefer to wait until after the three-month period before taking steps toward publication. They fear that, if the borrower reinstates within that time, the costs of publication already incurred will not be recoverable. As a consequence, they don't start preparing for publication until after three months, thereby delaying the foreclosure sale a month or more.

To get the trustee in motion, you'll probably have to guarantee payment of any unrecoverable publication expenses caused by the early start. The trustee will usually require a letter stating that you anticipate zero probability of reinstatement and that, if reinstatement does occur, you acknowledge responsibility for prematurely incurred expenses.

EXPEDITE THE PUBLICATION PAPERWORK

Publication of a notice of sale by a newspaper may involve a complicated routine of "galley proofs" of the notice and much mailing thither and yon. This usually causes delay of two weeks or more before publication. Depending on the distance to be traveled and the amount of money at stake, you may find it worthwhile to speed things up by hand carrying the paperwork to and from the newspaper.

Ideally, the first publication of the sale should occur the day following the end of the three-month reinstatement period. As a practical matter, this may be impossible because some newspapers publish their legal notices only once a week. By planning ahead, publication should nevertheless be possible with no more than a five day delay.

SELECTION OF THE NEWSPAPER

If you have several newspapers to choose among, you may want to investigate their peculiarities. Newspapers are by no means uniform in the way they publish legal notices. As mentioned before, some daily newspapers publish legal notices only on a certain day of the week. Weekly newspapers are automatically limited to a given publication date, which may not be compatible with your schedule. Each newspaper also has a certain deadline date for the acceptance of copy for publication, and the deadline for foreclosure notices may be set much further ahead than other copy.

Not often known is the fact that some newspapers in small communities take advantage of foreclosure publication requirements. They increase the amount of publication space by using larger type, and also raise their rates. This has a profound effect on those foreclosures involving a lengthy legal description of the property's boundaries. In such cases, the amount of space used can multiply by two or three times, with a corresponding increase in publication cost — an important factor if you end up with the property and the cost comes out of your pocket.

POSTING THE NOTICE OF SALE

The sale must be announced by posting a copy of the publication on "a conspicuous" part of the property at least 20 days ahead of time. If a house, the notice should be tacked to the front door. If tacking to the door is impractical, a sign stuck in front of the place will do; if the notice is subsequently torn down by the occupant, the requirements of the law are nevertheless served. Unimproved property, however remote the location, must also be posted — and sometimes at considerable expense. If the property is landlocked, posting is still required. If neighboring properties must be trespassed to do so, the posting is done anyway.

Posting is also required in a public place in the city or county where the sale is to be held. This part of the requirement is usually met by tacking the notice to a bulletin board in the local city hall or court house. Note that the posting is dictated by where the sale is held and not where the property is located. A sale of property located in the far reaches of the county, but auctioned in a city 100 miles away, must be posted in the city where the sale is held.

The services of "posting and publishing" experts are especially valuable in meeting the various posting requirements. These businesses save all the participants substantial travel expense by maintaining a network of local agents available to do the job.

SALE POSTPONEMENTS

Either the lender or the trustee can postpone the foreclosure sale at any time until the property is knocked down to the final bidder. All that is required is the trustee's announcement, at the scheduled sale, of the reason for the postponement and the new time and date. Subsequent postponements can be made in the same manner.

THE BORROWER'S RIGHT TO POSTPONEMENT

The borrower has a right to one postponement equal to "one business day, provided the reason for such request is to permit the trustor to obtain cash sufficient to satisfy the obligation or bid at the sale." The borrower's request must also be made in writing and, presumably, must state the source of funds. Most trustees will accept the postponement request even when submitted by a person claiming to be an agent of the borrower, regardless of whether a source of funds is given. Though the trustee is given a discretionary right to refuse any such request, denial is improbable given the broad judicial bias in favor of the borrower.

POSTPONEMENTS THAT REQUIRE REPUBLICATION

If you call a postponement, be careful the trustee understands there is a rational reason for your action. Trustees who figure the lender is playing games by postponement will either refuse to perform, or call for republication; if the trustee refuses to perform, you will have to substitute another trustee — who will also call for republication.

According to the civil code, republication is also required after three postponements. As usual, exceptions are provided. Exception is made if the postponement is at the request of the borrower. Postponements made in exchange for elimination of some part of the default are also excepted. And postponements brought about by operation of law (as in a stay of bankruptcy) are excepted.

HOW TO PROFIT FROM POSTPONEMENT

If delaying the sale is not otherwise adverse to your interests, you can arrange to profit from postponement. Postponement in consideration of the borrower's payment of cash separate from the amount due on the note is perfectly legal. It is also supremely desirable from the borrower's standpoint — it gives him time to put together that hoped-for sale or refinancing which always seems to be just around the corner.

ENFORCEABILITY OF POSTPONEMENT AGREEMENTS

Oral promises to postpone are not legally enforceable. The issue often arises from negotiations which lead to a number of proposals and counter proposals, and then misunderstanding (sometimes on purpose) as to what was said.

Also unenforceable are gratuitous promises to postpone. Arguments commonly pop up when a lender says he will postpone to give a borrower more time to solve his problems. The lender later changes his mind, deciding he doesn't like the borrower so much after all, and then the borrower throws a fit — disregarding the fact that he was not entitled to the postponement in the first place.

COURT-ORDERED DELAYS OF SALE

Foreclosure sales can also be postponed, and even permanently enjoined, by court order. Court orders usually first arrive in the form of a temporary restraining order (TRO), which directs the trustee to postpone the sale pending a hearing. Any trustor or other party with an equitable interest in the property is entitled to ask for this kind of court order. The ostensible purpose generally given for the procedure is to allow time to arrange an alternative to foreclosure. In most cases, bankruptcy is the anticipated alternative, despite contrary representations given the judge.

Depending on a wide range of variables, a restraining order can be a minor distraction, or an unmitigated disaster. The circumstances determining the degree of trouble caused, the procedural steps required, and the defenses you can employ, are described in the appendix on Special Strategies. If you suspect an attempt will be made to throw your foreclosure off stride by such an effort, you should review this portion of the appendix — there are certain preparatory measures you can take which diminish, or perhaps eliminate entirely, potential problems from a restraining order.

THE FORECLOSURE SALE

SALE PROCEDURE

A foreclosure sale may be held on its published date, but you can't count on its starting at the announced time. Usually the trustee waits until sale time to begin fussing with various related clerical matters. As a result, a half hour or more delay is common. If you want the sale to start promptly, you must ask the trustee to get his preliminary gyrations out of the way beforehand. You can also request that your sale be read first if the trustee expects to handle several sales at the time.

The auction procedure is called "crying the sale." It starts when the trustee reads the publication data and announces the amount the beneficiary (lender) has bid. Other bids are then asked of whomever happens to be standing around. If no one is present, the trustee still cries the sale. He reads the publication aloud and asks for bidders from the vacant space or wall in front of him, no matter how demented he may appear to passersby.

The trustee announces only the lender's opening bid. For this purpose, the lender does not have to be present. Any subsequent bids, whether by the lender or others, must be tendered by the bidders themselves; the prudent trustee won't do it for them.

SURPLUS CASH FROM THE SALE

Cash collected in excess of the amount due the foreclosing lender is paid to the junior lien holders in the order of their priority. Whatever is left then goes to the borrower. If the borrower cannot be located, the trustee holds the borrower's money in a separate bank account under a legislatively defined procedure. Small surpluses are fairly common because outside bidders overbid as little above the amount due the foreclosing lender as possible. As a consequence, trustees end up holding a lot of $1 and $2 surpluses for vanished borrowers — a benefit they would just as soon do without.

THE LENDER'S UNDERBID STRATEGY

If you bought your TD at a discount, there may be a tax advantage in bidding less than the full amount due at the foreclosure sale. This is because the IRS treats the difference between your cost of the TD and the amount you receive from the bidding as a taxable gain. If you find yourself in such a situation, and you are the only bidder at the sale, you should take advantage of the fact and bid less then the amount due from your TD. By underbidding at an amount equal to the TD's cost, you will be able to avoid a taxable gain. (For more on the tax affect of foreclosure, see the appendix on Income Tax Strategies.)

BID PAYMENTS

The law requires the trustee to accept all bids in the form of cash, cashier's check, or any cash equivalent designated in the trustee's notice of sale. If the cashier's check is made payable to the bidder, the trustee must (upon evidence of validity) accept it when the bidder endorses it over. If the check is in excess of the amount bid, the trustee refunds the difference. The trustee is not compelled to, and almost never does, make exception for bids made by lien holders junior to the foreclosing lender. Exception is made only for the foreclosing lender's bid. The foreclosing lender is entitled to credit bid up to the total amount due him at the time of sale. If he wishes to bid over his credit amount, he is subject to the same requirements on payment of the surplus as other bidders.

Despite the foregoing, the trustee has broad discretionary power over the form of bid payment. The law only defines the type of payment the trustee *must* accept. The trustee can otherwise accept postage stamps, a bidder's IOU, or a junior lender's credit bid — if he is willing to be responsible for the bid's conversion to cash. Almost never is the trustee willing to take the risk, and therefore bidders must expect to pay in the form of cash or one of its named alternatives.

JUNIOR LIEN HOLDERS DURING THE SALE

Once the sale starts, junior lien holders lose all right of redemption (as far as foreclosure is concerned, anyway). The junior is not entitled to stop a sale by paying the amount due the senior. The safest way for the junior to protect himself in this situation is to become an active bidder so that the sale price exceeds the amount due the senior. The surplus from the sale can then be applied to the junior obligation in the order of its priority.

The junior who has been cut off by a senior's foreclosure is termed "sold out." He can no longer look to the security for protection. If the sold out junior is classified a "purchase money TD" (see the Security Limits Appendix), that's the end of the line; the debt is automatically cancelled and the lender is unable to collect anything more. But if the sold out junior is not classified purchase money, he has one last card to play; if he acts within the time limits of the statute of limitations, he can still sue the borrower on the note alone, and then collect against the borrower's other assets. If the amount is small enough, the lawsuit can even be decided in a small claims court.

BID COMPETITION

Expect lots of bidders to show up at the sale if the property is close to a major population center, has a margin of equity, and is easily identifiable by address or legal description. Expect a reduced number of bidders on very large TDs or very small properties. Bidders also steer away from unimproved properties, no matter how valuable they are, because their location is not routinely identifiable; they have no address to work from and the property is usually identified only by a subdivision number which can't be readily located without a special map.

Subscription default services are a major source of bid activity in some counties. These are reporting services set up for the sole purpose of dispensing data on recorded defaults and prospective foreclosure sales. They normally are found in heavily populated counties with a high volume of real estate activity. Real estate investors hoping for a bargain are the principle subscribers to such services. Lenders and real estate brokers also subscribe. And, distressingly, so do lawyers hoping to solve the defaulting borrower's problems with bankruptcy.

If they've got the money to do so (see Bid Payments, earlier), junior lien holders are the most probable entrants in the bidding; it's the nature of the beast to hate to be cut off. Since surpluses generated from the sale pass on to the junior anyway, his entry in the fray is certain if the property is valuable enough.

You should also consider becoming an active bidder if the property is worth it. All the other bidders will be hampered by inexact information about the property. Most of them will not have a clear idea of the property's market value, and few will take the trouble to dig up exact information on its encumbrances. On the other hand, your information will be highly refined through prolonged association with the property. You can bid with much more confidence, while the others will sometimes hold back a bit to allow for unknowns. Indeed, you would be passing up a valuable source of income by ignoring this aspect of the lending business.

If you want to avoid owning the foreclosed property, you can stimulate competition by publicizing the sale. People such as former owners of property, neighboring property owners, lessees, and easement holders often are potential bidders and should be notified. Your follow-up among people who have inquired about the sale may encourage their bidding. For this purpose, the trustee may be willing to keep a log of callers who have inquired about the foreclosure. You can also pump up the bidding by keeping the potential bidders posted on changes in your information.

BIDDING WHERE THE UNEXPECTED IS NORMAL

Foreclosure sales that draw more than a few bidders are wildly unpredictable. The participants are often relatively ignorant about the property. Inexperienced bidders add to the instability because they are unfamiliar with foreclosure procedure. Bidding easily and often gets out of hand, even among experts, the competitive instinct is so strong. In some cases bidders forget they will have to finance the property's resale by carrying back a TD worth perhaps only 70% of its face amount — and thus overestimate the property's resale value. The more people present, the more likely someone will slip up and do something silly and therefore unexpected.

SALES CONTESTED BY JUNIOR TDS

Any foreclosure sale can be later set aside by a judge convinced that it was conducted improperly. A trustor, junior lien holder, or even an outside bidder has standing to sue for cancellation of the sale on this basis.

Junior lien holders are the greatest source of this type of conflict, and therefore everybody tends to be overly solicitous of junior interests. But the special position the junior enjoys in the affair is limited to the amount owed him on his note. If you are prepared to cover the amount owed the junior if he sues, adjustment of the sale to his whims becomes unnecessary.

DIRTY TRICKS

CHILLING THE BIDDING

Bidders at foreclosure sales used to discourage competition with a variety of tricks now considered illegal. They used to bid the property up until the competition quit and walked away. Then the bid was withdrawn, forcing a new auction at a lower figure. The law now says you cannot withdraw a bid; it is cancelled only by someone entering a higher bid, or by postponement of the sale. Bidders also used to pay their competitors "walking money" to induce them to go away; the tactic survives to some extent because the act is so difficult to prove. All such stunts are called "chilling the bidding" and, when proved, can lead to conviction as a felon.

THE TRUSTOR'S BID SCAM

A borrower with enough money to redeem his property may, instead, try to bid for it at the sale. The logic behind the maneuver stems from the fact that junior lien holders are cut off by a senior's foreclosure sale. Rather than redeem his property by paying the senior, the borrower enters the bidding through the aid of a strawman. If successful in buying his property back, he hopes to eliminate the necessity of paying the junior encumbrances. Enough borrowers have tried the stunt, however, that prohibition of trustor bid activity in these circumstances has found its way into case law (*Howell v Dowling* 52 Cal. App. 2nd 487).

If trustor bidding for purposes of eliminating a junior can be proven, the junior lien will remain an encumbrance on the property — in spite of the sale — and perhaps the sale will be set aside. You and the trustee should therefore watch carefully if the sale will result in a sold out junior, especially when the borrower shows up for the sale and looks like he might try to guide the action of a bidder.

CHANGES IN THE LOCATION OF THE SALE

Sales also used to be postponed to a new location. This was done primarily for shelter from inclement weather. No more. The law now forbids the practice as a result of a notorious case where the device was used to exclude bidders. The lender postponed a sale in Los Angeles to another site in Lancaster, 20 minutes later but over an hour's drive away. The lender's father-in-law was already at the new site ready to cry the sale free of bothersome bidders. They didn't get away with it, but they did cause new law to be created in memory of their imagination.

THE PHONY BANKRUPTCY

As explained elsewhere, bankruptcy can intrude and stay a foreclosure sale anytime before the property is knocked down to the final bidder. The trustee then has to postpone the sale, or abandon it. Some borrowers take advantage of this and gain postponement by a last minute claim of bankruptcy. The trustee will then generally postpone until he can determine the truth of the matter; to proceed might otherwise put him in violation of the law. If two postponements have already occurred, republication will be required even though the claim of bankruptcy is later found to be false.

POSTPONEMENTS TO DISCOURAGE BIDDING

Some lenders try to discourage bidders by a last minute postponement of the sale. The logistics of getting the money together and then getting to the auction site at an appointed time forces many bidders to drop out after this kind of postponement; especially when the bidder has no assurance his bid will be the highest anyway. The three-postponement limit mentioned earlier does much to stop the tactic. It nevertheless is still used to some extent by basing the postponement on a deal with the borrower to "save the property." Since postponement is then at the behest of the borrower, it is not included in the three-postponement limit. Trustees who suspect the lender's motives in such instances either refuse to act, or cancel the sale and call for republication.

AFTER THE FORECLOSURE SALE

If you have no competition in the bidding and end up with the property, it may be because the foreclosure has fallen at the bottom of a cycle in the property's value. To attempt to resell in such a mushy market is nearly impossible, except at giveaway prices. It's also frustrating beyond belief. If you find yourself in such a situation, you can save needless thrashing around (and pick up gratifying profits) by simply holding the property until the cycle turns. Major lending institutions are forced to ignore this fundamental reality of the market place; they have to get foreclosed property off their books as quickly as possible — much to the joy of sharpshooting real estate investors.

According to California law, a junior who forecloses on a property has the right to assume all senior liens. He can also assume a senior lien if he takes the property by a deed in lieu of foreclosure. The right is supposed to persist even in the presence of an enforceable due-on-sale clause in the senior. This privilege was expressed in an appellate court case: *Pas v Hill* (1978) 87 CA3d 521. However, according to federal law in the form of the "Garn Amendment," the state's authority on the issue has been usurped. In certain circumstances the senior lien holder may demand payment of the entire TD upon transfer of the property to the junior by foreclosure. For more on this, see the Due-On-Sale section of the Clauses Appendix.

Ownership of the property is one thing. Obtaining possession after foreclosure is another. If the property is encumbered with a lease which is senior to your TD, you will be obligated to comply with its terms. If the lease is junior to your TD, the lessee will nevertheless be entitled to a 30-day notice to move out — despite the fact that your foreclosure has severed the lease. Without a lease (i.e., the rental agreement had no provision for a fixed length of occupancy), the notice period to move out must be as long as the tenancy period (month to month, in most rental agreements).

CHAPTER 13

Other Approaches to TD Investment

TD investments are not limited to the approaches described earlier in this book. If you want to be free of all management detail, you can still find your niche in TDs through the alternative investments given in this chapter. On the other hand, if you enjoy being active in an investment, you may find satisfaction in TDs susceptible to the yield-boosting devices discussed later. If you like to gamble for high profits, TDs can satisfy this desire too when you poke among the higher yielding speculative property loans. Whatever your persuasion, you can always find a place in this market if you know where to look.

ALTERNATIVE FORMS OF INVESTMENT

1911 ACT BONDS

1911 Act bonds are an extremely useful, little known, alternative to TD investment. The "1911 Act" portion of their title refers to the year in which enabling legislation was enacted permitting their issuance. The bonds enjoy much the same right of access to their security as trust deeds. Unlike trust deeds, interest income earned from them is free of federal income tax. Perhaps because they have such weird characteristics, they are also unique to California.

The 1911 Act bond's security is rooted in the fact that it is issued for purposes of subdivision improvements. Unlike other bonds, designated lots in the subdivision are used to back each individual bond. For instance, the developer of a tract of 1,000 lots may finance the sewer system by arranging for a bond offering sufficient to cover the costs of the system. Each bond is then secured by a lot in the subdivision and has the same seniority as a tax lien. If the property owner fails to make his payments, the bond holder can call a default and initiate foreclosure in much the same way as on a trust deed.

The quality of security of each bond is generally high because the value of the improvement, which was the source of the bond in the first place, adds to the value of the lot. Any subsequent structural improvement, such as a house, adds still more to the security. Any subsequent lender against the security is junior to the bond and, in the event of default, must step in and cover the bondholder to avoid being cut off by foreclosure.

Detracting from the security's value is the fact that 1911 Act bond issues are small by comparison with the usual public issue. This translates to a higher original cost of sale of each bond. The quality of the security is thereby weakened because less money is left to spend on the subdivision's improvements. Furthermore, the developer sometimes fails to sell all the lots in the subdivision because he misjudges the demand for them. If that happens, the bondholder may find himself in possession of a subdivision lot with over-priced, bond-financed improvements that nobody wants.

142

Investors in 1911 Act bonds enjoy better rates of return than other municipal issues. The investor sacrifices something in exchange, however. Apart from the risk of an occasional failure to sell the subdivision, he also may have to accept a substantial discount if he wants to sell his investment. This is because most of these bonds are originally sold from a high pressure, "boiler room" type sales office; after the initial sales effort, the market tends to subside, and so do the prices. Most bond dealers try to compensate for this by promising to "make a market" in the bond following its original issue; that is, to repurchase the bond at an amount roughly comparable to your purchase price. But, such promises are chancy, and you should not lean too heavily on that type of support.

The most efficient way of investing in this type of bond is to buy those which have been in existence for several years and then only in large quantities. By buying seasoned issues you avoid the "boiler room" premium built into the original sales price. You also have a better perspective on the success of the subdivision. Purchase in quantity gives you a wedge by which a discount on the sale price may be pried loose. And if later you have to sell the bonds, the large quantity will be a bargaining tool for reduction in the resale commission.

With such precautionary measures, these bonds should provide a rate of return 20% or more higher than other municipals. If you crank in the fact that the income is partially tax-free, your investment may earn more than many trust deeds.

TRUST DEED PARTNERSHIPS AS AN ALTERNATIVE

Occasionally, limited partnerships are formed with the aim of specializing in trust deed investments. When properly managed by an expert, such partnerships can be extremely profitable. An expert manager can take advantage of the interest rate cycle to extract a return far beyond that of the normal investor. By using his knowledge of the real estate market, and switching back and forth between real estate and trust deeds, he can sometimes more than double the rate of return obtained by others.

The honesty of the manager (usually the general partner) is the principal concern in this approach. The manager's natural desire to satisfy his partners' demand for ever higher rates of return is also a problem. The limited partners usually are inexperienced investors who complain if the partnership does not earn as much as the rates advertised in newspapers. In order to meet demands for higher performance, the manager may go for higher risk TDs and thus bring down the whole organization.

If the partnership is honestly and competently managed, the inexperienced small (less than $100,000) investor gains in many ways. The investment may provide liquidity, not ordinarily available in TDs, if limited withdrawals or additions are allowed in the partners' capital accounts. Such partnerships are also better able to invest in higher yielding TDs with erratic payment patterns; with a large pool of such trust deeds, they can still maintain enough cash flow to meet their daily expenditures and pay regular dividends to the partners.

PARTICIPATING IN INDIVIDUAL TRUST DEEDS

This newest fad in TD investment is called "fractionating." It's born of the fact that the larger the trust deed, the higher the rate of return. By selling only parts of a trust deed (participations), a loan broker can also bring a greater number of small investors into the fold.

Participations have an advantage over the partnership approach described above because you can evaluate the TD before you put up your money. You thereby lessen, to a degree, the reliance that must be placed on the manager; a modicum of supervision by California's Department of Real Estate is also provided when the manager is a real estate broker. Participations are also sold by state regulated thrift institutions and may therefore be safer because the manager or sponsor is required to meet higher standards of financial reliability.

Participations should be avoided unless you have the utmost confidence in the manager's honesty and reliability. They should also be avoided unless you can be happy with short term TDs. The manager in a participation TD profits from the commission he receives with each loan origination. It's therefore to his advantage to take on short term TDs; i.e., to "churn" your funds as often as possible so he can create more commissions.

Participation agreements must necessarily try to allow for the prospect of foreclosure of the TD, and this can also be a problem. Most such agreements provide for the manager's repurchase, of the TD in such circumstances. But, if the manager does not repurchase, the various participants could find themselves in joint ownership of the security, and from that all sorts of complications can flow.

Perhaps the biggest disadvantage in fractional investments rests on the fact that participatory interests are notoriously difficult to unload. The other participants, or the manager, are the only people who would want to buy you out. The manager may not be able to, even though the participation agreement says he must; and you can be sure the other participants will discount their offering price in direct proportion to the paucity of buyers.

144

WAYS TO BOOST TD YIELDS

Most TD investors treat their loans as static things. Their TD's rate of return is established at the beginning. If there are no defaults or prepayments, the investment cranks out a precalculated profit for the life of the loan. You can, however, sometimes improve a TD's yield by tinkering with it. Indeed, some investors purchase trust deeds with this objective in mind. When they do, the results can be spectacular.

Basically, there are two ways in which yields can be improved. One is to attack the structure of the note itself and try to create a change in the terms which would increase the effective rate of return. The other is to promote a prepayment of all or part of the amount due.

TO TEMPT A MODIFICATION

Sometimes a TD can be made more profitable by offering the borrower cash, or an alteration of the note's terms, in exchange for a faster payoff. In this case, most borrowers will be attracted to an offer of an even lower interest rate because they have an exaggerated view of its importance. If you can reinvest your money at a higher yield, the value to you of the accelerated payoff can easily exceed the cost of the change in the note.

You may also be able to wipe out a loan with unfavorable payment terms by offering a new and larger one. As an existing lender, you already know the security's value and the borrower's payment habits. To make a new loan, you don't have to go through the throes of appraisal, credit reports, etc., that other lenders are faced with. Most borrowers are in need of money and would find a new and larger loan attractive if you pass these savings on in the form of favorable loan terms. In doing so, you can eliminate a loan with too low an interest rate or an abnormally stretched payment schedule.

INDUCEMENTS TO PREPAYMENT

Not all prepayments are advantageous. Even if the prepayment results in a windfall profit, you may lose when the payoff dumps you into a period of low prevailing interest rates. You also may find yourself unable to spend the time on reinvestment and will therefore have to temporarily park the payoff money at reduced rates.

It helps, then, if you give careful thought, make some calculations, and do a little research before making a proposal. Consider beforehand the borrower's financial condition and his plans for the property because these affect the kind of deal you can make. The borrower may also be too dumb to understand the various alternatives, and any time spent on the effort will be wasted.

Prepayment can be encouraged by selling your TD back to the borrower at a discount. The discount will have to be enough to make it worth the borrower's while, but most borrowers are willing to settle for a lower discount than the rest of the market.

Prepayment can also be encouraged by helping the borrower find a buyer for his property. If you sweeten the sale by financing part of it, you may still be ahead if most of your original loan is paid off.

If the borrower is afflicted with an overpowering ego, your insistence on his adherence to the exact terms of the TD may force a prepayment; fear of reprimand will probably torment him enough that he will refinance the loan to get you off his back. Many people of this personality are shiftless in their payment habits, and thus are especially susceptible to this maneuver.

PLAYING THE INTEREST RATE CYCLE

As anyone who has bought a house knows, interest rates fluctuate, usually with a period of more than five years between extremes in the cycle. In recent years the swings in market rate have become wider as the nation's economy adjusts to the accumulations of governmental excess. If your investment strategy doesn't try to accommodate these conditions, you're not doing justice to the earning capacity of your capital. You ignore supply and demand as a factor in your earnings; you neglect the most important factor, the engine by which any enterprise for profit turns.

Those unwary enough not to pay attention to what is going on in the economy may even lose money on their TD investment. Inflation can offset, or even exceed, the rate at which interest is earned. Losses can also be incurred as a result of property taken back by foreclosure in a collapsing market. To meet these conditions, you need to forecast several years ahead, and try to change the composition of your portfolio accordingly.

THE REAL ESTATE OPTION

Every business, whether TDs, real estate, some form of manufacturing, or other, undergoes cycles of profitability. They all have periods of depression during which profits are absolutely lousy, and other (less frequent) times of unimaginable gains. As a consequence, the Johnny-one-note investor who rides out the entire business cycle can only hope to perform efficiently half the time.

TD investors are fortunate in their ability to avoid the limitations of their cycle by switching in and out of real estate. Except during periods of catastrophic change, such as a "great depression," real estate's cycle is usually a

146

slightly delayed reverse of the TD interest rate cycle. Periods of peak profitability in trust deeds tend to be followed by low points in the real estate business, and vice versa. Real estate is also convenient to the TD investor. The close relationship of the two provides the TD investor with a reservoir of knowledge which helps him build expertise in real estate — information which reduces the risk of loss that would otherwise accompany a switch to another business. As a private party investor, you have the inherent flexibility to make such a major change in your strategy. Your competitors, the major financial institutions, are too muscle-bound to make other than token changes of this sort.

You can begin to take advantage of the cycle when you perceive interest rates on the brink of a decline. High interest rates are the consequence of a shortage of money. The greater the shortage, the more it flushes out bargains and distress sales among thinly capitalized real property owners. Real estate prices decline, and continue to do so, well after interest rates start down — sometimes continuing as much as six months past the approximate bottom in TD interest rates. Entry at any point along this part of the TD cycle's curve provides an exceptional profit opportunity: The lower the interest rates fall, the greater the supply of money available to real estate. Yet bargains in real estate persist during the initial part of the low point in the interest rate cycle. Only afterwards does the increased money supply affect property values and real estate prices start to drive upward again.

In the imperfect world of economics, nothing ever happens in a fully predictable manner, and the above can only be an approximation of events; there will always be departures in timing and scale. Furthermore, you will only sometimes have a surplus of money at just the right time, when just the right real estate investment happens along. Therefore, the real estate option may not always be at hand or be appropriate. But you must never ignore it, for it doubles the number of alternatives for profitable investment.

USE OF THE CYCLE TO LEVERAGE TD PROFITS

If you prefer to stick with TDs throughout their interest rate cycle, you can still find opportunities for additional profit by adjusting to changes in the cycle. The aforementioned brink of a decline in interest rates can, for example, produce extra profits if you invest in long term TDs. As market rates of interest go down, natural economic forces place enormous pressure on the borrower. He will make every effort to pay off a long term loan in order to get out from under the burden of a high interest rate. As interest rates decline, he will also find sale of the property more feasible, and this further increases the chance your loan will be paid off. A smart TD investor can develop his strategy to profit from these conditions:

147

- The most difficult to obtain, but still the best method to profit from a need to refinance is to simply eliminate the privilege of early payoff when the TD is written. As explained elsewhere, the right of early payoff, with some exceptions, exists only if the note provides for it. If the borrower wishes to prepay, then the lender is in position to demand additional compensation for the privilege.

- The easiest and most common device used to profit from the payoff is to negotiate a prepayment penalty into the TD (see the appendix on Clauses). Borrowers seldom see far enough down the line to spot reasons for objection to such a clause, even though the charge may cover the equivalent of six month's interest or more.

- Points charged at the inception of a loan are another means of accomplishing the same task. The TD is written at a slightly less than market interest rate, and points are charged to compensate for the difference. To make the arrangement palatable to the borrower, the points are usually added to the loan amount. Then, when the note is prematurely paid off, you gain from a shortened amortization of the points.

- A discount purchase of an existing trust deed accomplishes the same purpose as charging points on a new loan. It also has the advantage of bypassing the borrower in determining the number of points. Here you are dealing only with the previous owner of the TD, and additional discount points therefore come easier.

SHORT TERM LOANS AND THE INTEREST RATE CYCLE

If you find yourself with surplus cash while in the trough of the interest rate cycle, short term loans are your best option. Short term loans generally command higher interest rates. They also set you up for a cash surplus later on, when the loan is paid off and TD rates are higher. Nothing is so frustrating as to be locked into a low interest, long term loan of, say, 12%, when everybody else is doing business at 18%.

You must guard yourself against increased risk in loans made during this period. Sound borrowers are hard to find in times such as these because there is more competition for them among lenders. Furthermore, it seems to be more difficult than at other times to sort out the bad apples. The borrower's quality must also be a grade or so higher when short term loans terminating with a balloon payment are involved. Too often, the borrower miscalculates the impact of the balloon payment requirement. Rather than lose the property by foreclosure, he goes into bankruptcy — leaving you stuck with the loan for another year which, by then, may carry you into another low interest rate market.

Special Problems in Appraisal

CONDOMINIUM APPRAISAL

Condominiums are a method of dividing the ownership of real estate by granting owners title to a specific portion of a building (an apartment unit, for example). If residential condominium units are arranged side by side, each on a separate plot of land, they are also sometimes called "townhouses."

Except for "common area," each unit owner usually receives title to nothing more than the interior surfaces and air space included within the unit's perimeter walls, ceiling and floor. Title to the common area is held in the form of undivided equal fractional interests spread among all the unit owners. The portion owned in common is all that part of the property not considered part of the individual condominium units; i.e., driveways, space between the walls, landscaping, etc.

A condominium development is technically a subdivision and, like any other subdivision, a map is prepared showing the location of each unit. When the map is recorded at the county recorder, the development becomes a legal subdivision. Unit ownership changes are thereafter identified simply by their map reference.

CONDOMINIUM CC&Rs

Condominium developments are governed by a set of rules which act as a sort of constitution for the development's owners. These rules are recorded at the county recorder concurrently with the subdivision map and are called "covenants, conditions and restrictions," or simply "CC&Rs."

CC&Rs supply the wording necessary for establishment of a "condominium association." They provide for election of a board of governors by the unit owners, a method of levying monthly dues for maintenance and operation of the development is established, and the board is given authority to enforce collections. Guidelines instructing the board of directors how to manage various aspects of the development are also sometimes included.

If it were not for the CC&Rs, condominium appraisal would be no more difficult than that of a house; easier, perhaps, because condominium units are more uniform, and therefore comparisons between sales are less complicated. But the CC&Rs add a new dimension to the property's value. In a condominium, the CC&Rs are the very foundation of the development's management. They influence every single decision regarding the development's maintenance and operation. Furthermore, because of characteristics inherent in the condominium concept, CC&Rs are seldom amended; defects in the original document generally remain in place for the entire life of the project.

CHECKING OUT THE CC&Rs

Short term lenders (three years or less) seldom need be concerned about the CC&Rs; a valuation based solely on the condominium unit's comparable sales is usually sufficient because the market price won't change much during the life of the loan. But if your loan is expected to last longer, you need to examine the CC&Rs for flaws. Certain defects can cause cummulative damage to the security and affect the quality of your protection. Don't rely on the opinion of others in this regard. You can't tell who has enough practical experience in condominiums, even among institutional lenders, to rely on the judgement of others. You must make your own examination.

As a lender, you need be concerned with only a few danger spots. Though condominium CC&Rs are an appallingly thick bundle of legalistic jargon that only a lawyer could love, they usually follow a pattern of well-defined headings. You need not wade through the entire mass. Knowing which headings to look for, you should be able to complete your review with less than 15 minutes' reading.

Look at the voting rights section of the CC&Rs. Some developments have such stringent voting requirements that association members find it nearly impossible to govern their affairs. The CC&Rs may require, for instance, approval by 80 percent of the association's members before its monthly dues for maintenance can be changed. As a consequence, the dues remain unchanged despite gradually inflating costs and growing deterioration of the project. The CC&Rs may also require 70 percent of the owners present before the association can vote on any measure; but condominium associations are seldom able to muster more than 55 percent of their members for a vote, and such a clause may prevent them from voting on anything. Without the ability to vote, the association's members can't elect a board of directors, and all the development's services can eventually grind to a halt. Democracy may be one of the greatest organizational devices invented by man, but in this case too much of it can make your security virtually worthless.

Look also in the CC&Rs for a section which defines the powers of the board of directors. Some CC&Rs require general membership approval of the most trivial actions, making the board powerless to accomplish anything substantive.

Look for a section which permits the board to levy fines for failure to comply with association rules. Many CC&Rs do not grant such authority because there is currently much diversity of opinion as to its enforceability. But, even though fines are difficult to enforce, the apparent right to do so is important. A condominium association is not like the landlord of an apartment building; it cannot evict one of its members for destructive conduct. It needs every enforcement tool it can get in order to back up its rules, and the potential for levying fines has an electrifying effect in this regard.

Perhaps the silliest requirement some lenders make is that the CC&Rs carry a "mortgagee protection clause." That is, a clause which gives TDs priority over the homeowner association's lien for dues. Without such a clause, the association's dues are generally senior to any TD secured by the condominium units. In theory, the association can then cut off the lender's security by foreclosing a lien for delinquent dues. But the concern is overdrawn. All deeds of trust permit the lender to step in and pay the dues to protect his security. The lender can foreclose on the advanced dues just as in nonpayment of real property taxes.

WHAT ELSE TO LOOK FOR IN A CONDOMINIUM DEVELOPMENT

Condominium developments occupied by a disproportionate number of renters are not a good source of security. Renters naturally do not display the same dedication and interest in maintenance of the project as do owners living on the premises. Furthermore, because a homeowners association does not have the authority of a landlord, whatever antisocial tendencies the tenants have tend to go uncurbed. As a consequence, most authorities on condominiums regard occupancy by more than 30 percent renters as a sign of serious trouble. As a lender, you do not need to be so limited. You should, however, regard with caution any development which has more than 50 percent occupancy by renters.

Check whether the day-to-day operation of the condominium is under the care of a professional management company. Some condominium associations try to save money by eliminating the services of professional management; the association's board of directors undertakes the task themselves, instead. If the project is a small one, this may be all right. But when the condominium has 20 or more units, the arrangement ultimately ends in disaster. The non-management portion of the membership then delights in taking a whack at other members who are in authority. The visibility of the directors as day-to-day managers makes them an especially easy target, leading to discouragement and deterioration of the project. Loans in these circumstances should therefore be made only with a higher security margin than normal.

WHAT TO LOOK FOR IN RESTAURANTS

If the property is a restaurant or similarly specialized commercial structure, ask whether its equipment has been included in its valuation. People in such businesses have a deceptive habit of valuing their enterprise as an operating entity; that is, with all the kitchen equipment and dining facilities included. They also increase their valuation of the premises to include an element of goodwill. (In other words, they include the value of the business' good reputation among its customers.) But if you have to foreclose, you will be able to claim only the land and buildings as your security. Movable items, such as kitchen equipment, will most likely be owned by a restaurant supplier; the seemingly built-in dining room furniture will turn out to be highly portable and hocked to the same supplier; and the goodwill the business once had will have evaporated. If you end up with the property, it will be little more than a shell, and an ugly one at that, since little care will be taken in removal of the equipment.

LEGAL DESCRIPTIONS

A "legal description" is a formal method of describing the location of a parcel of real estate, whether a condominium unit, house, land, or an easement over land. It is used any time parties to a real estate transaction wish to accurately describe the location of the property involved. Without a proper legal description, many agreements in real estate (including trust deeds) become uninsurable, are refused for recording, and are unenforceable.

Legal descriptions fall into three broad categories:

(1) **Subdivision Map Reference:** Identification of a property by its reference number on a map which has been recorded at the county recorder. Anybody who wants to find the property's exact boundaries can easily do so by

152

looking at the map, a copy of which the county recorder will supply for a nominal fee. Because almost every division of land in California is now considered a subdivision, nearly all newly divided parcels of California real estate are identified in this manner.

(2) **Geographical Survey Description:** Description by reference to identifying points on a U.S. Geographical Survey map; that is, by township, range, and section number. Many older properties in California (especially acreage) are still described in this manner. As time progresses, the method will become less and less prevalent due to the further division of land and consequent description by subdivision map reference. If you do not know how to read a property's location by its geographical survey references, ask an experienced real estate broker or title officer for assistance. Once you get the hang of the system, you seldom will need help.

(3) **Metes and Bounds Description:** A method of explaining the location of a property by first describing the position of a point in its boundary by one of the two previous methods. Commencing with this beginning point, the perimeter lines of the property are each described, one after the other, by their compass direction (called course) and length (distance), until they return to the start. This kind of description is usually accompanied by a surveyor's map of the parcel. If you don't know how to use a compass, you may need the assistance of a surveyor to find the property's boundaries by this method.

LEGAL SUBDIVISIONS

The appraisal of any TD's security, especially raw land, requires investigation as to whether it is "legal" or not. If the property is the result of a division of real estate not sanctified by law, the local building department may not issue a permit for construction on it. Without a building permit, most public utilities will refuse to serve the property. Furthermore, the illegality of the property's creation can be used as a defense against any foreclosure you might undertake. If you do complete foreclosure of such a parcel, all you end up with is a property unmarketable except by deception.

Illegal divisions of real estate are quite common. The division of most real estate requires various governmental approvals. Because such approvals are accompanied by demands for compliance with numerous regulations, property sellers (especially of land) frequently try to avoid the law. They devise tortured schemes which they confidently expect will circumvent the need for governmental approval — schemes often considered successful by the participants only because no one has yet bothered to challenge them.

With few exceptions, every division of real property in California which occurred after March 1, 1975 must be accompanied by an approved subdivision map in order to be "legal." The requirement applies whether the property is broken up into two, four, or a hundred pieces; it applies whether the division is for purposes of sale, financing (as by trust deed), or lease. The requirement also applied to many divisions of property prior to March 1, 1975, but the number of allowable exceptions were then much higher.

Determination of whether your security is "illegal" is simple and it is most easily done during your verification of the property value:

- Any property which is identifiable by a subdivision map reference can be assumed to be "legal."

- Any parcel with a structure on it having a building permit dated *after* the parcel was created will probably be legal. (Municipal building departments generally refuse to issue a building permit if they suspect the parcel is "illegal.")

- Call the local planning department for assistance in verifying the legality of any other parcel, especially land or a parcel created after March 1, 1975.

LEGAL ACCESS AND EASEMENTS

The route by which a property owner gains access to his property also affects its value. Unless the owner has a legal right of access, he must necessarily trespass on his neighbors in order to reach his property. Unless the property owner also has exactly the *right kind* of legal access, he may find himself unable to subdivide his land, unable to get a building permit for construction, and will be denied municipal utility services.

The issue of legal access most often crops up during appraisal of rural property, where land parcels are of acreage size. Because of the vast amount of misinformation adrift about the subject (as well as its complexity), many parcels of raw land are inadvertently created without legal access. But, because greater governmental attention has also been given to the matter, the lack of access has become a more important factor and many properties have declined in value.

EASEMENTS

All properties which front on a public road have an automatic right of access (unless the roadway happens to be restricted, as in a freeway). If another person's property intervenes, however, legal access can only be obtained by an "easement" over the intervening property.

154

An easement can take many forms. It can be limited to specific individuals (a nearby property owner and his invitees), or for specific purposes (an electric company for its power lines). Most easements are also limited as to their location, though they can be so general as to grant right of passage over any part of a property.

One of the greatest difficulties people have with easements stems from their failure to realize that an easement is not necessarily permanent. An easement can have an automatic expiration date, or it may be revocable at the option of the owner of the property over which it passes. Also, an easement recorded subsequent to a TD on the property is automatically cancelled if the TD's beneficiary forecloses.

MISINFORMATION ABOUT EASEMENTS

There are a lot of land investors running around with a false but absolute conviction of their right of access. In some areas buyers and sellers of land have erected an entire body of law of their own on the subject. They happily pass around rules of access based on "common knowledge," because it's easier than looking for the actual limitations on their property.

Many take solace in the belief that everyone has an automatic right of passage along geographical section lines (see Legal Descriptions, earlier in this chapter); therefore, the story goes, any property owner fronting on a section line has a legal right of access to his property. Another fallacy stems from dependence on a statute (which everybody has heard about but never seen) that says nobody can deny an owner access to his property. And almost everybody is convinced that an automatic right of access exists via any preexisting path or road over intervening properties.

The fact is, easements over any property exist only when they are granted in writing by the property owner, or when established by judicial decree.

Prescriptive easements are among those which may be granted by a judge. Until the judge renders his decision, however, there is no easement, and people who conduct themselves otherwise can theoretically be halted on the basis of trespass. On the other hand, if sufficient evidence of the following is brought to court, the judge will grant a prescriptive easement which is limited to people who have had: (1) passage over the property for a period of five years; (2) open and notorious usage; (3) use which was continuous and uninterrupted; and (4) use which was hostile and adverse to the owner. If passage was with permission of the owner, even if revocable, the prescriptive right fails test No. 4.

An easement of necessity is another form of access which can be decided by a judge. "Necessity," in this case, does not mean that you receive access just because you need it; it's granted because a property owner divided and sold some land, but neglected to provide a right of access to the property sold. If this be the case, the court will grant an easement over the seller's remaining property in order to provide access.

In each of the foregoing instances, judicial determination requires suing the owner of the property over which you claim a right of access. If the owner opposes the lawsuit, obtaining the easement can be time-consuming (a matter of years) and appallingly expensive. The judicial approach is therefore seldom sought unless the value of the access justifies the dollars spent — and then only after an unsuccessful attempt at direct purchase of an easement from the intervening property owner.

LEGAL ACCESS, GOVERNMENT STYLE

Any property owner who applies for a building permit must prove to the governmental agency of jurisdiction that the property has "legal access." And "legal access," in this case, is whatever the government agency cares to make it. Furthermore, the agency's definition of legal access can vary from person to person, as well as from time to time. Most agencies are consistent in some respects, however. Frontage on a public roadway is, of course, unquestionably acceptable as a source of access — if there are no barriers such as those along a freeway. The person who reviews your application will also look for such things as: whether your easement is revokable by the owner of the property over which it passes; whether the easement is wide enough (an easement for a footpath won't be wide enough for a truck); whether the easement's wording includes all prospective users (an easement granted to a specific individual will be useless to public utility personnel trying to bring service to a property); and whether the easement is of record, so that its existence can be insured by a title company.

PROPERTY VALUES AFFECTED BY EASEMENTS

A property which lacks legal access would normally seem useless, and therefore be unmarketable. Yet such properties may carry a surprisingly high sales price. One reason is that most investors overpay for their land, largely because they don't have enough information to reasonably judge its value. Most of them buy by mistake, and misunderstanding their rights of access is one of their more common errors.

Even if people do realize that a property is landlocked (that is, lacks a right of access), they still buy, albeit not at as high a price. The desire to own real estate is so fundamental to human nature that many people buy just to

156

be able to say "this land is mine." Furthermore, though a permit to build on such property may not be obtainable, owners often bootleg their construction; they trespass over their neighbors and build regardless of the law, thereby gaining limited use of their land. Also, many buyers of landlocked property do so in the expectation that in time access will become available; they hope that access routes to a public roadway will be created during the course of the division and sale of intervening properties.

Easements also affect the value of property through which they pass. An easement across the middle of a property destroys much of its usefulness. You can't build over the easement, because you will have to tear down the building whenever the easement holder wishes to exercise his right of access. A potential for assertion of prescriptive easement rights over a property can also damage its value; the mere possibility of having to fend off such an attack in court would rattle the nerves of any knowledgeable land investor. On the other hand, if a public utility (a water company, for example) has an easement along the perimeter of a property, its market value will rise because of the close proximity of service.

ENCROACHMENTS AND PROPERTY LINES

If you see any structures located near a property's evident boundries, the job of appraisal will require some precise measurements. Property lines must be accurately identified, and their distances from any structures must be measured. If you don't do so, you may later discover a substantial chunk of value has disappeared from what otherwise seemed to be a perfectly good property. You can't afford to be wishy-washy in this situation.

SETBACKS AND THEIR EFFECT ON VALUE

Municipal ordinances commonly specify the distances a structure must be located from property lines. These are called "setback ordinances." If a property owner builds too close to his boundries, the municipality may demand that the building be torn down, or that the owner apply for a "variance" to the ordinance. The cost in either event can sometimes exceed the value of the structure itself.

The values of oddly shaped, unimproved lots are especially subject to damage from setback ordinances. In order to cope with setback requirements, any construction on the property may have to take on such a peculiar shape that it becomes impractical. Only an adjacent landowner will be able to make use of the property in these circumstances, and its market value will decline accordingly.

ENCROACHMENTS

An encroachment is the projection of a structure onto an adjacent property, or into the airspace of an adjacent property. It may ripen into actual ownership of the encroached property if all the following conditions are met:

(1) The adjacent property must be occupied, and the occupation must be under such circumstances that the property's owner receives actual notice of it.

(2) The occupation must be continuous and uninterrupted for five years.

(3) The encroachment must be hostile and adverse to the owner's title.

(4) It must be open and notorious.

(5) It must be done under some claim of right or color of title.

(6) The claimant must continuously pay all the real property taxes on the encroached property for five years.

THE EFFECT OF ENCROACHMENTS ON PROPERTY VALUE

Given the number of requirements necessary to convert an encroachment into ownership, its effect on property value would seem negligible. Not so. The probability that an encroachment will lead to argument over ownership is so high that any occurrence affects property value. In fact, the value of both of the properties involved is affected. The cost of removing the encroaching structure is one element. The fact that any action taken by either party must be thrashed out in court is another. Restrictions on use or sale of both properties during the period of argument is most damaging of all; the cost of litigation may then be only the smallest part of the expense.

MECHANICS LIENS

As a lender, you must also require that any investigation of a property include examination for "mechanics liens." Such liens affect the amount you can claim as security. Visual inspection of the property is necessary for this purpose, and your visit for appraisal purposes is a convenient time to do so.

THE MECHANIC'S LIEN AS A CONSTITUTIONAL RIGHT

A mechanic's lien has nothing to do with the repair of automobiles or other machinery. Instead, it is the constitutional right of certain individuals to claim payment for improvements on real estate by liening the property upon which they perform their work. Subject to various procedural limitations, the lien holder can foreclose on the property in order to enforce his right to be paid.

Only certain classes of persons are entitled to a mechanic's lien. They are defined by California Civil Code Sec. 3110. They include materialmen, architects, surveyors, subcontractors, laborers, prime contractors, and wreckers who break up and haul away unwanted buildings.

THE EFFECT OF MECHANIC'S LIENS ON LENDERS

A mechanic's lien has priority over a lender's TD if the lien work was commenced, or materials were delivered, before the TD was recorded. Hence, a general contractor's delivery of $1,000 worth of lumber, just before your TD is recorded, can establish the priority of $100,000 worth of subsequent construction. Though the construction may not be finished until a year after your TD's recording, the entire unpaid cost of the work remains senior to the TD. Depending on a complicated set of rules regarding notices and filings, the lien may be asserted any time up to 90 days after completion of the work. If the mechanic's lien holder is not paid, he can foreclose by judicial process, and cut off the TD's claim to the security.

HOW TO PROTECT YOURSELF FROM MECHANIC'S LIENS

When you look at the property, watch for evidence of recent improvements, or delivery of materials. Should anything of this sort show up, start asking questions. You may or may not be looking at mechanic's liens which later turn into a problem, but you can't afford to ignore the possibility. Look for things such as surveyor's stakes, piles of building materials, recently erected structures or alterations, changes in landscaping, grading of dirt, recently installed water or utility lines, holes newly dug or filled, or newly bared foundations left from a building which has been hauled away.

You can also ask for title insurance, which will trigger the same sort of inspection and protect you from mechanic's liens. If you demand the ALTA form of insurance (see Best Title Insurance, in the appendix on Escrow), the inspection for mechanic's liens will be done for you. The title company will send their own representative to look at the property before insuring you against risk of loss by mechanic's liens.

If you discover that the property is encumbered with a mechanic's lien which is senior to your TD, you need not necessarily turn the deal down. You can protect yourself by requiring lien releases from each of those with a potential claim to the property. Be sure the release is not conditioned on the receipt of a payment (a device commonly used to satisfy lenders, but which invalidates the release). You can also require that reserves sufficient to cover the cost of later construction be set aside from your loan amount. This latter procedure is complicated, however, and is best left to those familiar with the intracacies of the mechanic's lien law.

159

If a mechanic's lien holder with rights senior to your TD asserts his collection after your TD is in place, you will be entitled to protect yourself by paying the amount due. The amount advanced can then be added to your claim against the property and be used as a basis for your own foreclosure action. The amount advanced may not be wasted money; the improvements generally make the property more valuable, though not in an amount equivalent to their cost.

APPENDIX B

Trust Deed Clauses and Forms

The main consideration to keep in mind about trust deed clauses is that you can never completely rely on them. The fact that a lender and borrower agree to certain loan conditions often has no significance. The legislature — in its efforts to protect the borrower despite himself — may completely emasculate the effectiveness of a clause by statute. The courts may also mandate changes based on a turn of philosophy laymen consider remote from the issue.

Clauses that appear in the standardized forms of TD provided by title companies are no more reliable than others. Delay brought about by the logistics of printing and issuing the forms prevents them from reflecting the most recent changes in the law. Though the clauses are drafted by attorneys expert in the subject, they are no more determinant of results than other versions of the TD.

Unless you are a specialist, such as an attorney who devotes all his attention to real property security matters, you can never hope to keep track of all aspects of TD clauses. The constant stream of change in the law is simply too much to cope with. You can only try to be aware of those clauses most susceptible to interpretation, so you may know when to seek the advice of an expert.

THE NOTE

The note portion of a TD evidences the agreement between the borrower and the lender regarding the payment terms of the loan, the money part of the deal. The note may also contain bear non-monetary portions of the agreement as a precaution against misunderstanding conditions of special importance. Indeed, the law requires that some clauses, such as a "due-on-sale clause," appear in both the note and the deed of trust in order to be enforceable.

The note is tied to the deed of trust by reference. Sometimes the reference is a simple statement that the note is secured by a deed of trust, and a title company is named as trustee. In this case, the deed of trust need not come into being at the same time as the note. It can be added later, pursuant a separate agreement between the parties. Some versions of the note attempt to be more exact in their reference by identifying the deed of trust as of "even date," or of a given date. This latter form tends to be less confusing when the borrower and lender use the same trustee for multiple notes and deeds of trust. If the note bears no reference to a deed of trust, it will be unsecured except in very narrow circumstances.

THE DEED OF TRUST

PURPOSE OF THE TD

The deed of trust transfers technical ownership of the note's security to a trustee. Because the deed of trust is also a pledge of the security, it is cross-referenced to the note. Various clauses are included which embody the agreement between the parties regarding treatment of the security during the period of pledge. Failure of the borrower to comply with any one of his promises (called "covenants") can theoretically trigger a foreclosure.

The front of the deed of trust contains a description of the pledged security. In order to create a valid pledge, the description must conform with established principles of identification (see Appendix A regarding Legal Descriptions). A legal description referring only to an assessor's parcel number is considered inadequate for these purposes (though it would probably cloud title to the property enough to give the lender some leverage in case of default).

SECURITY PLEDGES BY OUTSIDERS

A note can be simultaneously secured by two or more deeds of trust. Furthermore, each deed of trust can be a pledge of security against the note by parties (trustors) who are separate from the borrower. (Excellent illustration, incidentally, why the words "trustor" and "borrower" should not be used interchangeably.) For example, a relative interested in the borrower's welfare may put up his own real estate as additional security to the loan. Unless the relative also signs the note, his connection with the loan is limited to the security; he is not the borrower and you cannot go to him claiming an additional amount due if foreclosure of the security is inadequate to satisfy the note.

PERSONAL PROPERTY AS SECURITY

The security transferred in the deed of trust cannot include personal property. Personal property is money, goods, and rights of ownership in things which are movable — as opposed to "real property" or "real estate," which is not movable. If personal property is to be pledged as additional security, a separate legal instrument is required. The Uniform Commercial Code dictates the procedure in this case, and a different method of foreclosure is used.

If personal property is affixed to real property so that it is no longer movable, it ceases to be "personal;" it becomes part of the "real" property under a set of rules called the "doctrine of fixtures" (California CC 658 and 660). The rules defining fixtures are complex, but generally anything which is nailed to a building is considered part of the real property. Even if the personal property is attached after the loan is made, it becomes part of the real property which is security for the TD.

Once the former "personal property" becomes part of the real estate securing a TD, it can generally be foreclosed along with the rest of the TD's security. The rules of foreclosure become complicated, however, when a tenant installs trade fixtures, or if the fixtures were purchased by conditional sales contract. If you wish to foreclose on fixtures under these conditions, you should do so only with the aid of an attorney experienced in the matter.

SHORT FORM DEEDS OF TRUST

Most deeds of trust are called "short form" because only the front side is recorded at the county recorder. The TD's back side is incorporated by reference to an earlier recorded fictitious deed of trust bearing the back side's wording. The front limits itself to the basic wording necessary for creation of a deed of trust, plus those portions of the TD which change with each transaction. (The security's legal description, for example.) The back side contains "boiler plate" embodying the bulk of the agreement of a routine nature.

THE POWER-OF-SALE CLAUSE

The power-of-sale clause is considered the guts of the deed of trust because it enables foreclosure by nonjudicial means. Absent the clause, you're stuck with judicial foreclosure, even though the deed of trust transfers the security to a trustee and contains all the other elements associated with a TD.

The power-of-sale clause usually starts with:

Upon default by Trustor in payment of any indebtedness secured hereby or in performance of any agreement hereunder, Beneficiary may declare all sums secured hereby immediately due and payable by delivery to Trustee . . .

Both the note and the deed of trust bear elements of this wording, which appear to accelerate the entire loan's due date upon a default in the payment. The clause is misleading, however, since default does not make the entire loan due and payable, whatever the TD says to the contrary. Unless the note's maturity is also at hand, the borrower always has a right to revive the loan during the first three months of nonjudicial foreclosure.

GUARANTORS

Sooner or later, every TD investor receives an offer of a guaranty as a substitute for insufficient security or poor credit background. Usually, the proposal comes in the form of an offer to "cosign the note." The cosignor's signature is supposed to be a general pledge of all his net worth.

On a practical level, cosignatures are usually worthless unless backed by a pledge of specific assets. Sometimes a friend or relative's unsecured cosignature will help keep the borrower straight for fear of displeasing the cosignor, but even that incentive tends to melt as the size of the obligation rises. A guaranty backed by a pledge of specific assets is infinitely better than a general pledge, and it can be easily implemented via a separate deed of trust signed by the proposed guarantor (see Security Pledges, earlier in this appendix).

LIMITS ON GUARANTY ENFORCEMENT

The enforcement of unsecured guarantees is subject to a number of limits which, while logical, can produce unexpected results. Therefore, any attempts to collect on a guarantor's general pledge should first be discussed with an attorney experienced in this portion of the law.

Basically, the limits on enforceability of unsecured guarantees stem from the antideficiency rules governing TDs (see the Security Limits Appendix). The difficulties start with the fact that, in the case of TDs, the guaranty is tacked onto a secured loan. This creates a problem because California law then permits the guarantor to insist on exhaustion of the security before his guarantee is activated; the property must be foreclosed and sold before the guarantor is approached. But if you foreclose by nonjudicial means, you're checkmated by a second obstacle. The law says that no deficiency judgement is obtainable after a nonjudicial foreclosure; the lender is cut off from all other claims, including that against the guarantor.

EXCEPTIONS (OF A SORT) TO GUARANTY LIMITS

If an unsecured guaranty (i.e., a cosignor's general pledge) backs a junior TD which has been cut off by a senior's foreclosure, the security need not be exhausted in order to activate the guaranty. In this case, the junior TD is termed "sold out," and the law permits him to sue the borrower (and therefore the guarantor) for direct collection from their other assets; a deficiency judgement can be obtained without first resorting to foreclosure.

If your sold out junior is classified "purchase-money," an interesting turn of events is produced: You may be able to collect from the guarantor, even though the borrower has no further obligation in the matter.

If your TD is non purchase-money or is one of the unrestricted classes of purchase-money loans, judicial foreclosure can be used to obtain satisfaction from a guarantor. Foreclosure through the courts satisfies the "exhaustion of security" requirement in the law. Therefore, all you must do to collect a deficiency is include the guarantor in the judicial foreclosure lawsuit. But, as is pointed out elsewhere, judicial foreclosure is an awkward and often impractical procedure. It requires the presence of dollar amounts large enough to justify the effort, a guarantor who will be around a year or more later when the matter comes to trial, as well as a guarantor with a net worth large enough to assure collection once the judgement is received.

You can short-circuit the limits in the general pledge form of guaranty if the guarantor waives his right to "exhaustion of the security." The need to foreclose is thereby eliminated, you can go directly to the guarantor to collect the amount due. The guarantor, in turn, has a cause of action against the borrower for collection of the payoff amount. Under a process called "subrogation," he also has the alternative of stepping into your shoes and foreclosing against the security on his own.

Waivers of the right to exhaustion of the security are often used by institutional lenders, and they work — if the guarantor is a large and responsible organization. Most private lender guarantors are individuals, however. Such guarantors easily find reasons for not meeting their promise when faced with the reality of paying off a loan. You then have a lawsuit on your hands just as though you were forced to exhaust the security through judicial foreclosure, and nothing is gained by the waiver. Faced with such a choice, most lenders decide to collect what they can by nonjudicial foreclosure rather than chase the guarantor. They simply accept their losses as the price of greater wisdom.

LATE CHARGE PROVISIONS

Late charge clauses appear in the note and not in the deed of trust. Given the option, you should insist on a clause approximating the following:

The maker(s) acknowledge(s) that late payment to payee will cause payee to incur costs not contemplated by this loan. Such costs include, without limitation, processing and accounting charges. Therefore, if any installment is not received by payee when due, maker(s) shall pay to payee an additional sum of . . . % of the overdue amount as a late charge. The parties agree that this late charge represents a reasonable sum considering all of the circumstances existing on the date of this agreement and represents a fair and reasonable estimate of the costs that payee will incur by reason of late payment. The parties further agree that proof of actual damages would be costly or inconvenient. Acceptance of any late charge shall not constitute a waiver of the default with respect to the overdue amount, and shall not prevent payee from exercising any of the other rights and remedies available to payee.

The effectiveness of late charge clauses, as well as the rules by which they may be applied, are explained in the chapter on Administration. One major concern is that late charges are supposed to cover actual damages only. The above form may reduce the chance that this will become an issue.

Theoretically, a late charge clause does not give the borrower an implied right to make late payments. Unless the TD contains an express waiver to the contrary, default presumably can still occur the day after a payment is due.

BENEFICIARY FEE CLAUSE

Civil Code Sec. 2943 permits the borrower, or other entitled party, to demand a statement of the condition of the loan from the beneficiary. (See also Beneficiary Statements, in the chapter on Administration.) As of Jan. 1, 1983, demands for a beneficiary statement may also require attachment of copies of the note and deed of trust. The code was therefore amended to permit the lender to charge a fee of up to $50 for the beneficiary statement, *but only if the TD specifically allows such a charge.*

At this writing, no publicly distributed standard form deed of trust carries such a provision. Because preparation of beneficiary statements can be a monumental pain, you should ask for the addition of an appropriate fees clause whenever possible:

The Beneficiary hereunder shall be entitled to a fee for any statement regarding the obligation, requested by the Trustor or any other entitled party, which fee shall be in the maximum amount provided for in Civil Code 2943 and 2954 at the date of such request.

THE ATTORNEY'S FEES CLAUSE

The attorney's fee clause need only appear in the deed of trust in order to be effective. Nevertheless, it is also customarily included in the note, though not necessarily in the same phrasing. Standard phrasing in the deed of trust (reverse side, fictitious deed of trust form) reads:

To protect the security of the Deed of Trust, Trustor agrees: To appear in and defend any action or proceeding purporting to affect the security hereof or the rights or powers of Beneficiary or Trustee; and to pay all costs and expenses, including cost of evidence of title and attorney's fees in a reasonable sum, in any action or proceeding in which Beneficiary or Trustee may appear.

The clause is handy when bankruptcy or condemnation matters arise. It provides a basis to claim reimbursement for your attorney's fees when he attempts to extract the TD from jurisdiction of the bankruptcy court. If your security comes under condemnation, it permits you to charge the borrower for your attorney's fees upon successful defense of your right to the condemnation proceeds.

COSTS OF ENFORCEMENT CLAUSE

The lender's actual costs of foreclosure are rarely limited to trustee's fees and expenses alone. To foreclose, you may have to hire the advice of an attorney, run up a large telephone bill, pay for an appraisal, and incur substantial travel expenses. Only the trustee portion of the charges are recoverable under the standard forms of deed of trust. The trustee will not permit you to add the other costs to the amounts due from the foreclosure. Unless the deed of trust makes express allowance for such charges (and few do), they become your expense.

The wording necessary to convince the trustee that you are entitled to recover these expenses varies. Some trustees require a greater degree of specificity than others. Wording such as the following may be sufficient:

(Trustor agrees) that either the Trustee or Beneficiary, with or without suit, may exercise or enforce the terms of this agreement at the Trustor's expense, whether or not judgement be entered in any action or proceeding, and that either may retain counsel therein, and take such action therein as either may be advised, and for any such purposes may expend and advance such sums as either may deem necessary.

167

Ideally, the clause should be submitted to the trustee for approval ahead of time, before the deed of trust is executed. (And preferably after review by an attorney.) Cost and lack of time often stand in the way of such perfection, however.

THE PREPAYMENT PRIVILEGE

Except as altered by statute, the borrower has no right to prepay his loan unless there is an express provision in the note permitting him to do so. Most notes allow prepayment by adding the words "or more" after the monthly payment amount. The privilege is also created when the note calls for payment "on or before" its due date. More complicated clauses are often employed which permit prepayment, mostly for purposes of limiting the amount which may be prepaid at any one time.

As elsewhere, whatever the intent of the borrower and lender, the law has its own say in the matter:

- If the loan is secured by a single family, owner occupied dwelling, and is arranged by a loan broker, Business and Professions Code Sec. 10242.6 grants an automatic right of prepayment despite any contrary phrasing contained in the TD.

- If the loan is not arranged by a loan broker, but is secured by residential property of four or fewer units, Civil Code Sec. 2954.9(a) also permits prepayment, regardless of the note's phrasing.

- If the loan is the result of a purchase money transaction, the law does not interfere during the first calendar year of the loan's existence — whatever the property's occupancy. After the first calendar year, the lender under purchase money TDs secured by four or fewer units may not forbid prepayment.

- The foregoing rules apply only to currently executed TDs. Older TDs may be subject to different prohibitions against prepayment if the loan was made while different restrictions were in place; in such cases you'll need to consult an attorney to determine the applicable rule.

PREPAYMENT PENALTIES

Although the note portion of a TD may not forbid the borrower's prepayment of the obligation, it may exact a penalty for doing so. A penalty equal to six months interest on the prepaid portion of the loan is typical.

STATUTORY LIMITS ON PREPAYMENT PENALTIES

All loans made by lenders under the jurisdiction of the Federal Home Loan Bank Board are regulated by federal law in their application of prepayment penalties. Private investors in California TDs don't usually encounter this type of loan and therefore must look to state law for limitations on their exercise of the penalty.

As in the case of the prepayment privilege, B&PC Sec. 10242.6 defines the penalty that can be charged for payment of loans arranged by a real estate licensee, which are secured by a single family, owner occupied dwelling. The rules applicable in this situation are very specialized and are best obtained from a loan broker of known competence, as the need arises.

Prepayment penalties are completely forbidden, except under rare conditions — if the loan involves a variable interest rate and security containing four or fewer residential units. For a more exact definition of the application of variable interest prohibitions, see Contingent Interest in the appendix on Usury.

All other notes secured by residential property of four or fewer units are guided by CC Sec. 2954.9 as to the amount of prepayment penalty. The penalty is then limited to no more than the equivalent of six months interest on the prepaid principal if the prepayment occurs during the first five years of the TD. Free prepayment of up to 20% of the original loan during any 12-month period is also allowed during the first five years. No prepayment penalty may be charged after five years.

All purchase money TDs, to a maximum of three per lender in any calendar year, are exempt from the above restrictions, as are all other TDs not secured by four or fewer residential units. Their borrowers and lenders may agree on whatever prepayment penalty they desire, without interference.

EVENTS WHICH TRIGGER A PREPAYMENT PENALTY

Prepayment penalties may only be applied on a borrower's voluntary act which causes the prepayment or upon involuntary activation of a contingency provided for by written agreement. If prepayment is at the election of the lender (as in the application of fire insurance proceeds or condemnation awards), no prepayment penalty may be charged.

Prepayment penalties currently seem possible when a lender accelerates a payment due date in accordance with provisions in the TD. Exceptions abound, however. A prepayment penalty cannot be charged, for instance, when the acceleration is based on a due-on-sale clause if the loan was originally secured by residential property of four or fewer units. Nor can penalties be collected from due-on-sale accelerations of other properties, unless the TD contains the borrower's express waiver of shelter from the penalty. (After Jan. 1, 1984, the waiver also must be separately signed or initialed by the borrower and must be accompanied by payment of consideration.)

PREPAYMENT PENALTY PITFALLS

Unless your right to collect a prepayment penalty is clear cut, consulting a lawyer expert on the subject is wise before attempting its collection. The wrong moves here can get you in a peck of trouble.

If you erroneously include a prepayment penalty in the foreclosure of a TD, the entire procedure will be contaminated. To complete the foreclosure, you may have to start all over again — and you won't be able to collect costs sustained during the previous effort. Even if inclusion of the prepayment penalty in the foreclosure is not in error, its mere presence may give the borrower enough of a handle to obtain restraint of the proceedings until the matter can be sorted out in court as much as a year later.

If you incorrectly demand a prepayment penalty during the course of a prospective sale of the security, the borrower may claim "intentional interference" in his contract with the buyer. You then may be held liable for actual damages to the parties, and perhaps punitive damages.

PREPAYMENT PENALTY GAMESMANSHIP

Borrowers can sometimes avoid a prepayment penalty by taking advantage of its prohibition when there is a due-on-sale clause acceleration of the loan. If the borrower voluntarily pays the lender off, the loan's prepayment penalty will be activated. But if the borrower can convince the lender that the property is to be sold, and can trap the lender into an action evidencing acceleration of the loan, the prepayment penalty can be avoided.

For purposes of the foregoing, the lender's commencement of foreclosure may or may not be necessary to evidence acceleration under the due-on-sale clause. A beneficiary demand for the full payment of your loan may void the prepayment penalty when sent to a sale escrow for the property. Correspondence referring to fees for assumption of the loan may be evidence of acceleration, as may any other action taken which shows your intent to exercise your right to require full payment of the loan.

To escape evidencing acceleration in such circumstances, some lenders communicate their intent to accelerate orally, and send the sale escrow only a statement of the loan balance. Knowledgeable borrowers counter such tactics by mailing the lender a return receipt confirmation of the oral demand. If you're convinced that the circumstances of sale of the property would result in payment of your loan anyway, a letter waiving the due-on-sale acceleration in the current transaction may be sufficient to quell a potential challenge to the prepayment penalty. Otherwise, retention of the prepayment penalty may be an impossible task, especially if the borrower obtains experienced advice.

THE SUBSTITUTION OF TRUSTEE CLAUSE

As beneficiary of the TD, you usually will be able to change trustees by simply recording a notice of substitution. With the exception of some TDs executed before January 1, 1968, substitution does not require the consent of the borrower (trustor) or anybody else, not even the trustee. Unless a notice of default has been recorded, the only required notice of the substitution is its recording; neither the trustor or trustee need be informed. If substitution is undertaken after a notice of default is recorded, the procedure remains the same, except that all those who were entitled to a copy of the NOD, plus the former trustee, must also be informed of the change in trustees.

The beneficiary's privilege of unilateral substitution is granted by CC Sec. 2934a. It is effective for all TDs executed after January 1, 1968, whatever their phrasing to the contrary. If the TD was executed prior to that date, the substitution procedure is dictated solely by the terms of the TD. If the TD was executed December 28, 1967, for instance, and carries no substitution clause, the beneficiary has no privilege of substitution; he must have the borrower's consent before changing to a new trustee.

DUE-ON-SALE CLAUSES

Due-on-sale clauses are used to accelerate the maturity of a TD upon changes in form of ownership of the security. The clause is important, because you have no control over who borrows your money without it. As pointed out elsewhere, the character of the borrower is almost as important as the quality of your security. Without an effective due-on-sale clause, anybody can buy the security and step in as borrower, and then loot the property, go into bankruptcy, or do any number of things which jeopardize the loan.

Because of its social impact, the due-on-sale clause has become such a battleground that details of its future enforceability are unpredictable. At this writing, federal law, via "The Garn Amendment," has been enacted which is supposed to settle the matter once and for all. The subject is so politically sensitive, however, that further tinkering is bound to occur. Furthermore, refinements in the law's application are inevitable; acceptance, for example, of

TD payments after a change in the security's ownership has been construed a waiver of the clause in some instances. Reference to a knowledgeable source of information, as each occasion for enforcement arises, is therefore necessary.

Regardless of its enforceability, you should always try to have the clause included in your deed of trust and note. If you're investing in a new TD, its inclusion usually costs nothing, and the winds can change so that part or all of it can later become enforceable. Its presence may also permit you to throw up so much dust before a change of ownership that you can control the borrower on a de facto basis.

If you find the clause is included in a senior TD, its significance is multiplied. The above mentioned Garn Amendment may be used as a vehicle to override California law. Despite state law, the senior may be able to call the loan due upon change of title from the junior's foreclosure (and sometimes when a junior TD is merely recorded against the property). The junior then must pay off the senior loan, or try to purchase the senior's consent to its assumption. Given the usual circumstances, both objectives will be difficult to achieve, and the junior may be wiped out by the senior's subsequent foreclosure.

Typical wording for the clause reads:

In the event the herein described property, or any part thereof, or any interest therein is sold, agreed to be sold, conveyed, leased, or alienated by Trustor, or by operation of Law or otherwise, all obligations secured by this instrument, irrespective of the maturity dates expressed therein, at the option of the holder thereof and without demand or notice shall immediately become due and payable.

RELEASE CLAUSES

Most standard form deeds of trust contain a worthless release clause. The clause says that the trustee shall reconvey or release the security from the encumbrance upon written request of the beneficiary. The reason for its inclusion is inexplicable, since the trustee cannot act without the beneficiary's direction anyway. Moreover, even though the clause provides for release at the sole direction of the beneficiary, the law prohibits the beneficiary's unilateral release; any release requires the trustor's consent, either specific to the instance or through compliance with the terms of the TD. Release without the trustor's consent could otherwise be used to circumvent the antideficiency portion of the law described in the Security Limits Appendix.

Special form release clauses are written for borrowers who want to be able to liberate part of their property from the encumbrance of the trust deed. Without the clause, the lender can insist on payment of the entire debt before releasing any part of the security. Land developers, in particular, require partial releases so they can borrow, build, and sell from portions of the property while continuing the loan on the remainder.

JUNIOR LIENHOLDER CONSENT MAY BE REQUIRED

Normally, reconveyance of part of the security pursuant to a release clause does not require the consent of junior lien holders. But if the clause is a modification of a TD which was recorded *after* the junior, or if the release is independent of any clause, junior consent is required.

The junior consent requirement is known as the "two fund rule" and is found in CC 2899 and 3433. It protects junior lien holders secured by only a part of a property blanketed by a senior TD. The junior needs to make sure the senior does not issue partial releases without appropriate reduction in the senior debt. If a disproportionate amount of senior debt remains encumbering the junior security, the junior would find himself squeezed out of his protection.

FORMS OF RELEASE CLAUSE

The following form of release clause is typical of those used in acreage size properties:

It is expressly agreed that a partial reconveyance may be had and will be given from the lien or charge hereof, of any parcel, upon payment of a portion of the principal balance then remaining due on said note in an amount equal to the ratio between the area of the property to be reconveyed and the total property then encumbered.

Notwithstanding anything in the foregoing to the contrary, no reconveyance or release shall occur during default in any of the covenants contained herein or in any of the payments due on the promissory note secured hereby. Further, that the Trustor or record owner agree before release of any parcel to create legal access to all the remaining encumbered parcels and that any release or partial reconveyance given shall be in accordance with state and county regulations and at the Trustor's or record owner's expense.

Due to the diversity of transactions, there is no single ideal method of release. The dollar amount of the release can be, as in the above example, proportionate to the acreage released. It can also be based on lump sum payments matched to the release of predetermined parcels. Each situation seems to require adjustments to the needs of the parties involved.

SUPPLEMENTAL RELEASE PROVISIONS TO ASK FOR

To make sure that a partial release does not damage the quality of your security, the remaining property should retain legal access to a public road. As described in the appendix on Appraisal, landlocked property is worth only a fraction of property with the right kind of access.

Equally important is the need to make sure the property remaining after the release continues to front on a utility service line, public road, railroad, or other elements of value — or that a compensating reduction in the principal amount of the loan is made instead.

A proviso that any release be made in accordance with state and county land division regulations is important. Unless the release is based on a legal subdivision, the remaining property will be unmarketable among knowledgeable investors. (For more on this, see Legal Subdivisions in the appendix on Appraisal.)

FIRE INSURANCE CLAUSES

FORM OF CLAUSE AND COVERAGE

Fire insurance clauses commonly read:

To protect the security of this Deed of Trust, Trustor agrees: To provide, maintain and deliver to Beneficiary fire insurance satisfactory to and with loss payable to Beneficiary. The amount collected under any fire or other insurance policy may be applied by Beneficiary upon any indebtedness secured hereby and in such order as Beneficiary may determine, or at option of Beneficiary the entire amount so collected or any part thereof may be released to Trustor. Such application or release shall not cure or waive any default or notice of default hereunder or invalidate any act done pursuant to such notice.

Few forms of the clause attempt to extend the insurance requirement beyond fire protection. Risk of loss through vandalism, theft and catastrophe are ignored. Fortunately, the insurance agent's pursuit of a higher premium, and the property owner's self interest, leads to protection of the lender against these risks also — most fire policies carry an "extended coverage" endorsement covering these hazards, and the lender is caught up in the protection as well.

INSURANCE THAT DOESN'T PROTECT THE LENDER

Note that the sample clause makes it optional, on the beneficiary's decision, whether the proceeds of the insurance will be applied against the loan.

Literal interpretation of the wording seems to leave distribution of the proceeds up to the lender. But this is another case where the law bends the agreement to what it considers equitable treatment.

California courts have found that the insurance clause contains an implied "covenant of good faith." Therefore, the reasoning goes, a lender may not demand the insurance proceeds when there has been no impairment of his security. Even when the security *is* impaired, the lender still may not claim the proceeds if the borrower intends to use the money to rebuild the property (81 CA 3d 75).

Some lenders attempt to circumvent the problems of interpretation inherent in the "covenant of good faith" by altering the clause's standard phrasing. They make mandatory the application of insurance proceeds against the note in hopes that a clear statement of contractual intent will overcome any argument. Nevertheless, it's still probable that a determined property owner can successfully resist turning over the insurance money when the loan remains secure.

THE CONDEMNATION CLAUSE

The intent of the condemnation clause is much the same as for fire insurance. In this case, the purpose is the application against the amount due on the TD of any money received from a public taking of the security . Again, as in the fire insurance clause, the "implied covenant of good faith" prohibits collection of the proceeds when the quality of the security is unimpaired.

The question of the amount of security that can be taken before your loan becomes unsafe complicates matters. A reduction in the security may not bring its value below the amount due on the TD, yet still jeopardize the safety of the loan. If the loan ratio becomes unbalanced, the TD will be unsafe, but few experts can agree on the definition of a safe loan ratio. A lot of strategy and maneuvering can therefore accompany this type of situation, a subject dealt with extensively in the appendix on Condemnation.

THE "WASTE" CLAUSE

Because lenders need to be able to prevent loss of security value through the borrower's improper management, deeds of trust include wording such as the following:

To protect the security of this Deed of Trust, Trustor agrees: To keep said property in good condition and repair; not to remove or demolish any building thereon; to complete or restore promptly and in good and workmanlike manner any building which may be constructed, damaged or destroyed thereon and to pay when due all claims for labor performed and materials furnished therefore; to comply with all laws affecting said property or requiring any alterations or improvements to be made thereon; not to commit or permit waste thereof; not to commit, suffer or permit any act upon said property in violation of law; to cultivate, irrigate, fertilize, fumigate, prune and do all other acts which from the character or use of said property may be reasonably necessary, the specific enumerations herein not excluding the general.

Foreclosure based on the above clause is inhibited because it attempts to include a number of covenants unrelated to protection of the security. Features such as agreement to comply with all laws affecting the property, for example, probably cannot be used for a foreclosure based on waste.

When there is evident waste of the security, the method of foreclosure is theoretically dictated by the type of waste that occurs. The law distinguishes whether or not the waste is "bad faith" or not. If the waste is in bad faith, nonjudicial foreclosure is possible. But a nonjudicial foreclosure for bad faith waste is susceptible to challenge on whether the waste has been cured or not. Such defaults are not easily reduced to dollars and cents and are not as reliable as failure to pay on the note. Therefore, judicial foreclosure is the route most often chosen when waste is the source of default.

The standard form waste clause could actually be dropped in its entirety from the deed of trust with little change in its enforceability; CC 2929 already imposes the requirement that the trustor refrain from "any act which will substantially impair the mortgagee's security." This section of the civil code can only be used to obtain an injunction against waste, and not for foreclosure; but then, an injunction may be a more practical means of enforcement anyway.

THE ASSIGNMENT OF RENTS-AND-PROFITS CLAUSE

This clause is automatically included in most deeds of trust; in fact, most deeds of trust are entitled "Deed of Trust and Assignment of Rents." The clause usually appears on the front of the document, with supplemental wording of great length on the reverse. Typical wording includes the following:

Trustor also assigns to Beneficiary all rents, issues and profits of said realty reserving the right to collect and use the same except during continuance of default hereunder and during continuance of such default authorizing the Beneficiary to collect and enforce the same by any lawful means in the name of any party hereto.

JUDICIAL CONSENT IS REQUIRED

The usual phrasing of the rents-and-profits clause appears to give the beneficiary right to grab the trustor's "rents and profits" directly upon default. Again, the wording in the agreement does not necessarily accomplish the fact.

The mechanics of collecting rents and profits operate against activation of the clause. In order to collect, possession of the property is a practical necessity. But if you attempt to take possession of the property by other than peaceable means (i.e., if forceable entry is required), you can be held criminally liable as a trespasser.

The real value of the rents-and-profits clause is its authority for gaining possession of the security's proceeds by judicial means. It gives you the right to ask the court to appoint a receiver who will undertake specific performance under the deed of trust — that is, to collect rents and profits and to manage the property so to reduce waste during the foreclosure period.

Absent a rents-and-profits clause, you still have a right to appointment of a receiver, but the proofs necessary to the accomplishment are much more stringent. (Even with the clause, the proofs necessary to get some courts to appoint a receiver are so stiff you may not be successful.)

The legal procedure necessary for appointment of a receiver costs time and money, a cost you may not be able to recover from the borrower; only if you are successful can you tack the legal expenses onto the amount due under the TD.

TRAPPED BY AN HONEST TRUSTOR

Sometimes a borrower surrenders his rents voluntarily in order to fulfill his obligation under the rents and profits clause. If this occurs, you must be very careful to do nothing which might create the impression you are in possession of the property. Otherwise, you may be tagged as having performed "possessory acts" which make you a "mortgagee in possession." As such, you may be held liable to the owner of the property (and junior lien holders and any others with an equitable interest in the property), for real or imagined errors in its management.

THE ABSOLUTE ASSIGNMENT OF RENTS

The rents-and-profits clause is sometimes amended to assign all rent collections to the beneficiary as of the inception of the loan. This is called an "absolute assignment of rents" and is appended separately to the deed of trust.

It is a highly effective means of encouraging payment of a loan — except that it shares the same danger of making you a mortgagee in possession, along with the accompanying liability.

FUTURE-ADVANCES CLAUSES

The front portion of many trust deeds contain a future- advances clause buried in a recitation of the purpose for the security:

> *. . . for the purpose of securing payment of the indebtedness evidenced by a promissory note, of even date herewith, executed by Trustor in the sum of $_____, any additional sums and interest thereon hereafter loaned by Beneficiary to the then record owner of said property, which loans are evidenced by a promissory note or notes, containing a recitation that this Deed of Trust secures the payment thereof.*

Though there once was considerable argument over a TD's ability to secure future advances, the dust has now pretty well settled on the issue. Since enactment of CC 2884, lenders have had conclusive authority to enforce such a clause. In fact, the code now permits a deed of trust to be created without any currently existing debt; you can fill in the note portion of the TD later, when the money is needed.

ADVANTAGES OF FUTURE-ADVANCES CLAUSES

A TD without future-advances phrasing should not necessarily be cause for distress. Wherever you have the option of requiring the clause, however, you should ask for it; it's a handy thing to have around.

If the trustor wishes to borrow additional amounts against the security, the clause permits you to add to the loan without need of a new deed of trust. The expense of additional title insurance and escrow activity can thereby be avoided. A borrower who needs money for improvements to the security, or to relieve a tight spot in his cash flow, will be more easily accommodated. Some lenders whose rules prohibit lending under 2nd TDs also use the clause to include subsequent loans under their 1st TD.

The clause is *not* necessary to add advances to a loan when the purpose is protection of the security (as for taxes). Other provisions in the trust deed, as well as the Civil Code, permit addition of this type of advance to the loan.

EFFECT OF ADVANCES ON JUNIOR LIEN HOLDERS

Advances under the clause may or may not take priority over junior lien holders. Their priority depends on the payments' timing, on the clause's wording, and the methods the parties use to give one another notice. If a 1st TD carries a clause which calls for obligatory payments, its advances will be senior to any junior TD. On the other hand, if the clause only calls for optional advances (as in the sample given earlier), the payments will be senior only if made before creation of the junior TD or when the 1st TD is unaware of the junior's existence.

The above framework affords opportunity to play all sorts of games. The question of what is obligatory, for example, can make the 1st and 2nd TDs' lawyers rich if the lenders decide to fight about it. On this issue alone, a scrappy junior may be able to scare a timid senior away from further advances, and thereby negate the effect of the clause. Construction lenders are especially susceptible to this kind of argument. So many ways are available to interpret such obligation that the potential for dispute can only be avoided by scheduling the advances with great precision.

The question of proper notice can also lead to a squabble over priority. A 1st TD's advances which are clearly optional aren't necessarily subordinate to a preexisting junior, unless the 1st has actual knowledge of the junior. Apparently lenders are not supposed to consider the recording of the junior lien as notice to the senior in these circumstances. Direct written notice from the junior to the senior may or may not be required, dependent on the mood of the judge, if the junior wishes to avoid subordination to a senior's later optional advances.

DRAGNET CLAUSES

Dragnet clauses are an expansion of the future advances concept. Instead of limiting the security to future loan amounts, a dragnet clause pledges the property against all monetary debt between the borrower and lender. Every conceivable obligation between the two, whether past, present, or future, whether secured or unsecured, is gathered under the protection of a deed of trust containing a dragnet clause. Even such diverse matters as the borrower's checking account overdrafts and credit card purchases are secured by the TD if the lender happens to be carrying those accounts.

Dragnet clauses are usually created by appending wording such as the following to a future advances clause:

. . . And for the purpose of securing any other indebtedness or obligation of the Trustor, or any of them, and any present or future demands of any kind or nature which the Beneficiary or its successor may have against the Trustor, or any of them, whether created directly or acquired by assignment, whether absolute or contingent, whether due or not, whether otherwise secured or not, or whether existing at the time of the execution of this instrument, or arising thereafter.

A WARNING ABOUT DRAGNETS

Private party investors don't ordinarily come across dragnet TDs. If you are offered such a TD, be sure to examine the reason for its presence — it could be a clue to a weak borrower. The original lender may have started with an unsecured loan which the borrower had difficulty paying. It's considered smart in such circumstances to maneuver the borrower into a secured position (usually by offering an extension on the loan in exchange for the pledge of security). By nailing down the security, the lender hopes to beat out other creditors in their race to attach the borrower's assets. Unless you are prepared to treat the TD as a way of purchasing the property by foreclosure, any infirmity in the borrower should therefore be taken as cause for its rejection.

LIMITS ON THE CLAUSE'S USEFULNESS

Use of a dragnet clause is subject to literal interpretation of its wording. Its implementation must also match the parties' actual expectations at the time the trust deed was executed. The lender cannot, for example, later go around buying up unsecured obligations of the borrower in the expectation of including them under the dragnet TD's protection.

An unsecured lender's position is not always improved by use of a dragnet TD. By taking on the security, the lender becomes unable to force collection by any procedure other than foreclosure (CCP 726). As explained in the appendix on Security Limits, he gives up any practical chance of obtaining a deficiency judgement if the security is too weak. On the other hand, as an unsecured lender he has the ability to attach any or all the borrower's other assets while in pursuit of payment.

SUBORDINATION CLAUSES

Subordination clauses derive from priority of TDs under the rule of first in time (of recording) is first in right (of claim against the security). (CC 2897.) With a subordination clause, the borrower sets aside the rule, so that a later recorded TD may step into 1st priority. Without the priority created by such a clause, most institutional lenders would be unable to finance construction improvements.

The clause was once dynamite to unsophisticated land owners. Lured by an unexpectedly high offer for his property, an owner would sell his acreage to a developer. In his eagerness to sell, the owner would agree to take back a TD as part of the sale price. But buried in the TD would be an agreement to subordinate it to a later recorded construction loan. If the seller questioned the arrangement, his fears were usually allayed by claims that the construction loan improvements would bring about a corresponding increase in the property's security value. But many property sellers failed to recognize that the clause effectively compelled them to assume all the risks of the development and share in little of its profits. If the development was successful, the seller would be paid off according to the terms of his TD. The developer would then receive the bulk of the profits. If the project failed, the developer could walk away from his obligations — and leave the seller to absorb the losses when the construction lender foreclosed him out.

As junior lien holders, subordinated lenders have the right to cure a default in a construction 1st in order to prevent being cut off by foreclosure. But few property sellers have the financial capacity to do so. Furthermore, by the time the construction lender gets around to foreclosure, the project is usually in a mess. The construction loan money also used to be sometimes siphoned off for other purposes. Worse yet, partially completed projects are invariably worth only a fraction of the money put into them. Therefore, most subordinated junior lenders have to let the property go upon default in the senior loan.

So, to protect the subordinated lender in spite of himself, the law has been changed to do his thinking for him — and, in the process, nearly eliminated the clause's effectiveness.

SUBORDINATION REQUIREMENTS

To make sure inexperienced lenders are given fair warning, any loan of less than $25,000 must contain a large-print notice of its subordination. The clause must also spell out the actual terms of the prospective senior loan, whatever the size of the TD. Subordination clauses must furthermore be fair, and they must stipulate the use to be made of the senior money. The required description of the senior TD must include the clauses to be used in its deed of trust, as well as the interest rate and scheduled payments. Failure to meet any of these requirements either invalidates the subordination, or limits it so much it becomes useless.

LIMITS ON SUBORDINATIONS

In recent years, the judiciary has tended to impart enforceability to the subordination clause by retaining the specificity requirements. Nevertheless, an effective clause still cannot ordinarily be written unless the new senior loan is also right at hand, ready to be recorded. Property development based on a subordination clause is not feasible until construction financing has been set up. Title companies are in such a dither over the exactitude of the law that they limit use of the clause still further; they refuse to insure unless the construction loan is either recorded before that of the subordinated lender (in which case the subordination clause is no longer necessary), or a subordination agreement in immense detail is drawn up and executed as a separate instrument.

Gone also are the days when construction loan money could be bled off by use of imaginative bookkeeping. If the TD is to be subordinated to a loan for the construction of improvements, the money can be used only for items directly identifiable with the project. The developer cannot pay administrative overhead, interest, or loan fees out of the construction loan.

INVITATION TO A LAWSUIT

If a subordinated lender becomes unhappy with the treatment he receives, he can taint everyone connected with the transaction. He may not be able to bring about cancellation of the senior lender's priority (even though there is misappropriation of funds), but he can sue for damages. For this purpose, he can join both the construction lender and the developer (borrower) in the action. Third parties, such as an escrow, have also been dragged into such squabbles on the basis of their failure to protect the subordinated lender.

On the other hand, the subordinated lender is also open to lawsuit under some versions of the clause. In an attempt to avoid the specificity requirements of the law, some construction lenders require a clause which compels the seller of the property "to execute such further documents as are necessary to a later subordination." The seller then must cooperate as much as can reasonably be expected, given the intentions of the parties. But the participants never interpret their intentions the same way, and therefore the situation is rife with opportunities for dispute.

ALL-INCLUSIVE DEEDS OF TRUST

These TDs are also called "AITDs" or "Wraparounds."

An AITD is a TD which states that the dollar amount of its obligation includes (wraps around) a previously recorded TD secured by the same property. As part of the agreement, the AITD lender assumes responsibility for satisfying all the terms of the senior lien, including the payments. For this purpose, the AITD usually says: ". . . *the obligation for the senior encumbrance(s) is therefore that of the (AITD) lender.* . . ." Samples of the complete wording can be obtained from some of the title companies who have standard forms for this purpose.

An AITD can be written, for example, in the amount of $100,000, with interest at 10% and monthly payments of $1,000. It may wrap around an existing 1st TD of $50,000, 5% interest, and $500 a month payments. As part

182

of the agreement, the AITD lender assumes responsibility for the 1st TD's $500 a month payments, the property owner (AITD borrower) pays the AITD lender the entire $1,000 called for in his loan.

ADVANTAGES IN AITDS

AITDs are most frequently used to jack up the amount of interest collected by the AITD lender. The financing in the foregoing example could have been cast in the form of a 2nd TD of $50,000 on top of the $50,000 1st for a total encumbrance of $100,000. But by wrapping a $100,000, 10% interest AITD around the $50,000, 5% interest 1st TD, the AITD lender is able to pick up an additional 5% return on the initial $50,000.

AITDs are also written for their tax advantages. The borrower and lender can then simultaneously profit from use of an AITD. For instance, by playing around with the AITD's monthly payments, the parties can either reduce or increase their tax reportable income and expense, as suits their purpose. The variety of maneuvers that can be concocted by a tax consultant with a devious mind are almost infinite when AITDs are involved.

AITDs are sometimes also used as a sales device by people who wish to dangle attractive payment terms in front of prospective buyers of real estate. In this instance, the interest relationship given in the earlier illustration may be reversed: The AITD charges only 5% interest in order to attract a buyer, while assuming the obligation of making the 10% interest payments on the 1st TD.

PROBLEMS WITH SENIOR PAYMENTS

The most obvious defect in wraparound TDs concerns problems that arise if the AITD lender fails to keep up the 1st TD's payments. Most AITD forms attempt to defuse the problem by permitting the property owner to step in and cover the missing payments. The payments thus advanced are then deducted from the amounts due the AITD lender. But if the owner is not promptly informed of the AITD lender's failure to pay the 1st, the cost of curing a default can be significant. An AITD which permits the property owner to pay the 1st TD directly, and reduce the AITD payments accordingly, is therefore much better from the borrower's standpoint.

THE PROBLEM OF DIFFERENT AMORTIZATION RATES

The biggest defect in the AITD way of doing things results from the fact that the amortization rates of the AITD and 1st TD are almost never the same; one is always being paid off at a faster rate than the other. If the AITD is paid off faster than the 1st TD, it will become smaller than the 1st TD at some point along the line. When the property owner pays off the AITD according to its terms and asks for reconveyances to clear the encumbrances, a balance may still be due on the 1st. If the AITD lender does not have the cash to pay off the 1st, the property owner has a real problem.

BLANKET 1ST TDS / DEATH BY STRANGULATION

If Jonah had tried to swallow the whale, he would not have been much different from lenders who attempt to write an AITD which wraps around a much larger, blanket 1st TD. This situation crops up every once in a while in minor subdivisions. To avoid paying off a 1st TD covering all his property, the subdivider finances his sales by carrying back AITD paper. He makes each AITD subject to, and inclusive of, the blanket 1st TD covering all the lots. More often than not, the amount due on the 1st TD exceeds the individual AITD which is supposed to wrap around it.

To mask the apparent impossibility of such a feat, the subdivider points to a release clause written into the 1st TD. In theory, the property buyer can liberate his land from the blanket 1st by paying a release amount which is only a fraction of the total due on the first TD. But most release clauses also say that the release privilege cannot be exercised if the TD is in default in any way (not just in the payments). If the developer stumbles and goes into default, the property owner becomes obligated for the entire 1st TD. He must cure the default himself, or pay off the subdivision's entire encumbrance to keep from being foreclosed. Either way, the cost can easily exceed the value of his individual lot.

The property owner, in this most screwy of all TDs, is in a poor position, but the AITD lender's predicament may be worse. Many trustees refuse to act on foreclosure of such TDs because of difficulties in obtaining title insurance; the possible necessity of paying off the much larger blanket TD would chill the bidding at the foreclosure sale, make the sale a sham, and therefore invalid. Any release clause contained in the blanket encumbrance would be useless to outside bidders, because it probably would not be transferable — an outside bidder would have no contractual relationship with the 1st and therefore insufficient standing (called "privity of contract") to demand a release. The AITD lender must therefore be prepared to pay off the entire blanket encumbrance in order to enforce his collections, or make sure his buyers never have reason to be unhappy with their purchase.

How to Calculate Yield

Investment yield rate is the amount of profit expressed as an annual percentage of the total dollars invested. Yield rate differs from TD interest rate because it accounts for additional variables such as prepayment penalties and discount points. Because yield calculations attempt to uniformly reflect the entire annual percentage profit earned, they can be used to compare all varieties of TDs. TDs for $1,000 are placed on the same footing as those for $100,000; and the performance of a six month TD can be measured against one which lasts for six years. Yield rates are, in fact, the common demoninator in comparing the performance of all forms of investment, whether TDs, shares of stock, or a chicken ranch.

In TDs, yield calculations are usually brought on by a need to measure the effect of discounts received in the purchase of existing TDs, or of percentage points collected for making a new loan. Many publishers provide tables which make the calculation easy so long as the TDs follow a pattern of regular monthly payments. An example of one of the tables, published by Contemporary Books of Chicago, Ill., is shown as an exhibit at the end of this appendix.

When TDs depart from the usual monthly payment configuration, most investors run into trouble. Yield rates may be the common thread that binds all trust deeds together, but investor inability to calculate yield in unusual situations is equally common. The use of rule-of-thumb estimates is widespread, and so are gross errors in calculated rates of return. Figuring the true yield is simple, however, once you understand the logic behind the calculation. With clear understanding, you can profit handsomely from the inability of others to cope with the situation.

RULE-OF-THUMB ESTIMATES

Most investors believe that you can approximate a TD's yield rate if you divide the percentage amount of the discount received by the number of years of investment, and then add the product to the TD's interest rate. But the formula is much more inaccurate than is generally realized.

For example:

A $10,000 trust deed bears interest at 10% per annum. It is offered at $8,000 (a 20% discount). No payments are required on the TD for 5 years, at which time the entire principal amount and accrued interest (a total of $16,105) become due.

The typical investor makes a quick calculation:

The amount of the discount is	20%
He divides by the number of years to final payment	5
Which gives an average annual discount of	4%
The annual interest rate, as per the note, is	10%
Therefore, his estimated annual yield is	14%

The smart investor takes only a little more time and finds the real rate of return through use of Compound Interest and Annuity Tables or from a calculator programmed for that purpose. In the above example, he would find his true yield to be very close to 15% per annum (see Sample Calculations, later) — a 7.3% difference in the rate of profit.

HOW TO CALCULATE TRUE YIELD

PRESENT VALUE AND FUTURE VALUE

A need to understand the twin concepts of "present value" and "future value" is central to understanding yield calculations. The logic behind these two values is simple, and once you pass this minor barrier the calculation becomes easy.

Present value is the current worth of something that is due in the future. For instance: A new $10,000 TD at 10% interest with a one-year maturity will (assuming there are no interim payments) pay $11,000 at the end of the year. In this case, the $10,000 beginning amount is the present value of the future $11,000 payment when the money is worth 10% per annum.

Future value works in a reverse manner. In the above example, the future dollar value of your initial $10,000 investment is $11,000 assuming the investment is to earn 10% per annum.

If instead of the above single payment you are the recipient of a series of payments, the concepts still apply. Each payment in the series has a separate value. The discounted price necessary to produce a given yield in a TD is, hence, the sum of the present values of all the payments.

AIDES TO CALCULATION

You don't have to actually calculate the present value of each payment in order to find the discounted purchase price necessary for a given yield. If the payments occur at regular intervals and in equal amounts, financial tables can draw all the separate present values into a single total for you so that the value of the TD may be reckoned in one simple computation.

With the use of calculators such as Hewlett-Packard's HP 12C or one of Texas Instrument's "Analyst" models, the calculation of present values becomes even more convenient. These calculators are small enough to be hand held and are beautifully programmed to solve in seconds just about every problem a trust deed investor might run into. Their operation can easily be learned from instruction booklets provided by the manufacturer — if you restrict yourself solely to those instructions dealing with yield calculations; trying to wade through the entire booklet can otherwise lead to confusion because the instructions also deal with a huge variety of calculations relative to other uses for these handy little devices.

A SAMPLE CALCULATION OF TRUE YIELD

Given the example of the TD described in the rule-of-thumb calculation earlier, true yield can be found by use of a calculator such as the HP 12C in the following manner:

In the upper left portion of the calculator, you'll find a row of six keys labeled [n], [i], [PV], [PMT], [FV], and [CHS]. Most financial calculators bear a set of the same or similarly labeled keys which perform the same function. These keys, along with the calculator's numerical key pad, are all you need for most TD calculations.

To calculate the true yield from a TD such as the example, you'll first need to figure the TD's final payoff amount. For this purpose, you need to enter:

The interest rate (10% per year in this case) with the [i] key.

The number of interest compounding periods (5 years in this case) at the [n] key.

The present value of the loan amount ($10,000) with the [PV] key.

If interim loan payments were called for, their amount (per [n] period) would be entered at the [PMT] key, with the [CHS] "change sign" key punched to indicate it is the borrower's outgoing negative payment. In this example, no monthly or other interim payments are called for so the [PMT] and [CHS]) keys go unused. To find the final future payoff amount, then, all you need do is punch the future value or [FV] key. After a few seconds of busyness during which the calculator blinks away at you, the borrower's final balloon (outgoing negative) payment of $16,105 shows up on the screen.

With the balloon final payment information at hand, you're now in position to find the TD's yield when purchased at a discount. For this purpose, you need only change the amount carried under the calculator's present value [PV] key from the former $10,000 to the new value of $8,000. All the previous entries (including the recently calculated final payment) remain unchanged in the calculator. To change the [PV] figure, all you need do is key in the $8,000 and the previous entry will be automatically displaced. This, in turn, causes the TD profit to increase because of the discount to be collected — and that forces the rate of return (yield) carried in the calculator under the [i] or interest key to automatically change. To recall the amount now carried under the [i] key (or from any of the other keys), simply push the appropriate key and the new interest (yield) rate of 15.02% will appear on the screen.

DISTORTIONS CAUSED BY MONTHLY COMPOUNDING

Technically, all references to yield are based on an annual percentage rate, or APR. This was the convention used in the foregoing example. It is supposed to be the common basis of comparison used by every investor and assumes that interest is collected annually. The convention is also required by the "truth-in-lending" statutes when you report to the borrower the actual rate of interest he is being charged.

But most trust deeds require monthly payments and stipulate that the payment "be applied first against interest and then against principal." The real result, then, is a monthly compounding of interest because the interest is collected monthly. Theoretically, the interest can be reinvested each month. In other words, interest is earning interest. This means that a note which reads 10% per annum will produce an effective annual percentage rate of 10.47% if it calls for monthly payments. The following table shows the impact of this under varying rates of interest:

"Per Annum" Interest Rate	Interest Rate When Compounded Monthly
6%	6.2%
8	8.3
10	10.5
12	12.7
14	15.1
16	17.2
18	19.6
20	21.9
25	28.1
30	34.5

Because the differences caused by monthly compounding increase as the interest rate rises, monthly payments can distort your calculation of a TD's yield. Conversion to a true annual rate can easily be made, however, with the aid of the instructions provided with most financial tables and financial calculators. A number of specialized tables are also available for this purpose. Investors not frequently in the market can probably obtain the same information by calling their banker.

HOW TO CALCULATE AITD YIELD

Calculation of the yield derived from an all-inclusive trust deed has always been a bugbear to investors. Each investor seems to apply a different brand of logic to the calculation. Some of the most reputable people in the business come up with formulas which differ wildly and which only roughly approximate the yield. But the reasoning behind AITDs is simple, and so is the calculation when done correctly.

The usual source of the trouble is the fact that AITD payments are collected according to one schedule, and then you must turn around and pay out money to senior TDs according to a different schedule. The solution to the difficulty rests in the logic used in all calculations for yield: You measure only the present value of the stream of cash which comes from the trust deed, in this case the net stream of cash. The interest rate shown on the note has nothing to do with the calculation, except as a means of figuring the length of time and amount of cash payments collected.

The following is a simplified example of the calculation needed:

An AITD is written for $20,000 at 12% interest and requires an annual payment of $3,000. At the end of three years, the entire balance comes due at which time the lender collects $20,975 (which amount includes the last year's accrued interest).

At the same time, the AITD wraps around a 1st TD in the amount of $10,000, 10% interest, and annual payments of $1,000 due roughly the same date as the AITD collections. The 1st also balloons at the end of three years, at which time the AITD lender must pay out $11,000 (including the last year's accrued interest).

The stream of cash collected is then:

END OF THE	AITD RECEIVES	AITD PAYS 1ST TD	NET CASH RECV'D
1st year	$ 3,000	$ (1,000)	$ 2,000
2nd year	3,000	(1,000)	2,000
3rd year	20,975	(11,000)	9,975
			$13,975

190

If you buy the above AITD at a discount of 10% of its equity, you will have purchased the above stream of cash for $9,000;

AITD balance	$20,000
1st TD	(10,000)
Net AITD equity	$10,000
Discount 10%	(1,000)
Purchase price	$ 9,000

Your yield calculation then resolves itself to finding the rate of return that produces a present value of $9,000 on the net cash collected.

A search in your calculator for present values [PV] at various [i] interest rates reveals that at 19% per period the following will be the value of the amounts collected:

The present worth of $2,000 collected 1 year hence is	$1,680
The present worth of $2,000 collected 2 years hence is	$1,412
The present worth of $9,975 collected 3 years hence is	$5,919
And the sum total of the present values is	$9,011

Since $9,011 closely approximates your $9,000 investment, the real rate of return must be 19% per annum.

Most AITDs call for payments on a monthly basis, rather than by the annual rate used in the above example. In that case, the foregoing method can be used without much distortion by lumping the monthly payments into more easily managed groups. For example, the payments for an entire year can be totaled and regarded as collected at the midpoint of the year.

For purposes of simplicity, the above example assumed that the payment dates of both the AITD and the 1st TD around which it wrapped were roughly the same. In the real world such perfection is only a dream, and you will be certain to come upon AITDs with radically different payment dates. As a consequence there will be periods of negative flow in the AITD's stream of cash due to payouts which are out of phase with collections. Your yield calculation during those periods is then reversed. The negative portion of the scheduled stream of cash is figured on the *future value* of the payout instead of the present value normally obtained. Each yield table contains both present and future value figures on the same line, and you can switch back and forth, depending on whether you have a negative or positive cash flow. The positive and negative values are then added together, just as in the original example, in arriving at the TD's present value.

To make the calculator easier to use, the procedure used in the example calculation used a trial and error search to find the yield. The time required for this kind of search is negligible because all the information is stored in the calculator; you can simply punch different keys to sort through various interest rates and their present values until you find the matching investment amount. However, with the use of a few additional keys most financial calculators are able to find the yield in such example situations with a single calculation. Learning this latter method is relatively easy once you find the appropriate explanatory page in the calculator's instruction booklet.

DISCOUNT %	MONTHLY PAYBACK RATE (%) (MONTHLY PAYMENT DIVIDED BY LOAN AMOUNT)										
	.83	.85	.90	.95	1.00	1.05	1.10	1.15	1.20	1.25	1.32
1.0	10.16	10.16	10.17	10.17	10.18	10.19	10.19	10.20	10.21	10.22	10.24
2.0	10.32	10.33	10.34	10.35	10.36	10.38	10.39	10.41	10.43	10.45	10.48
3.0	10.49	10.49	10.51	10.53	10.55	10.57	10.59	10.62	10.65	10.68	10.73
4.0	10.65	10.66	10.68	10.71	10.74	10.77	10.80	10.83	10.87	10.92	10.98
5.0	10.82	10.83	10.86	10.89	10.93	10.96	11.01	11.05	11.10	11.15	11.24
6.0	10.99	11.00	11.04	11.08	11.12	11.17	11.22	11.27	11.33	11.40	11.50
7.0	11.16	11.18	11.22	11.27	11.32	11.37	11.43	11.49	11.56	11.64	11.76
8.0	11.34	11.36	11.41	11.46	11.52	11.58	11.65	11.72	11.80	11.89	12.03
9.0	11.52	11.54	11.59	11.66	11.72	11.79	11.87	11.95	12.04	12.14	12.30
10.0	11.70	11.72	11.78	11.85	11.93	12.01	12.09	12.19	12.29	12.40	12.58
11.0	11.88	11.91	11.98	12.06	12.14	12.23	12.32	12.42	12.54	12.66	12.86
12.0	12.07	12.10	12.17	12.26	12.35	12.45	12.55	12.67	12.79	12.93	13.15
13.0	12.26	12.29	12.37	12.47	12.57	12.67	12.79	12.91	13.05	13.20	13.44
14.0	12.45	12.48	12.58	12.68	12.79	12.90	13.03	13.17	13.31	13.48	13.73
15.0	12.65	12.68	12.78	12.89	13.01	13.14	13.27	13.42	13.58	13.76	14.03
16.0	12.85	12.88	12.99	13.11	13.24	13.37	13.52	13.68	13.85	14.04	14.34
17.0	13.05	13.09	13.21	13.33	13.47	13.62	13.77	13.94	14.13	14.33	14.65
18.0	13.26	13.30	13.42	13.56	13.71	13.86	14.03	14.21	14.41	14.63	14.97
19.0	13.47	13.51	13.64	13.79	13.95	14.11	14.29	14.49	14.70	14.93	15.30
20.0	13.68	13.73	13.87	14.02	14.19	14.37	14.56	14.77	15.00	15.24	15.63
21.0	13.90	13.95	14.10	14.26	14.44	14.63	14.83	15.05	15.29	15.55	15.96
22.0	14.12	14.17	14.33	14.51	14.69	14.89	15.11	15.34	15.60	15.87	16.31
23.0	14.34	14.40	14.57	14.75	14.95	15.16	15.39	15.64	15.91	16.20	16.66
24.0	14.57	14.63	14.81	15.01	15.22	15.44	15.68	15.94	16.23	16.53	17.01
25.0	14.80	14.87	15.06	15.26	15.48	15.72	15.98	16.25	16.55	16.87	17.38
26.0	15.04	15.11	15.31	15.53	15.76	16.01	16.28	16.57	16.88	17.22	17.75
27.0	15.28	15.35	15.56	15.79	16.04	16.30	16.58	16.89	17.22	17.57	18.13
28.0	15.53	15.60	15.82	16.07	16.32	16.60	16.90	17.22	17.56	17.94	18.52
29.0	15.78	15.86	16.09	16.34	16.62	16.90	17.22	17.55	17.92	18.31	18.92
30.0	16.04	16.12	16.36	16.63	16.91	17.22	17.54	17.90	18.28	18.69	19.32
31.0	16.30	16.38	16.64	16.92	17.22	17.54	17.88	18.25	18.65	19.07	19.74
32.0	16.57	16.66	16.93	17.22	17.53	17.86	18.22	18.61	19.02	19.47	20.16
33.0	16.84	16.93	17.22	17.52	17.85	18.20	18.57	18.98	19.41	19.87	20.60
34.0	17.12	17.22	17.51	17.83	18.17	18.54	18.93	19.35	19.81	20.29	21.04
35.0	17.41	17.51	17.82	18.15	18.51	18.89	19.30	19.74	20.21	20.72	21.50
36.0	17.70	17.80	18.13	18.48	18.85	19.25	19.68	20.13	20.63	21.15	21.97
37.0	18.00	18.11	18.45	18.81	19.20	19.61	20.06	20.54	21.05	21.60	22.45
38.0	18.31	18.42	18.77	19.15	19.56	19.99	20.46	20.96	21.49	22.06	22.94
39.0	18.62	18.74	19.11	19.50	19.93	20.38	20.86	21.38	21.94	22.53	23.45
40.0	18.94	19.07	19.45	19.86	20.31	20.78	21.28	21.82	22.40	23.02	23.97
41.0	19.27	19.40	19.80	20.23	20.69	21.18	21.71	22.27	22.88	23.52	24.50
42.0	19.61	19.74	20.16	20.61	21.09	21.60	22.15	22.74	23.36	24.03	25.05
43.0	19.96	20.10	20.53	21.00	21.50	22.04	22.61	23.22	23.87	24.56	25.61
44.0	20.31	20.46	20.91	21.40	21.92	22.48	23.07	23.71	24.38	25.10	26.20
45.0	20.68	20.83	21.31	21.82	22.36	22.94	23.55	24.21	24.92	25.66	26.80
46.0	21.06	21.22	21.71	22.24	22.81	23.41	24.05	24.74	25.47	26.24	27.41
47.0	21.44	21.61	22.12	22.68	23.27	23.89	24.56	25.27	26.03	26.83	28.05
48.0	21.84	22.02	22.55	23.13	23.74	24.39	25.09	25.83	26.62	27.45	28.71
49.0	22.26	22.44	22.99	23.60	24.23	24.91	25.64	26.41	27.22	28.08	29.39
50.0	22.68	22.87	23.45	24.08	24.74	25.45	26.20	27.00	27.85	28.74	30.09
52.0	23.57	23.78	24.41	25.09	25.81	26.58	27.39	28.25	29.17	30.12	31.57
54.0	24.52	24.75	25.43	26.17	26.96	27.79	28.67	29.60	30.58	31.61	33.17
56.0	25.55	25.79	26.54	27.34	28.19	29.09	30.05	31.05	32.12	33.22	34.88
58.0	26.65	26.91	27.73	28.60	29.53	30.51	31.54	32.63	33.78	34.97	36.75
60.0	27.84	28.13	29.02	29.98	30.99	32.05	33.17	34.35	35.58	36.86	38.77
62.0	29.14	29.46	30.43	31.48	32.58	33.74	34.96	36.23	37.57	38.94	40.99
64.0	30.57	30.91	31.99	33.13	34.33	35.60	36.92	38.31	39.75	41.23	43.43
66.0	32.14	32.52	33.70	34.96	36.28	37.66	39.10	40.61	42.17	43.77	46.14
68.0	33.89	34.31	35.61	36.99	38.45	39.96	41.54	43.18	44.88	46.61	49.16
70.0	35.85	36.32	37.76	39.29	40.89	42.56	44.29	46.08	47.93	49.80	52.55
PERCENTAGE OF LOAN AMOUNT LEFT UNPAID AT DUE DATE											
	100.0	96.59	86.34	76.10	65.86	55.62	45.37	35.13	24.89	14.65	.00

Reprinted from Mortgage Yield Tables © by Delphi Information Sciences Corp. with permission of Contemporary Books, Inc., Chicago.

APPENDIX D

Usury

In California, usury is a form of price control authorized by Article XV of the state constitution. It's a codified limit on the price charged for temporary use of money, a concept which has been around since biblical times. Where in earlier days it was intended as a limit on the rapacious charges of some lenders, it now is primarily used as a means of aiding specific segments of our society.

All forms of price control lead to distortions in the market place if the prices depart from the realities of economic conditions. The flow of related trade tends to slow as restrictions on market values close down the profitability of various transactions. To continue doing business, many buyers (borrowers) and sellers (lenders) willingly join in complicated schemes of circumvention. In the case of usury, efforts at bypassing the law have caused some of the most imaginative and complex real estate transactions ever formulated.

If you are faced with usury questions which go beyond the bare bones sorted through here, you'll be smart to consult an attorney who is expert on the subject. An enormous body of law has grown around efforts to untangle the various schemes people have used while trying to avoid usury. Only someone close to the subject can fully deal with it. If your attorney tells you the law on usury is not clear relative to your transaction, drop the deal; even with the best legal advice, success is not all that predictable if you have to go to court.

DEFINITION

Usury requires the presence of the following elements: (1) taking an excessive rate of interest, (2) a loan or forebearance, and (3) wrongful intent.

The "taking of . . . interest" portion of the definition requires there be an actual payment of interest. An otherwise usurious note theoretically remains untainted if no interest has been paid.

For the non-exempt loans, the taking of an excessive rate of interest is defined as anything over 10% per annum — if the loan proceeds are used for personal, family, or household purposes. Non-exempt loans for other purposes may contain higher interest rates, so long as they do not exceed: 5% per annum, plus the discount interest rate charged member banks by the Federal Reserve Bank of San Francisco on the 25th day of the month preceding the earlier of (a) the date of execution of the contract to make the loan, or (b) the date the loan was made.

The federal discount rate may be obtained by called telephone number 213/683-8358 or 415/544-2535.

PENALTIES FOR USURY

If your loan is usurious you can be penalized an amount equal to all the interest paid against the loan (not just the usurious portion), plus a penalty equal to three times all the interest paid. Punitive damages can also be exacted if the court decides they are justified. If the usury was willful, it is a felony for which you can be imprisoned up to five years.

Even if the borrower knows at the beginning that the loan is usurious and willingly enters into the transaction anyway, he can still claim the penalities provided by the law. The amount he can claim is discretionary upon the court, however, and depends on his relative guilt. For instance, if the borrower is the sole instigator of a usurious loan, he's not entitled to profit from his own wrong and therefore shouldn't be able to recover treble damages.

The recovery of damages is also subject to a statute of limitations. Treble damages can be claimed only on the previous year's interest payments, and any claim for return of usurious interest is prevented after two years.

Contrary to frequent belief, the penalities for usury do not include prevention of TD foreclosures. Regardless of usury, you are still entitled to the protection of your security to the extent of the principal part of your loan. Nevertheless, foreclosure of a usurious loan can be difficult if the borrower has made payments against it. Opportunity is then given to attack your interpretation of the foreclosure amount by claiming the balance due has been altered by the penalties.

HOW TO CALCULATE THE AMOUNT OF USURY

Points charged for a loan are considered interest and therefore a part of any usury calculation — unless they are for reimbursement of the lender's expenses. Those expenses which can be reimbursed by points include such direct cost items as credit reports, title insurance, escrow, etc. An agent's commission for securing the loan *cannot* be included among the expenses applied against points; commission payments are excluded from the usury calculation only when they are paid by the borrower direct to the agent and not to the lender.

Late charges and prepayment penalties are not considered interest for purposes of computing usury. Generally charges such as these, which are within the borrower's control (i.e., self-inflicted), are safe from a borrower's complaint of usury.

An "all inclusive deed of trust" (see AITD, in the Clauses appendix), may or may not produce usurious interest. The question is a matter of frequent concern because the disparity between the interest rate collected on the AITD versus that paid the enclosed TD often results in a net return exceeding the usury limits. If the AITD is the consequence of a sale of a piece of property, as most of them are, it is automatically exempt from usury. Even if the AITD is not the result of such a transaction, it probably would not be considered usurious. But there is still much argument over the issue.

Monthly compounding of the interest can cause an otherwise safe note to be usurious if the rate of return, on an annual basis, exceeds the legal maximum: If the monthly interest is simply added to the principal of the note (causing interest to be earned on interest), the extra earned interest is included in the usury calculation. But if the monthly interest is paid out monthly, it is not included in the calculation — even though the lender turns right around and lends the collected amount back to the borrower on a new note.

LENDERS EXEMPT FROM USURY

Article XV of California's constitution was amended November 6, 1979, to exempt from usury those licensed real estate brokers who make or arrange loans which are secured by real estate — a classification so large that the burdens of the law were eliminated for a huge portion of the market.

Though there was some initial thrashing around in trying to define the breadth of the exemption, it's now established that: (1) only licensed brokers are included and not those people licensed as real estate sales persons; (2) the exemption extends to all subsequent purchasers of a loan made or arranged by a broker; and (3) the exemption includes licensed real estate brokers who lend their own funds, even though they are not acting in a brokerage capacity.

Other lenders exempt from the law are industrial loan companies, savings and loan institutions, banks, credit unions and agricultural co-ops. All of these are licensed organizations and their lending rates are regulated by other means.

The broker's exemption does not extend to loans made *to* brokers, unless the lender himself is exempt. Furthermore, a broker who borrows at usurious rates can easily find himself in hot water with the Department of Real Estate, whether the borrower raises the issue of usury or not. Brokers are required by B&P Code Sec. 10231.2 to report all instances of "self-dealing" to the DRE 24 hours in advance of accepting the money. Departmental regulations may then compel the real estate commissioner to suspend the broker's license.

The foregoing restrictions on interest rates in a selfdealing transaction apply only to real estate brokers. Other exempt lenders are permitted to borrow (take deposits on a savings account, for example) without regard to usury.

TRANSACTIONS EXEMPT FROM USURY

PURCHASE-MONEY TDS

"Purchase-money TDs," resulting from seller-financed sales of real property, are exempt from usury because they are not a "loan or forebearance" of money. They are, instead, considered delayed payment of part of the purchase price of the property. Though the seller of a property is a non-exempt lender, he can charge 25% interest when the maximum otherwise allowed by law is only 10%. Furthermore, he can turn around and sell the TD to another non-exempt lender who, in turn, inherits the exemption. And to assure himself of a buyer for his exempt TD, he can even make the sale of his property contingent on the other lender's concurrent purchase of the TD.

The purchase money exemption has one prominent exception. Some variable interest rate TDs are limited by statute. In this instance, all interest charges exceeding the defined maximums are usurious, even if they stem from seller financing. For more on the subject, see Contingent Interest, later in this appendix.

Of all the exemptions from usury, the purchase money variety is the most important to private lenders. So long as the loan is tied to the transfer of property, anybody can step in as a lender free of usury. Because most TDs are connected in one way or another with the transfer of property, virtually every investor has the opportunity to lend exempt from usury. All he has to do is be sure the transaction is structured properly.

TDS SOLD AT A DISCOUNT

Sale of an existing, non-usurious TD at a discount which boosts the rate of return above usury limits does not, of itself, make the loan usurious. The discount is considered a private matter, between the original lender and the TD's purchaser, and it has no connection with the borrower. The borrower's obligation remains isolated in its original, nonusurious state.

HOLDER-IN-DUE COURSE EXEMPTIONS

A TD purchaser who is a "holder-in-due-course" is also exempt from a claim of usury, even though the TD was usurious at its inception. This is a condition of the Uniform Negotiable Instruments Act, which permits the buyer of a note to look to the document itself for proofs of the obligation. The exemption works only if the TD buyer has no knowledge or suspicion of usury at the time of purchase, which is not usually the case. Also, there must have been no fraud involved in the issuance of the TD, and the words of endorsement transferring the TD must fit a certain standard (see Endorsements, in the chapter on Escrows).

CONTINGENT PAYMENT EXCEPTIONS

Usury requires the presence of a "loan or forebearance" (see Definition, earlier). To qualify as a "loan or forebearance," the principal sum of the obligation must be payable absolutely. If payment of the loan is contingent upon an event unpredictable at the time the deal was struck, there can be no claim of usury.

If only the payment of interest in a TD is contingent, the exception from usury can still apply — though the subsequent rate of return ends up grossly in excess of the maximums. If the loan's original potential for change in interest rate had no greater probability of falling above or below the usury level, and the avoidance of usury was not intended, the loan is not usurious.

The law expressly limits the contingent interest exemption in certain cases, however. The limits apply whenever the loan is simply variable in the amount of interest and:

"[the loan's] purpose is to finance the purchase or construction of real property containing four or fewer residential units or on which four or fewer residential units are to be constructed."

Variable interest rate loans blanketed by this portion of the law are limited as to the amount of change in interest rate, as well as the frequency of change. Prepayment penalties are also forbidden except under narrowly specified conditions. Both federal and state law play a part in defining the limits on these loans, but the phrasing is too tortured for inclusion here. Reference to the applicable code sections (CC 1916.5, 6, and 7, in California law), and/or a person knowledgeable on the subject, is in order before taking on this type of TD.

TYPES OF EVASION

Many forms of usurious transactions tend to have a life of their own. People active in real estate continually use them in the blithe assumption that the law has been circumvented, mostly because opportunities to test their belief never arise. The borrowers never complain because they too believe in the circumvention and are satisfied with the deal in any event. Everybody continues to regard the evasion as successful because of mutual ignorance.

THE DISGUISED SECURITY/CATASTROPHE IN WAIT

The "disguised security transaction" is the most complicated, and potentially the most harmful, of the many ways lenders and borrowers try to hide from usury. Both parties, realizing that the deal they want to make would create a usurious condition, try to avoid the problem by camouflaging the event to make it look like something other than a loan. They change the name and give it such titles as a "loan with option to purchase," or a "sale with option to repurchase" — and then decorate it with appropriate paperwork. But no matter what the form of transaction, no matter what name the parties attach to it, if the substance demonstrates an intent to lend, it becomes subject to the usury law.

The most damning part of a disguised security transaction is not the penalties but the fact that the instrument of debt becomes a mortgage. Absent those elements necessary to an effective deed of trust, such as a power-of-sale clause, the debt must be considered a mortgage — and, as a mortgage, enforcement by nonjudicial foreclosure is cut off. The only way the lender can foreclose is by judicial means which, as explained in the chapters on Foreclosure, is an extremely expensive process. If the borrower is backed by a savvy lawyer, he can then simply refuse to make his payments. The lender who wishes to extricate his investment will be forced to either pay the borrower off or undertake a judicial foreclosure costing many thousands of dollars.

Lenders in disguised loans often try to circumvent obstacles to foreclosure by excluding the borrower's interest in the property from the public record. For example, property representing the loan's security is deeded to the lender and the deed is recorded. At the same time, the borrower is given a separate document evidencing his option to "repurchase" the property at a price sufficient to pay off the loan plus accrued interest. The lender also deliberately avoids notarization of his signature on the repurchase agreement. Because county recorders do not accept documents for recording unless they are notarized, the lender believes he has prevented the agreement's recording. Presumably, only the lender's name — as per the deed — will appear on the property's record of ownership. Then, if the borrower fails to come up with the option price, the repurchase agreement simply expires, and the lender retains ownership without having to go through foreclosure.

But borrowers can jam the mechanism of such a scheme by assigning their repurchase option rights to a strawman. By obtaining notarization of their signature on the assignment, they are able to create a document which can be recorded — with the previously unrecordable repurchase agreement attached. Once the repurchase agreement becomes part of the public record, the lender's title to the property is clouded. He can do nothing of practical value with the property until he goes through judicial foreclosure to clear the title. Until then, the borrower can remain in possession of the property and successfully resist eviction.

OTHER TYPES OF EVASION

"Manufactured trust deeds" are another form of evasion. The device tries to take advantage of the fact that discounts given in the sale of a TD are supposed to be exempt from usury. A property owner in need of money executes a non-usurious note and deed of trust in favor of a relative, partner, or some other trusted strawman. The loan portion of the transaction is not initially consummated, however; at this stage, no money changes hands between the "borrower" and "lender." To collect the cash necessary to complete the "loan," the strawman turns around and offers the TD to a third party at a discount. On receipt of payment from the third party investor, the strawman passes the cash back to the borrower and steps out of the picture. To disguise the initial absence of cash, the transaction is sometimes embellished with a claim that the TD was given the lender in exchange for goods or services rendered. And sometimes the scheme is so shallowly constructed that the strawman doesn't even bother to put the TD up for sale; the borrower does it for him. Because the entire transaction is a sham, and because any common sense investigation reveals the possibility of a sham, such TDs have a high probability of being considered usurious.

The hidden rebate scheme is another way people try to avoid usury. This form of evasion is a favorite of those short term borrowers trying to borrow from a "friend." The borrower suggests that usury can be circumvented by an immediate kickback to the lender in the form of cash. Usury, it is claimed, is avoided because the proof of the loan's usurious nature is absent when there is no evidence of the kickback. But in order to avoid evidence of the kickback, the transaction cannot be passed through an escrow. And without an escrow, the lender may find it difficult to obtain title insurance. If the lender is willing to accept the hazards of no escrow or title insurance, he must still face the risk that the borrower has accumulated indirect evidence of the false nature of the transaction; something easily contrived if the borrower plans ahead and evidences the rebate with bookkeeping entries, matching bank deposits, cancelled checks and such.

The common defect that runs through all sham transactions, such as manufactured trust deeds and disguised rebate schemes, is the assumption that all courts are stupid. Judges with any amount of time on the bench are exposed to many more evidences of chicanery by litigants than the layman gives them credit for. No genius is required for a judge to recognize that borrowers and lenders can happily agree to certain facts in order to avoid usury, only to fall out later. Any protest to the contrary is certain to be subjected to a dab of judicial skepticism.

APPENDIX E

Bankruptcy

The risk of bankruptcy is the single greatest flaw in trust deed investment. In contrast to other variables associated with TDs, bankruptcy is only narrowly predictable — and when it does occur your array of defenses is limited. Most frustrating of all, in bankruptcy you lose effective control of your investment; your degree of loss becomes a function of someone else's decisions.

And make no mistake, bankruptcy *will* produce a loss, for rarely does the debtor manage to cure his defaults. If your TD is well secured, the property will often be milked to a pale imitation of its former self before you manage to lay claim to it. Even those bankruptcies which result in recovery of the full amount of the loan still produce a loss, because you must divert time and attention, and incur peripheral expenses, in defense of your investment. Furthermore, market shifts in interest rates may occur while your TD is frozen in bankruptcy, leaving you with earnings of, say, 10% interest while inflation is roaring along at a 15% rate. And if you have scheduled the maturity of your loan to meet your own cash needs, the bankruptcy may cause financial difficulties for you also, and you may have to sacrifice other properties in order to cope with the problem.

TYPES OF BANKRUPTCY

Bankruptcies fall into two broad categories: those aimed at the financial rehabilitation of the debtor, and those for the sole purpose of liquidating the debtor's assets in an orderly manner.

Bankruptcies with the goal of financial rehabilitation are authorized under two chapters of the Bankruptcy Act: Chapter 13 is restricted to individuals with a regular source of income (such as wages), whose unsecured debt does not exceed $100,000, or whose secured debt does not exceed

203

$350,000. Chapter 11 encompasses all non-individual debtors, such as corporations and partnerships, as well as individuals with over $100,000 unsecured, or $350,000 secured, debt. Lawyers sometimes play a game of semantics with Chapters 11 and 13 by labeling them a "plan of arrangement" rather than bankruptcy — seemingly in the belief that calling them something other than "bankruptcy" removes some of the stigma attached to the process.

Liquidation bankruptcies all fall under Chapter 7 of the Bankruptcy Act. Both individuals and non-individuals may file under this chapter. Chapter 7 proceedings are called "straight bankruptcy," again in an apparent effort to distinguish them from the presumably less objectionable reorganization type of bankruptcy.

To the secured creditor, the most important distinction between the forms of bankruptcy is whether they are "trusteed" or not. If the debtor's estate is managed by a trustee, the length of stay in bankruptcy is apt to be shorter. On the other hand, if the estate is managed by the debtor himself, the proceedings usually take longer, and they are conducted less efficiently. Chapter 7 proceedings are considered the most desirable form of bankruptcy because they are all trusteed. Since many Chapter 13 bankruptcies are accompanied by appointment of a standing trustee, these too tend to be more efficiently managed and hence more desirable. Chapter 11 proceedings are the worst; the bankrupt remains in control of his assets as a "debtor-in-possession" — whereupon he usually continues the sloppy financial habits that created the problem in the first place.

SPECIAL PROBLEMS CAUSED BY BANKRUPTCY

BANKRUPTCY STAYS OF FORECLOSURE

Immediately on filing bankruptcy, all civil actions against the debtor are automatically "stayed," or stopped. Notices of default recorded after the stay takes effect are automatically void; indeed, recording a notice of default in conscious violation of the stay is a crime.

Notices of default recorded before bankruptcy are valid. Upon removal of the stay, a new notice of default need not be recorded so long as all interested parties are notified of the change. If, however, your foreclosure has reached the redemption (publication) stage before bankruptcy, you may or may not have to republish when the stay is lifted; you'll have to consult a competent foreclosure trustee or an attorney expert in bankruptcy to find out which.

The reinstatement period clock set in motion by recording a before-bankruptcy notice of default may be allowed to continue running during the bankruptcy — but the borrower's reinstatement period is then extended up to an additional 60 days, dependent on a formula based on the type of bankruptcy. Much bickering surrounds the foregoing effect of a stay on the foreclosure time clock, and the rules may be changed. Some have successfully contended that the clock is "tolled," or frozen in place, and does not start again until the stay is lifted. Again, you'll need to consult a bankruptcy attorney to receive the latest bulletins on the struggle.

Whether or not a foreclosure started before bankruptcy is "tolled" will have much to do with your future planning. If the reinstatement period is allowed to expire during bankruptcy, start of publication can be arranged to coincide with relief of stay, and a foreclosure sale may be held some 21 days later. Under ideal circumstances, the bankruptcy may not delay the foreclosure at all if the reinstatement period runs unhindered during bankruptcy. Also, if the reinstatement period clock is allowed to continue, expiration of the three months will allow you to demand payment in full rather than accept continuation of your loan.

Note that in the foregoing, stays in bankruptcy apply only to actions against the debtor. They do not exempt cosignors of a TD from your collection efforts. Nor does a stay from the borrower's bankruptcy apply to your dealings with junior lien holders; a foreclosure already underway cannot be "tolled" against junior lenders, and expiration of three months will sever any rights the juniors may have to reinstate. (For more on this, see 1st TD Gamesmanship, later in this appendix.)

Stays of action against the debtor do not necessarily have to originate with the bankruptcy of the debtor himself. They may be triggered by the bankruptcy of parties outside the loan agreement. For example, 1st TD lenders are automatically stayed from foreclosure whenever a junior files bankruptcy. And the bankruptcy of anybody with a fractional interest in the property, no matter how minor, will also stay foreclosure. The personal bankruptcy of a general partner does not stay foreclosure against partnership property, however, though the law did at one time enforce a stay in such instances.

Surprisingly, foreclosure sales held in ignorance of a stay are considered valid if the property is sold to an outside bidder and the sale is conducted in a county other than the one in which the bankruptcy was filed. A provision in the bankruptcy code protects such sales when there is a "bona fide purchaser;" the lender, in this case, is not usually considered a bonafide purchaser.

The Bankruptcy Act requires the court to hear arguments within 30 days after a lender's petition for relief of stay. If the court fails to do so, the stay is automatically lifted. Most petitions are heard within the allotted time, and relief is denied if the security is of significant value to the estate. Loan brokers often brag that their investors are able to take advantage of the 30-day requirement and get stays lifted in little more than a month; the real reason for such short stays is that the judges find the properties of such little value over the encumbrances that they're not worth saving.

CRAM DOWN ALTERATIONS OF THE TD

To TD lenders, the most devastating of the bankruptcy court's powers is its "cram down" authority. The Bankruptcy Act permits the court to modify a trust deed for the betterment of other parties interested in the bankruptcy. The privilege is limited to reorganization type bankruptcies, and presumably can be used only when the modification involves property essential to the success of the reorganization. For instance, the court may substitute other property as security before allowing you to proceed with foreclosure. If the judge decides the security is in excess of your needs, he can direct subordination of your TD to other financing — i.e., change your 1st TD to a 2nd TD. If the judge deems your TD's payment schedule oppressive, he can modify the payments to a pace the debtor can more easily afford. And if the judge decides your $100,000 TD is secured by property worth only $80,000, he can reduce the amount of the obligation to the lesser figure.

SPECIAL TREATMENT FOR FARMERS

The Bankruptcy Act exempts farmers and eleemosynary institutions (churches) from being forced into "involuntary" bankruptcy. The consequences of this exemption can be disastrous.

Involuntary bankruptcies are conducted with the aid of a trustee. The trustee promptly sells the TD security so that its obligation can be paid off and surplus from the sale used elsewhere. But with inability to force involuntary bankruptcy, the judge cannot compel the debtor to accept a trustee; he must allow the debtor to sell the property himself. The only effective way the judge can force sale of the property is to lift the stay on the TD's foreclosure. But he's not likely to do that if the property's value significantly exceeds its encumbrances. The debtor is therefore under no pressure to sell the property, especially if the sale would bring about an end to the bankruptcy. He is perfectly happy to continue as before, because bankruptcy permits him to go about his business without being plagued by bothersome creditors. As a consequence, a TD secured by farm land can be tied up in bankruptcy for years — until the judge becomes sufficiently disgusted with the debtor's delay to lift the stay.

1st TD GAMESMANSHIP

The special circumstances of bankruptcy create unique opportunities for 1st TDs to escape its effects by bludgeoning junior lien holders.

If the 1st manages to get its Notice of Default (NOD) recorded before the bankruptcy, it can force junior TDs to cure the debtor's defaults. Bankruptcy does not stop the clock against 2nd TD holders; the 1st TD reinstatement period may be tolled only with regard to the bankrupt. The three-month reinstatement period following the NOD continues to run against the junior. At the end of the three months the 1st TD can refuse to accept a junior's tender of the defaulted amounts, and require full payment of the debt instead. If the junior expects to foreclose and wishes to retain the 1st TD financing, he must cure the senior default in the initial three months — even though both lenders are otherwise frozen by the bankruptcy.

A 1st TD can also push around junior TDs by attempting a more prompt release of stay. A senior's successful petition for release does not automatically transfer to junior lien holders. Juniors are expected to enter their own petition for release and fight their own battle. If a senior can get his petition and lift of stay in first, he will be able to put the junior that much further behind him in the procession toward foreclosure. Again, the junior may then be forced to cure the 1st TD defaults just to prevent being cut off by its foreclosure.

Seniors can beat up on hapless junior lien holders still further by repeated attacks against the stay in bankruptcy. According to the TD (see Attorney's Fees in the Clauses Appendix), the senior's legal expenses connected with the bankruptcy can be added to the debt. Each time the senior's attorney attacks the stay, the senior debt rises and diminishes the amount of security left to the junior. If the amount of security left becomes narrow enough, the junior may be stampeded into paying off the senior simply to stop further losses.

Junior lien holders are not without defenses to senior depredations. The junior can always stop the senior by curing the default. And if the cost of the cure is more than he can afford, the junior can go on the offensive himself. His attorney (at the borrower's expense, of course) can ask the court to prohibit the senior from holding a foreclosure sale ahead of the junior's sale. The junior's attorney might also be successful with an attack which claims the senior's legal expenses a capricious waste, that both the court's time and the debtor's estate are being wasted because the 1st is duplicating the junior's efforts.

DIRTY TRICKS — THE BANKRUPTCY WAY

Bankruptcy seems to stimulate levels of debtor creativity which, if employed earlier, would easily have eliminated the need for bankruptcy.

REPEATED BANKRUPTCIES

Contrary to popular belief, there are no limits on the number of times a person can file bankruptcy. The code provides that Chapter 7 debtors can be discharged from their obligations no more than once every seven years. Many lenders, especially unsecured ones, take comfort from this. But Chapters 11 and 13 debtors are not subject to the limitation. Furthermore, the law does not prohibit the *act* of filing bankruptcy, regardless of the form of chapter proceeding employed — and it's the filing of bankruptcy that triggers the automatic stay. A growing number of debtors are using this loophole to stop foreclosure; after a stay of foreclosure is lifted, the debtor immediately refiles bankruptcy in another court, thereby reinstating the stay. The stunt has been employed so often that judges have become increasingly sensitive to it and little is needed to get the new stay lifted.

POST FORECLOSURE BANKRUPTCIES

Although bankruptcy filed after a foreclosure sale is not supposed to affect the validity of the sale, some bankruptcy attorneys try to claim the foreclosed property anyway. The trustee's deed officially transferring property ownership after a foreclosure sale is frequently not recorded until a month or more after the sale. Some attorneys try to take advantage of the delay and claim mechanical matters, such as recording the trustee's deed, are stayed. They threaten the trustee with dire consequences if he records the deed, and much of the time will be successful with the approach; few trustees are so confident in this situation that they are willing to risk a lawsuit. But most of the time the deed is already prepared. It simply awaits miscellaneous paper shuffling connected with tidying up the sale. If the successful bidder of the foreclosure sale stops by the trustee's office, picks up the deed, and delivers it to the recorder himself, the impasse can be broken.

TRICKERY WITH PHONY TITLE TRANSFERS

Debtors whose property is under foreclosure can take shelter under the bankruptcy law without filing bankruptcy themselves. By deeding a part of their property to a prospective bankrupt, foreclosure on the entire property can be stayed. This strategy is popular among co-signers who have guaranteed the debtor's obligation by executing a separate deed of trust as additional security. Transferring a minuscule portion of the property to the pending bankrupt stays forclosure and prevents effective enforcement of the guarantee.

The "off record deed" is another variation of the phony title transfer trick. Knowing a person who may file bankruptcy, a defaulting borrower, as a contingency measure, deeds his property to the other party. The borrower has the deed notarized, but then keeps it and fails to record it. If the other party later files bankruptcy, the borrower then tries to stay foreclosure by flourishing the deed. And the trick usually works — until the bankruptcy court gets around to unraveling what happened.

LENDER STRATEGIES IN BANKRUPTCY

Once you receive word that bankruptcy has been filed, the best strategy is to attack. Attack loudly and vigorously. The lender who fails to assert his rights in protection of his security can face a loss where none existed before. Furthermore, the secured lender with the highest profile, who gets up and waves his arms the most, has the best chance of gaining relief; this is one instance where the old saw about "the wheel that squeeks the loudest . . ." is true.

For this purpose, you should always check the bankruptcy papers filed by your borrower. Look especially for the valuation given your security in the "debtor's disclosure statement," and protest its accuracy if you believe it to be materially in error. Too low a valuation may be used to cram down a reduction in your TD amount (see Cram Down, earlier), and too high a valuation may prevent obtaining a lift of the stay.

PROVE YOUR CLAIM

Always file a "proof of claim" with the bankruptcy court. One school of thought says that since your TD is already a matter of public record, no further proof is necessary, that there is nothing the court can do if you just sit tight. All of which may or may not be true, but one thing that filing the proof can do is put you first in line for cash distributions during bankruptcy. This is an important factor if the bankruptcy drags on very long. Filing the proof also establishes your presence with the court and puts on record the amount you claim due, matters which are frequently botched by the debtor.

The proof of claim is submitted on a form obtained from the clerk of the court. You can fill out and file it yourself if you don't want to get an attorney involved at this stage. Be sure you adequately describe your security when you fill out the form; failure to fully describe the security has been, in some instances, considered a waiver of claim to property omitted from the description.

GET A GOOD LAWYER

Selection of proper legal representation in court is perhaps the most important element in your strategy. A lawyer expert in the local bankruptcy court is necessary. He should be a bankruptcy specialist, because bankruptcy law tends to be exclusive unto itself; the best bankruptcy attorneys stick to bankruptcy and nothing else. Local representation is also desirable because bankruptcy courts tend to be closed communities. Everybody knows everybody else and they soon learn to accommodate one another if they expect to regularly do business in the same court. Judges are often former bankruptcy attorneys, and attorneys are sometimes former bankruptcy judges, switching back and forth on either side of the bench. Attorneys local to the bankruptcy court also tend to be cheaper; some court jurisdictions are so large, geographically, that importing an outside attorney may cost travel of as much as 300 miles from the attorney's regular place of business.

Finding the right attorney may not be easy. Some courts are located in communities with so few bankruptcy attorneys that one law office will handle 70 percent of the bankruptcies, virtually all on the side of the debtor. You may then be forced to use an inexperienced local attorney, or bring in an outside expert at correspondingly greater expense.

Sometimes it makes sense to represent yourself in bankruptcy court rather than use an attorney. The value of your security may be so low that you will be unable to recover the attorney's fees from sale of the property. If so, representation "in pro per," (from the words "in propria persona") is the best approach. Since bankruptcy courts tend toward informality and pragmatic solutions to problems, efforts of this nature are usually tolerated. Such appearances are limited, in a practical sense, to issues already before the court (such as opposition to a senior's petition for an independent lift of stay). If you contemplate introducing a new subject, you will have to file your own petition, a matter best handled by an attorney.

PETITIONS TO LIFT THE STAY

Left to its own devices, the bankruptcy court will continue to stay your foreclosure until it decides your security is not worth keeping or until the debtor is discharged from bankruptcy. In some cases this may take years. To speed things up, you must petition the court for relief from the stay. If the court decides to hear your reasons for lifting the stay within the 30 days allowed (see earlier), it must either (1) deny your petition, (2) lift the stay, (3) continue the hearing for another 30 days, or (4) otherwise modify or extend the stay.

210

Among the issues the court will consider for a lift of stay are: whether the debtor has equity in the property worth saving by sale within a reasonable time, whether the property is vital to the debtor's reorganization efforts (under Chapter 11 proceedings), and whether you are adequately protected if the stay remains in place.

Property not worth saving is the most common reason for lifting the stay. Attacks based on this issue hinge on evidence of the property's value, a matter always subject to dispute. If your existing proofs of value are not clear, you may need the services of an expert appraiser as a witness. The appraiser should be someone accustomed to testifying in court. It takes a certain kind of personality to do a good job in a courtroom atmosphere, and appraisers who testify generally specialize in the work. Their fees are correspondingly higher, too.

Stays can also be lifted for cause. Justifications for relief based on cause include: evidence that the security does not really belong to the bankrupt, lapse of an unreasonable length of time in disposal of the security, and poor management or waste of the security. The judge may also be more willing to grant relief based on evidence of the debtor's deceptive or dishonest behavior. He then may lift the stay at an ex parte hearing; that is, without the debtor or his attorney present. Evidence of repeated filings by the debtor to avoid foreclosure, or that your borrower transferred his security (see Dirty Tricks, earlier) to the bankrupt simply to stay your foreclosure, may get you ex parte relief.

LENDER "DROP DEAD" STRATEGIES

You should have alternative proposals ready in case the court decides your security is worth keeping and refuses to lift the stay. Your best approach in this case is to ask for "drop dead" stipulations based on the bankrupt's failure to perform as promised. For instance, if the bankrupt promises prompt sale of the property and payment of the debt, request a stipulation for automatic relief of stay if the sale isn't completed by a certain date. Your chances of success in gaining the stipulation may be improved if you also describe the amount of additional grace period provided by the foreclosure process after the stay is lifted.

Often the judge will not trust the bankrupt's competence any more than you do and therefore be unwilling to chance a deadline. If so, ask that the bankruptcy be converted to the relatively rapid Chapter 7 (liquidation type) proceeding, so the property can be sold by a trustee.

OTHER STIPULATIONS TO ASK FOR

Every time your attorney appears before the bankruptcy court, he should ask for stipulation that his fees be added to the balance due on your TD. Although the TD already gives you the right to claim such charges, you won't be able to collect them during bankruptcy unless the judge consents.

If your security is income property, ask for appointment of a receiver who will manage and distribute its income toward cure of the defaults in your TD. You are entitled to make the request because your TD gives you a claim against rents and profits in the event of default. Unless he amends the agreement (see Cram Down, earler in this appendix), the judge must theoretically comply with its terms. For more on this see Assignment of Rents, in the Clauses Appendix.

WHERE BANKRUPTCY HELPS THE LENDER

Sometimes a debtor's bankruptcy benefits his secured creditors as well. Though bankruptcy courts are governed by federal law, they have broad power to decide issues based on state law. For instance, they can decide quiet title actions connected with the bankrupt debtor's estate. Furthermore, hearings are held within a relatively short time, and in an atmosphere favorable to the bankrupt and his creditors. In state courts, a landowner may not be able to perfect prescriptive rights of access (see Legal Access in the Appraisal Appendix) to his property for a year or more. But if the proofs are clear enough and the derivative easement is important to disposition of the estate, a binding decision can be obtained from a bankruptcy court in as little as a month.

Such powers are accessible to the bankrupt's lenders also. So long as your TD is under the jurisdiction of the court (i.e., until the stay is lifted), you can file a complaint for relief from problems related to the TD. You can promptly settle such diverse disputes as the TD's ownership, encroachments on the security, as well as problems of access to the security. If the bankrupt's attorney fails to file an action to clear up a clouded title, you can do so instead — and thereby upgrade the value of your security before foreclosure.

Condemnation

Like bankruptcy, condemnations can lead to investment losses where none existed before unless you stand up for your rights. Unlike bankruptcy, you may sometimes gain from condemnations — but may have to run a game of bluff in order to do so.

Condemnation, in this context, refers to the taking of private property for public use by a governmental or quasi-governmental agency. This differs from condemnation in which a building is "condemned" and occupancy prohibited because it violates minimum standards of health or safety. The condemnation considered here is a constitutional right given government agencies to "take" property against the wishes of the property owner, provided there is an appropriate need for the property, and provided the property owner is justly compensated.

Acquisitions of properties by condemnation always result in transfers "free and clear" of all equitable interests. If the property is encumbered by a trust deed, the TD must be paid off or eliminated from the record of title in some other manner.

VARIETIES OF CONDEMNATION

Condemnations arise when a public agency's planned purchase of real estate is disputed. If the property owner disputes the price offered (or if the ownership itself is disputable) a condemnation action must be filed to settle the matter.

Most condemnations involve the property's lenders only marginally because the loan amounts are well defined. Disputes with property owners are common, however, because public purchases are generally limited to the property's appraised value. Settlement at a price materially different from the appraisal is illegal. Opportunities to negotiate differences of opinion over value are therefore limited and the matter often ends up in court.

PARTIAL TAKINGS

A government agency's condemnation of only part of a property is called a "partial taking." It's during partial takings that TD lenders most often find themselves drawn into condemnation wars. Much case law says encumbering lenders may not claim condemnation proceeds if their loan remains adequately secured by the property remaining after a partial taking. As might be expected, everybody has a different view as to the amount of security needed by the lender. Unless the lender also joins the combat, his opinion of the required amount of security will be hindmost. (For more on this, see later in this appendix.)

INVERSE CONDEMNATION

Inverse condemnation occurs when a public body "takes" real estate by indirect means. For example: A city announces its intent to take a property, but then delays the taking for an unreasonable length of time. If, in the meantime, the property declines in usefulness and/or market value due to the city's failure to act promptly, an inverse condemnation will have occurred, and those with an interest in the property will be entitled to recovery of their losses.

Numerous efforts have been made in California to link "down zoning" to inverse condemnation, so far without result. Down zoning occurs when an ordinance is passed altering the permissible use of a property, making it less valuable. For instance: A property's zoning is changed from permitted use for three-story apartment buildings to use only for single family residences on 10,000 sq. ft. lots. An encumbering TD's security may in this way be destroyed with the drop in the property's market value, and there will be little that anybody can do about it.

PRIVATE CONDEMNATION

Naturally, California has found a way to introduce its own variation in eminent domain (condemnation) law. Civil Code Sec. 1001 says that if a "great necessity" plus certain other requirements exist, individuals are entitled to a take a "public utility easement" over their neighbor's property. "Public utility," for this purpose, is defined as water, gas, electric, drainage, sewer, or telephone service. Roadways for owner access are not included in the definition. Before this type of condemnation can be initiated, a local legislative body (such as a city council) must find that all the elements necessary to satisfy CC 1001 are present.

214

THE EFFECTS OF CONDEMNATION ON TD LENDERS

Most eminent domain proceedings work to the encumbering lenders' advantage. Just about any action which results in prepayment of your TD is inherently desirable (though, in this case, you won't be able to extract a prepayment penalty). If you bought the TD at a discount, or received "points" as an incentive to make the loan, condemnation is especially welcome because it provides early collection of these amounts when the loan is paid off. And if the condemnation is only a partial taking, you may be able to collect more on your loan than the offset reduction in security, leaving your TD more well protected.

LENDER'S RIGHTS IN CONDEMNATION

Encumbering lenders' rights in condemnation are much the same as those of owners of the property. Lenders cannot collect more than the amount due under the terms of their note and deed of trust, however. Lenders also differ because they have a right to be paid first (except in partial takings), with only the remainder going to the owner.

The lender's rights in condemnation stem from a clause contained on the reverse of the deed of trust. The typical clause reads:

It is mutually agreed that any award of damages in connection with any condemnation for public use or injury to said property or any part thereof is hereby assigned and shall be paid to Beneficiary who may apply or release such moneys received by him in the same manner and with the same effect as above provided for disposition of proceeds of fire or other insurance.

Note the optional character of the clause. If the clause contains an unequivocal proviso accelerating payment of the entire loan upon the taking of any part of the security, it might be more enforceable; whether it is or not is difficult to determine without the aid of an attorney abreast of all the changes in condemnation law.

If several trust deeds encumber a property, their rights to condemnation proceeds are based on their order of priority — 1st TDs collect first, then 2nd TDs, and so on until the money runs out. This is an important distinction when some of the TDs differ by including other pieces of property in their security, or when the funds from a partial taking are insufficient to cover all encumbrances. Without this rule, there could be a real cat fight over entitlement to condemnation proceeds.

CONDEMNATIONS WHICH WIPE OUT THE LENDER

In a partial taking, the lender who fails to defend his right to condemnation proceeds can lose all but a fragment of the security necessary for his protection. To be sure that the security remaining after condemnation is enough to protect the debt, TD lenders must always be prepared to defend themselves in a partial taking.

A lender can also be eliminated from the proceeds if he is named in a condemnation complaint and fails to respond. While the division of condemnation money in most cases is relatively simple (settled by issuance of a joint check among the participants), some situations require great caution. Each party must then prove his right to be paid. To accomplish this, an "apportionment" section is added to the lawsuit so that the right to payment can be decided in court. All possible interested parties are named as defendants. Those beneficiaries who fail to respond to the lawsuit will be eliminated from the payment by default and may be left with only an unsecured note.

LENDER STRATEGIES IN CONDEMNATION

DECISIONS TO BE MADE IN A PARTIAL TAKING

Some effort should be made to define your objectives before making any move in a partial taking: You may not want the condemnation proceeds applied against your TD, even though you have less security after the taking. Perhaps forcing payments to be applied against the TD will dump you into a low-interest market unsuitable for reinvestment. Or maybe the balance due on your TD is so small it's not worth fighting for a better position.

Crucial to any decision is whether you can expect to win legal actions connected with your effort. If you do win, you will be able to collect your attorney's fees under the terms of the deed of trust. The borrower will be obligated to pay these costs because he has promised "To appear in and defend any action or proceeding purporting to affect the security hereof . . . and to pay all . . . attorney's fees . . . in which the Beneficiary may appear. . . ." On the other hand, the borrower will not be responsible for your attorney's fees if they are incurred chasing enforcement of non-existent obligations in the deed of trust.

Part of your decision to act may hinge on whether or not you should try to run a bluff on an otherwise questionable right to payment. Many property owners under condemnation hire an attorney not expert on the subject — an attorney unaware that the payment allocation is a function of the endangerment of the security. The attorney relies instead on the terms of the deed of trust which say the proceeds must be applied to the TD. He may also be influenced by fear that, if he opposes you, the borrower may have to pay your separate legal expenses under the aforementioned attorney's fees clause. It's possible, therefore, that the borrower and his attorney may be gulled into defending your position, even though it's against their interests.

LENDER'S STRATEGY OF DEFENSE

If you decide to play an active part in a condemnation action, you are required to transmit your expectations to the property owners and any other parties of possible interest. The "may", or optional portion of the clause cited earlier, requires this. At the same time, you may help your cause by taking the opportunity to remind the borrower of his obligation to defend you in the action and to pay your attorney's fees.

If you have been named a party in the eminent domain complaint (lawsuit), you must also file an answer within a specified time or be considered in "default." Filing an answer requires an attorney. If you and the borrower are not in dispute at that point, the most efficient approach is to use the borrower's attorney. The addition of your name to the borrower's answer to the complaint is a relatively simple matter; if the borrower believes he will otherwise have to pay your attorney fees, he will jump at the chance to save the money. Later, if a dispute arises, you can substitute your own attorney.

If you must substitute your own attorney, be careful. Like bankruptcy, eminent domain law is so utterly foreign to the practice of most attorneys that the best ones specialize in condemnation and little else. Furthermore, any use of an appraiser should be limited to a person who specializes in expert witness testimony on condemnation cases; in condemnations, the appraiser is the key element, and the attorneys play only a secondary role. Though your role in the condemnation will otherwise be relatively passive compared with the property owner, you will still want the very best in both cases, because your losses can be just as great.

INCOME TAX STRATEGIES

TDs are commonly thought to have only a limited potential for tax saving. For that reason, investors with aggressive tax avoidance objectives generally look to other forms of investment, such as real estate.

But taxes on TD income can be minimized, and in ways just as good as in real estate though not quite as numerous. In fact, TDs exceed real estate's tax advantage in one respect: Most people who invest in real estate for its tax benefits pick up their biggest deductions when they must write off part or all of their investment as a loss.

Because TDs are perceived a poor tax shelter, they have become a better investment for those who most need them. Market rates of return are higher because of the reduced supply of investors, yet they are exceptionally safe if proper care is taken. Retired people, and others not so concerned with tax savings, are able to fulfill their basic need for safety while picking up much higher yields than otherwise available from sources such as savings accounts.

TAX SAVING DEVICES

KEOGH PLAN TAX SAVINGS

When invested in trust deeds, Keogh type personal pension plans are as good a tax shelter as any to be found. Such plans are a perfect match for trust deeds because they permit individuals with self-employment income to take advantage of the private money TD's inherently higher yields, while deferring or eliminating the debilitating effects of income taxes.

Keogh plans allow taxpayers to set aside a portion of their self-employment income each year, and to deduct that amount from their taxable income. The money set aside goes into a trust account under the care of an independent trustee. An administrator is also appointed and the trust funds are invested under his guidance. All income then earned by the trust fund is free of income tax. Only when the taxpayer (called the "trust beneficiary") withdraws the funds is there a tax, at which time the withdrawn amount is taxed as though it were ordinary income. Presumably, withdrawal will occur only in the taxpayer's retirement years, when the tax damage is lessened due to his lower income and increased medical expenses.

After age 59½, Keogh funds can be withdrawn any time and in any size increment the taxpayer wishes. If he withdraws before age 59½, however, he must pay a penalty in addition to the ordinary income tax paid on the withdrawn funds. The penalty for premature withdrawal tends to reduce the plan's value as a "rainy day" reserve, but the damage can be minimized by timing the event to match a low income year. The effect of the penalty is also offset by the opportunity to earn interest on amounts which would otherwise have been paid for taxes during the plan's existence.

The self-employment income on which Keogh contributions are based covers a surprisingly large range of people. Professional people such as doctors or lawyers are not the only ones covered. The income earned by painters, handymen, surveyors, authors, accountants, musicians, members of a corporation's board of directors, and any type consultant, is also eligible for Keogh benefits — if the person is not classified an employee. Eligibility is also extended to owner-employees of businesses which provide personal services (such as doctor's offices). If the person's ownership is more than 10 percent of a partnership, or if the business is a sole proprietorship, and if the plan meets certain minimum standards (such as inclusion of employees), the business' net profit is eligible for calculation of Keogh contributions.

The key to effective use of a Keogh plan is to be sure the plan is of the "self-directed" variety; that is, a plan which permits you to direct the investment of the funds. Most plans advertised by savings and loans and other institutions try to lock the taxpayer into one form of investment, an investment which serves the operator of the plan more than it profits the taxpayer. Self-directed plans, on the other hand, are operated by administrators who do so simply for the fees they collect with each transaction. A number of large, reliable organizations are available for this purpose, and they can usually be found from their advertisements in the financial section of newspapers. They are also a convenient source of detailed information about tax laws governing Keogh plans.

Investors disappointed by the operation of a particular plan or its administrator can take the plan's assets and hop over to another organization any time they wish. Many savings and loan and other institutional personnel try to discourage this by pointing to the IRS penalty on withdrawal. Nothing could be more deceptive; you can always "roll over" your plan into another organization, free of penalty, if you do not siphon off the plan's assets during the transfer.

IRA PLAN SAVINGS

IRAs are another form of pension plan, somewhat akin to Keogh plans. IRA refers to the Individual Retirement Act, which is aimed at helping the employed individual. Currently the amount of permitted contributions to IRAs is not as great as the Keogh variety, but the two plans otherwise function along the same lines.

Because IRA contributions are relatively limited, more time is required to bring the fund to a level high enough to invest in TDs. An employee starting an IRA is therefore better off beginning with a plan administered by a savings and loan or other institutional lender; institutional fees are lower with relation to the size of plan than administrator fees in self-directed plans. After the account rises to an amount large enough to efficiently invest in TDs ($10,000 or more, by most standards), the institutional plan can be rolled over into the self-directed variety, as described earlier.

The very best and most efficient use of the self-directed IRA occurs when an employee retires, quits, or is fired from an organization in which he has a substantial pension account. In these cases, the employee is usually given the opportunity of withdrawing from the company plan. The withdrawal is then taxed as ordinary income, unless the money is rolled over into another plan. This is where the selfdirected IRA shines. A high tax bracket executive with a pension balance in the hundreds of thousands of dollars can avoid showing so much as blip on his tax return by rolling over into a self-directed plan; and the size of his plan will permit him to invest in those extremely profitable private money TDs in the $50,000 to $100,000 range. The profits he receives under the new setup can easily exceed twice his earnings under the company pension plan.

TAX-SAVING BY POSTPONEMENT OF INTEREST

The impact of taxes on your TD investment can be postponed or eliminated if the TD is appropriately structured. Most people are cash basis taxpayers. That is, they report taxable income only when it is collected in cash. If a TD carries interest at a 10% rate, for example, but is written so the interest is payable only at the end of four years, the taxable income is correspondingly postponed — and the foundation for all sorts of tax-saving maneuvers is thereby established.

By postponing the collection of interest, time is given to devise offsetting deductions, such as lump sum interest payments, and arrange for them to arrive in the year of the TD's income. The TD's postponed income can also be made to coincide with retirement, and the then lower tax bracket. And with the aid of an expert tax advisor, you sometimes can avoid taxes on the income altogether by giving the TD to your low-income offspring's trust fund, just before the postponed payment is collected.

A tax-saving device which has no economic purpose other than to save income taxes, and which results in a material distortion of your income, can be disallowed by the IRS. This rule was not violated in the preceding example because an economic purpose can be shown for the transaction — such deferred payment trust deeds usually command higher rates of interest and the transaction therefore has a legitimate business purpose. But if you don't have your documentation set up to evidence this, or if the postponement is so extreme (like 20 years) as to be void of economic purpose, the tax treatment would be certain of defeat on audit.

CAPITAL GAINS AND LOSSES FROM TD INVESTMENTS

TDs are not usually looked on as a source of capital gains treatment on tax returns; they are instruments of debt, and interest income is the dominant purpose of the investment. But if you buy a trust deed at a discount and it is later prepaid, the unamortized portion of the discount represents a windfall profit — and therefore a capital gain taxable at a much lower rate than interest income.

TD's have a flip side, however. They can also lead to capital losses. If, for example, you are saddled with a low interest TD which you want to convert to cash, you will probably have to sell it as a discount. If the discounted sale price is less than the amortized cost of your investment, you will have a capital loss of limited deductability on your tax return.

HOW TO REPORT THE TD ON YOUR TAX RETURN

HOW TO REPORT POINTS

The most frequent tax question asked with regard to trust deeds concerns the treatment of "points." Here, the rule is that points charged by a lender for expenses incurred, or for services performed in connection with the loan, are income in the year received. If the points are simply an adjustment of the TD's face interest rate, they must be amortized into the investment's income stream along with the interest earned, just as though the points were a discount received on purchase of a TD (see below).

REPORTING DISCOUNTS

Discounts received in purchase of a TD also must be reported as income in your tax return. If you are a cash basis taxpayer (see Postponement of Interest, earlier), the income is reported only as you collect payments against the TD. For tax purposes you can otherwise amortize the discount in any rational manner if it's uniform in treatment.

Breaking the discount into equal amounts corresponding with the number of the TD's scheduled payments is the simplest way to amortize. So long as there is no undue distortion of the TD's true income picture, the IRS will accept the method.

Amortization of the discount as a percentage of the amounts paid against the principal of the loan is also acceptable and somewhat more accurate. For instance, if you buy a TD at a 10% discount, you can report the discount portion of its taxable income at the rate of 10% of the principal amounts collected during the year.

Methods of amortization which treat the discount as an adjustment of the interest rate shown on the note are the most accurate of all. If a TD shows a 10% interest rate on its face, but was bought at a discount which yields 14%, each payment collected can be divided between principal and interest as though it were a 14% note. In this case, the TD's face interest rate and loan amount are discarded; for tax purposes, the TD's discounted purchase price is used as the loan amount, and its 14% yield rate becomes the interest rate.

REPORTING PREPAYMENT PENALTIES AND LATE CHARGES

The IRS regards loan prepayment penalties and late charges as a form of adjustment of the note's stated interest and therefore taxable as income in the year collected. Though prepayment penalties are a windfall collection based on premature payment of the TD, they do not qualify as capital gains.

THE WOES OF FORECLOSURE

If you end up with the security after a foreclosure sale, you may be faced with a taxable gain even though you have lost money by the foreclosure. The source of this peculiarity is a grotesque distortion of the logical calculation of foreclosure results, brought about by IRC Sec. 1038.

If you acquired your TD at a discount, income from the discount is deferred by spreading it over the life of the TD, as described earlier. But if a foreclosure sale is held, the IRS regards the TD as paid because it no longer exists; and because the TD has been paid, taxes on the discount income then become due — in spite of the fact that you've only received the property back and have not been paid in cash.

Having to pay taxes on a hypothetical gain is bad enough, but being compelled to pay taxes on a loss is worse. Borrower waste of the security is common. If the waste is deep enough, the property may be worth less than the cost of your TD, thus creating a loss when you lay claim to your security through foreclosure. But the IRS refuses to recognize such losses until the property is resold; you're still obligated to pay taxes on the unamortized discount when you foreclose the debt.

The foregoing problems can be avoided if you open the foreclosure sale bidding with an amount less than that due under the deed of trust, "underbidding," as described in the chapter on Foreclosure. You can then substitute the underbid price as the TD's payoff amount and show that no taxable profit occurred. (You can't, however, use the underbid to show a tax deductable loss.) For instance: a note which has a balance due of $10,000, but which you've purchased at an amortized price of $6,000, would produce a $4,000 gain if you bid the full $10,000 due. But if you bid $6,000 instead (and nobody bids higher), you can show zero gain on your tax return.

APPENDIX H

Sources of Information and Assistance

No decision is better than the information on which it is based is an oft quoted truism. If possible, the rule is even more true in trust deeds than with other forms of investment. Ready access to reliable information is crucial to even the smallest TD investment.

The trust deed investor's information sources need not all spring forth full flower immediately upon entry into the business. They can be developed as the need arises. This is fortunate, because some of the most important sources are also suppliers of services further down the line — people who can afford to be very liberal with free advice in order to attract future business.

ATTORNEYS

As a trust deed investor, you should be comfortable with attorneys and the law, because legal matters comprise the greatest number of risk-variables in the business. This does not mean you must become expert in the law. But the subject should not produce an allergic reaction either.

HOW TO FIND THE RIGHT ATTORNEY

Title companies are probably the best lead to attorneys expert in trust deeds. Most title companies have their own "in house" counsel, who naturally become acquainted with attorneys of similar interest. The title company attorney's advice is especially appropriate because, as employees, they have been taken out of the legal market place. They are able to make recommendations uncluttered by overtones of competition or pressures of ego. A senior title officer, one who has been in the business a long time, is also a good reference. He inevitably becomes expert in portions of the law himself, is acquainted with a lot of attorneys, and is exceptionally qualified to point out those who know what they are talking about.

An excellent place to look for the expert trust deed attorney is among those articles written about trust deeds in the local bar association's law review. (See "Libraries," later in this appendix.) The author of an article on some part of trust deed law will be certain to have a good knowledge of the business. Moreover, he may be trying to attract your type of business, or he would not have written the article in the first place. Your local public law library usually stocks copies of law reviews, or will be able to order an index of trust deed related articles for you.

Acquaintances who are attorneys or real estate brokers should not be counted on for reference to an expert TD attorney. More reliable recommendations can be found in a publication called "Martindale and Hubble," which lists attorneys and their specialties. All attorneys, and all public law libraries, have copies of this book. When listing their specialties for the book, attorneys tend to claim too many areas of expertise to permit that part of the book's listings to be a guide. But the publication does rank law offices in a very revealing system operated by the attorneys themselves. Attorneys are periodically canvassed as to their assessment of the competence of other law offices that they have dealt with. Some law offices tend to attract uniformly high grade talent and to receive consistently high ratings. Therefore their claim to expertise may be more reliable.

THE "BUSY" ATTORNEY

For reasons not entirely explicable, an attorney who is slipshod with your time will always prove to be incompetent. The phenomenon shows itself among lawyers who take days to return your telephone calls, fail to keep timely appointments, make you wait inordinately long periods during appointments, or who do not deliver papers to you when they say they will. Blessed with this type of attorney, you're better off facing up to the fact that you'll lose by dealing further with him. No matter how far along you are in your endeavor, you should dismiss such an attorney and try another.

THE HOME TOWN SYNDROME

If you're confronted with the necessity of trying an issue in a court some distance from your regular attorney's offices, you should consider employing the services of a specialist local to that particular court. Time is important and it can be expensive for everybody, especially if much travel is involved getting to and from a distant court. Furthermore, you may be "hometowned" even if you do have a local attorney; an opponent's local attorney may have enough of a social relationship, or at least enough of a working relationship, with the judge to give him an edge in the case.

You can also be hometowned where the distance is not great. Attorneys and judges sometimes see each other so often, across the bench in the same courtroom, that they learn how to accommodate one another just to get their business done as efficiently as possible. Outsiders appearing against local attorneys then must have a much stronger case than normal if they are to count on success. Otherwise they may not be able to predict the judge's reaction to the arguments presented, much less overcome the nuances of cooperation maintained with other attorneys in the court.

HOW TO EMPLOY AN ATTORNEY

Dissatisfaction with the law and with legal services received is almost axiomatic among most people when they attempt to make use of an attorney. Part of the problem stems from public failure to realize that the law is far more complex than it appears to be. Only a lawyer who specializes in the most finite part of the law can hope to keep up with its changes and their effect on real life situations. Efficient use of an attorney rests on employing only the most specialized part of his knowledge. Whenever use is made of his services beyond that, a whole host of problems, apart from bad advice, ensues.

The key to successful employment of an attorney is to make sure that you direct the attorney, rather than the other way around. When dealing with an attorney, many investors seem impelled to shed whatever common sense defensive mechanisms they possess; they limply accept everything their attorney tells them as gospel. Attorneys, for their part, are so accustomed to this phenomenon that they too begin to believe in their own divinity and then dispense advice beyond their competence. To keep things in perspective, you must limit the attorney to issues involving only his specialty, and maintain a rigorous separation from the rest of your problems. Anytime a legal issue is raised which does not sound quite right, you should sort out its logic to determine its degree of applicability to your situation. No one can know as much about your business as you do. Even if you cannot articulate your reasons for disagreement with your attorney, you should stick with your own conclusions in such instances.

Attorneys are often labeled "deal killers," and the above described problem of proper use of their services is the reason. A conscientious attorney's main objective is defense of his client. This means that, if the attorney spots a legal issue that represents a danger, he feels driven to advance the risk as a certainty (which also, incidentally, tends to polish his importance). Some attorneys are more accustomed to this approach than others, because of the number of nitwit schemes brought to them by their clients. But your objective is to make a profit, and the legal issues represent only part of the picture. You should measure the size of the risk and selectively ignore the attorney's advice rather than abandon a profitable deal or alter it to protect against an improbable contingency.

That your position, as the one paying the bills, gives you authority to direct the attorney's actions should be self-evident. But many people lose sight of that fact. They think that once an attorney has been engaged, they are obligated to stick with him through the end of the affair, and therefore they have little control over him. This is not even remotely true. Few situations are so complicated that a competent attorney, an expert on the subject, cannot pick up where another left off with very little loss to the client — and discharge of the former attorney does wonders for the performance of the latter.

Reduce the cost of the attorney by accumulating your questions so they can be asked during a single telephone conversation. Most attorneys bill their time on a "unit basis." That is, they'll bill you for their time in 15-minute increments (some use 30-minute intervals). Discussions which take only seven minutes of an attorney's time cost just as much as those where you group several items which occupy the full 15 minutes. At the rates attorneys charge, this kind of saving adds up quickly.

If you are dissatisfied with the attorney's bill because of his miserable performance, don't hesitate demanding an adjustment. If he refuses, ask for its review by the bar association's arbitration department; he'll be obligated by law to comply with your wishes. Unless the attorney has been an outright thief, you probably will not win an adjustment, but the effort will cost you little. So repugnant is the procedure to some attorneys, that you may even be able to convince him that he should settle with you ahead of arbitration.

ON LEGAL SELF-HELP

At various points later in this appendix, methods of doing your own legal research are described. Some lawyers tend to be contemptuous of people who engage in this kind of legal self-help. But, the better your grasp of the fundamentals of trust deed law, the less you will have to run to a lawyer for trivia. Also, lawyers and their clients have a much better chance of communicating effectively in the presence of some knowledge by the client. And, most important of all, greater knowledge of the law helps you figure out whether the attorney you are dealing with has taken you for an ignoramus and is trying to bluff his way through the job.

TITLE COMPANIES

Perhaps the most important information leg a trust deed investor needs is a good title company.

Title companies are required to charge a fee for the information they provide, unless it relates to a title matter at hand or which will soon be at hand. Whether a separate fee is charged or not, any information provided will be a bargain.

TITLE OFFICERS

A title officer is usually the first contact point in any effort to order title insurance. It is he who has the primary responsibility for shepherding the record search on a property through to the final title policy. Because the cost of error is so great at the title officer level, unbelievably high standards of competence are sometimes found among these people. They often are also unsurpassed as a source of miscellaneous other information required when investing in a TD.

Among their many charms, experienced title officers are a good source of a lot of the law relative to TDs. Their knowledge of real estate law generally exceeds that of all but those attorneys who specialize in the subject — sometimes to the point that a non-specialist lawyer will seek a title officer's opinion rather than spend time researching the law himself. Moreover, if the legal question goes beyond the title officer's knowledge, he has the power to ring in the title company's in-house counsel for an answer at a still higher level of expertise.

If so inclined, a good title officer can provide valuable insights far beyond a particular title problem. Because of their frequent contact with many people in the real estate business, they are privy to much of the gossip that goes on. Experienced title officers can also point out the best real estate lawyers. They know who the best escrow officers are, as well as the commercial history behind a surprising number of properties. Sometimes they can even give you a run-down on the character of the people you are dealing with.

You can increase the degree of cooperation you get from your preferred title officer by trying to pass as much of your title work through him as possible, and by making him aware that you are doing so. To this end, when you open an escrow that requires title insurance, you should insist that the escrow place the title order with your designated title officer, and that he be informed that you requested him. And, if the title officer moves to another title company — as they often do — be sure to track him down at his new location. Such loyalty will attract his attention and ensure his greater cooperation.

TITLE CUSTOMER SERVICE DEPARTMENT

Title companies accumulate huge quantities of data in support of their business. The more complete the history on the properties they insure, the less the chance they will have to pay an insurance claim. The data gathered goes far beyond recorded deeds and deeds of trust. They also have copies of assessors' maps, tax rolls, abstracts of judgement, and anything else that might influence their determination of the condition of title. They can provide you with copies of any recorded document you may need if you provide them with the identifying recording number. They can give you the probable ownership and owner's address of an adjacent parcel by looking it up on their copy of the tax roll. If they want to, they can get copies of documents in the mail to you by the end of the next working day.

You can draw on this information via the title company's customer service department. If the data required is related to a current or anticipated title matter and is complicated, you should make the request through your selected title officer. Other requests, especially simple ones, should be directed straight to the customer service department to save the title officer's time.

FORECLOSURE TRUSTEES

A cooperative trustee can also be a source of valuable information relative to TDs, especially if it concerns foreclosure. Every move relating to a trustee's foreclosure or reconveyance (payoff) is influenced by activities which transpire during the life of the trust deed. Because of this, supervisors in some trustee offices end up knowledgeable in many ways valuable to TD investors. If you become known to the trustee as a result of past or anticipated future business, you can often draw on this experience.

PUBLICATIONS

Of all information sources, published data is the least likely to be biased. It is also, all things considered, the cheapest. For these and many other reasons, TD investors who expect to continue in the business should try to build their own information library — gradually, as the need arises — or learn where to look for the same information at other locations.

LAW BOOKS

The best single, all encompassing legal publication on California real estate is a six-volume set issued by the Bancroft Whitney Co. called *Current Law of California Real Estate,* written by Harry Miller and Marvin Starr. The set is updated periodically with pocket parts, and sometimes volumes are retired in favor of others which are more detailed and up to date. Apart from the set's real estate coverage, those portions on TD law are as thorough as any to be found. The books are very easy to read, considering the complexity of the subject. The set is expensive, by layman standards, and a part-time investor probably would not find it economical to own one. It can be found, however, in virtually every county law library and a great number of the larger city libraries.

The University of California Board of Regents, through its Continuing Education of the Bar (CEB) section, publishes a large number of books on real estate law. These are discussed later in this appendix. For the TD investor, the publications' most valuable characteristic is their focus and extraordinarily complete analysis of very narrow portions of the law, TD law being one of these.

The bulk of our law stems from legislation, which is subsequently codified and reduced to bound volumes sold by various legal publishers. These "codes" are the purest source of information about the law on any particular issue. However much other publications clutter the subject, the code in its original form will always be the best and clearest reference you can turn to.

An unannotated (that is, without interpretive comment) code is not expensive. Paperback copies can be purchased from Parker Publishing Co., and hardcover versions can be bought from Deering as well as West Publishing, among others. For a full time trust deed investor, just a copy of the Civil Code alone will suffice most of the time. The Business and Professions Code will answer most of your remaining needs.

ESCROW BOOKS

Title companies all have escrow departments and sometimes the activity becomes substantial enough for them to prepare a procedures manual to guide their various escrow officers. These manuals are sometimes available to the public for a fee. Because most escrow transactions involve trust deeds in one manner or another, they are a goldmine of actual "hands on" information about TDs. Among other things, the escrow manual will display copies of various forms related to TDs, and give the escrow officer step-by-step information on how to fill them out. Rudimentary legal application of the forms is also provided.

APPRAISAL AIDES

Marshall and Swift Publication Co. provides a *Marshall Valuation Service* as an aid to appraisal. The company is located at 1617 Beverly Boulevard in Los Angeles. Their service, in book form, pictures representative architectural styles, which are then translated to a cost-per-square-foot figure. Regional variables and alternate methods of calculating a building's value are also provided. To keep the data current, the publisher has a subscription service which sends out a monthly update.

Thomas Brothers Maps publishes street atlases of the more populated counties in California. Most investors are already aware of them as an aid to property location by address. They are, however, also helpful if the property is remotely located and is identified by township, range and section; the maps, in those instances, picture the section lines as well as those of township and range.

The U.S. Government publishes topographic maps of California through the Geological Survey. The maps show the contour of the land and sometimes even animal trails. Locations are identified by township, range and section numbers. The maps are priceless if you wish to identify the location of property in a rural area, when you have only a legal description given in geographic terms. The maps can be ordered by mail through the local regional office of the Geological Survey or, at substantially greater cost, from local map stores and surveyor supply stores.

THE "REFERENCE BOOK"

The California Department of Real Estate sells what it calls the annual *Reference Book*. The department also publishes another book called, simply enough, *Real Estate Law,* which is a compilation of those parts of the various codes and regulations that the real estate commissioner thinks pertinent to the real estate brokerage business. The *Reference Book* is intended to give members of the real estate profession the commissioner's views as to the conduct of their affairs. It also contains a lot of related information and practical advice. The book is a miracle of efficiency, because it manages to discuss exactly those questions or problems which people involved in real estate are most likely to confront. Though small in size, it does an exceptional job of describing a wide range of real estate issues.

Both books have to be among the best bargains around, and every real estate investor, whether in trust deeds or not, should have copies of them.

FINANCIAL TABLES

The best, most comprehensive book of financial tables is a three-inch-thick volume called *Financial Compound Interest and Annuity Tables*. It is published by Financial Publishing Co. of Boston, Mass. Because the book requires some study, it is not much in demand and your local book store will not ordinarily carry it. Though the book may have to be ordered, it will be worth it if you do not use a financial calculator; there is no other substitute for calculating the yield on trust deeds with complicated payout schedules.

Contemporary Books of Chicago, Ill., publishes a series of books entitled

Mortgage Yield Tables. These are quick and easily read compilations of tables for the calculation of yield on those discounted notes which call for monthly payments. The tables can also be used to approximate the yield when payments are quarterly or semiannual. These books are better than most others available, because they cover a wider range of interest rates and variables. The tables cannot be used if the note calls for intermediate "balloon" installment payments, or similar gimmicks in the life of the TD.

INCOME TAX REFERENCES

Invest in trust deeds long enough and you'll ultimately be inspired to an occasional investment in real estate. Especially if you follow the strategies suggested in the Other Approaches Chapter of this book. If you succumb, you'll need good tax references because real estate investment is entwined with some of the most complicated provisions in the tax code.

From the standpoint of practical applications, your most valuable reference could then be an extraordinary book called *Aggressive Tax Avoidance for Real Estate Investors,* by John Reed, available from Reed Publishing Co. of Danville, California. The book is simply written and does a very good job of making the dull business of income taxes actually sound interesting. Its greatest usefulness, however, lies in its demonstration of innovative ways of avoiding income taxes. It shows how professionals in real estate investment go about reducing the burden of, and sometimes eliminating completely, income taxes.

For explanation of the income tax law alone, without an overlay of tax avoidance strategy, your best reference is the *US Master Tax Guide,* published by Commerce Clearing House. The same company also publishes a similar book, called *Guidebook to California Taxes,* which describes the state income tax structure. Both Commerce Clearing House books — as much as the complexities of the law permit — explain income taxes in plain terms accompanied by an abundance of examples. Although they don't go into all the vagaries of the law, they should be sufficient for most transactions. In fact, most professionals in the business, CPAs and tax advisors alike, use these books as their primary reference.

CEB (CONTINUING EDUCATION OF THE BAR) INFORMATION

CEB PUBLICATIONS

The Board of Regents of the University of California, in conjuction with the California Bar Association, publishes a number of books for the aid of attorneys in search of the most recent thought on given portions of the law. The books are surprisingly easy to read and contain instruction on such practical matters as how to fill out various sample forms, with accompanying comments on the applicable law regarding the forms. The books are supplemented when sufficient changes occur to require an update of the information. They are of more than passing interest to TD investors, because some of them contain a microscopic examination of those areas of the law related to trust deeds.

At this writing, the following CEB books are of interest to the trust deed investor:

California Mortgage and Deed of Trust Practice, Bernhardt, 1979.

Ogden's Revised California Real Property Law, Bowman, Vol. I, 1974; Vol. II, 1975.

California Real Property Sales Transactions, Graham and Scott, ed., 1981.

Next to the Miller and Starr set on real estate law mentioned earlier in this chapter, the Bernhardt book is currently the most comprehensive compilation of TD law — and it's a lot cheaper.

The CEB also publishes a monthly bulletin called the *Real Property Law Reporter.* It endeavors to cover all real estate law changes of importance in California. Though you must filter out the parts not pertinent to TDs, you'll still find a subscription to the publication worthwhile if you do TDs very often.

The easiest way to get on the mailing list for the announcement of publications such as these is through your attorney. The CEB will then send you notices of the books and their supplements as they come out. When you purchase a book, you are given the opportunity to sign up for the automatic mailing of supplements as they occur. Once on the mailing list, you will also be sent an annual CEB catalog of the available books, supplements, and lecture tapes.

CEB SEMINARS

The CEB also sponsors a series of traveling seminars hosted by local bar associations. Schedule announcements are regularly sent all addressees on the CEB mailing list. The seminars generally are held on weekends or in the evening, at locations convenient to the largest number of attorneys in the area. They are valuable if you have a legal question in TDs, because they enable you to ask questions and receive answers from experts on the panel and in the audience. Because the panelists are, or try to be, experts in the seminar's subject, you also have a chance to evaluate them in case you need an expert TD attorney in the future.

Tapes of some of the more popular seminars are made, and they can be bought along with the CEB publications. Their availability is announced in the annual CEB catalog.

LAW LIBRARY INFORMATION

Most counties have one or more law libraries, which are available to the public as well as attorneys. The libraries are usually located in or near a courthouse, and can be found in the white pages of the local telephone directory under the county listings. Other law libraries accessible to the public may be found at nearby publicly endowed colleges which have a law school. If you have trouble digging up the answer to a question at any of these libraries, there will usually be one or more people on hand who can point you in the right direction.

INFORMATION FROM LOCAL GOVERNMENTAL AGENCIES

COUNTY RECORDER

Each county has an office, at the county seat, which is required by law to accept certain documents for recording. When recorded, the documents are considered legal evidence of constructive notice of the events they describe. To record a document, the county stamps it with identifying characters, dates it, takes a picture of it, and then mails it to the addressee given on the document's face. Deeds, deeds of trust, leases, abstracts of judgement, easements, assignments, and a host of other documents contributing to the history of a property must be accepted for recording.

All this information is theoretically available to whomever wishes to search it out. To help with the search, the county stations people about the premises to answer questions. The quality of help varies, however, and only the simplest type of search is practical, unless you have expert advice. In some of the larger counties, such as Los Angeles County, search may be impossible due to overcrowding of the facilities. Even in the smaller counties, without experience, hired search may be the most profitable approach.

COUNTY ASSESSOR RECORDS

Each county has an assessor's office which is responsible for placing a valuation for tax purposes on all real property in the county. To this end, the assessor maintains certain records which are also available to the public. As with the county recorder, the information is stored at a central office located in or near the county seat. The assessor in the larger, more populated counties will also have branch offices for greater efficiency in dealing with local properties. The branch offices contain records relative to property in their region only.

The county assessor maintains maps of each and every parcel of property in the county. The maps show property lines, dimensions, acreage and much other valuable information. Easements and roads are sometimes also shown. The maps also show each parcel's assigned assessor's number, and this provides a handy means of identification of the property (though it's no substitute for a legal description). Copies of the maps may be bought at the assessors office for a nominal fee.

The assessor's office also carries copies of the tax rolls, and these too are available to the public. Tax rolls show the ownership, address of the property, address of the owner, the assessor's valuation of the property, and other data of occasional use. The property valuations tend to be out of date, depending on how much staff the assessor has relative to the amount of the county's real estate activity.

If you are the owner, or have some other legal interest in a property, you can question its valuation by the assessor, and the staff will sometimes show you comparable sales in the area in support of their figure. Otherwise, the assessor's valuation data is not supposed to be used as a substitute for your own appraisal efforts.

DEPARTMENTS USEFUL FOR APPRAISAL

City and county planning departments can help you with zoning records, as well as other information pertinent to the security's valuation. Zoning maps are always available, along with lists of the permitted uses for each zone classification.

Each improvement to a property in a municipality also requires a building permit and, to implement the task, the building department maintains a record of the improvements for which a permit has been issued.

A detailed explanation of the application of both planning and building department information is given in the Appraisal sections of this book.

INFORMATION FROM ELECTRONIC CALCULATORS

Financial tables are mentioned earlier in this appendix as necessary to the calculation of yields and other information about a trust deed. A few handheld electronic calculators, such as Hewlett Packard's HP 12C or Texas Instrument's Analyst Series, supply all the information found in the financial tables, and do it much faster. Furthermore, cost of a suitable calculator is not much more than the purchase price of the printed tables you would otherwise use. To learn how to use the contraption does require some study, however, and if you invest only occasionally, the printed financial tables will be more convenient.

236

INFORMATION SOURCES THAT DON'T WORK

Escrow officers are generally not good sources of information, unless they happen to be very well acquainted with you. Though the best ones have an impressive knowledge about the technicalities of real estate, their need to remain independent tends to make them shy of offering advice. Furthermore, they always stand in fear that one of their customers will claim interference based on unlicensed legal or real estate advice.

Real estate sales people are also a poor source of information about TDs. Much of the real estate profession is appallingly ignorant on the subject. As a consequence, information from this source is often flawed. Very few real estate licensees go out of their way to study trust deeds; most learn from their individual experiences as they go along, or from gossip and hearsay among their brethren. Only when you get to the loan brokerage portion of the profession do you begin to find any depth of knowledge about TDs, and even then this usually occurs just in the supervisory end of the business.

Ignorance aside, all information, no matter what its source, is also likely to be self-serving of the informant's needs and should therefore be discounted to some extent.

APPENDIX I

Security Limits

ANTIDEFICIENCY LAW

In a practical sense, your ability to collect on a defaulted TD is limited to its security. If you foreclose by nonjudicial means (i.e., through a trustee), you cannot pursue the borrower's other assets if the security proves insufficient to cover the loan. Only when you abandon the nonjudicial process and foreclose judicially (by going to court) can you look beyond the TD's security for protection. As a result, California lenders generally regard a trust deed only as an encumbrance on the security and not as a direct obligation of the borrower.

The foregoing is the outcome of what is known as "antideficiency" legislation and especially that part of the law called "the one-action rule."

THE ONE-ACTION RULE

The "one-action rule" forbids your foreclosure on a trust deed by both nonjudicial and judicial process. It states that you may foreclose only as a mortgage (judicial), or only as a deed of trust (nonjudicial). You cannot do both. Because judicial foreclosure is so cumbersome, the nonjudicial process is almost always chosen. Therefore, as long as the borrower is willing to sacrifice the TD security, he can usually duck out of his obligation. In such an event, the borrower does not even suffer damage to his credit, since foreclosures are not regularly picked up by credit reporting agencies.

PURCHASE-MONEY LIMITATIONS

Under certain rare circumstances you might choose judicial foreclosure in order to pursue all the borrower's assets rather than merely a TD's security. But even that approach may be denied if your TD is considered "purchase-money." (See Purchase-Money in the Fundamentals Chapter.)

All purchase-money TDs which are vendor (seller) financings are forbidden collection of deficiency in the security's ability to cover the loan. With the exception of certain federally guaranteed loans, all third party purchase money lenders are also prohibited deficiency judgements — if the loan is secured by four or fewer residential units, one of which is occupied by the borrower. Subject to the aforementioned one action rule, all other third party lenders are free to pursue judicially the borrower's assets for security deficiencies.

PRIORITY RIGHTS TO THE SECURITY

The TD's recording date determines the seniority of its claim to the security. This rule applies to all instruments recorded against the property, whether they be judgement liens, other TDs, or non-monetary items such as easements.

TD priorities assume special significance in the event of foreclosure. Foreclosure of a senior TD wipes out all junior interests in the security, including later recorded easements — unless the junior steps in and covers the default in the senior beforehand (see the chapters on Foreclosure for more on this). Though the borrower's obligation to pay a junior loan may continue after senior foreclosure, he may have insufficient other assets to make collection enforceable, causing the junior TD to become worthless.

As might be expected, the rule of "first in time is first in right" has exceptions. Normally a judgement lien recorded ahead of a TD has prior claim to the TD's security. However, when the seller of a property finances part of the sale by taking back a purchase-money trust deed, the trust deed so created is superior to any judgement, regardless of their respective recording dates. Furthermore, all TDs are junior to certain governmental liens, such as real property taxes, no matter when the TDs come into existence. Likewise, mechanics liens for works of improvement on a property which were started *before* the TD's recording are senior to the TD.

Special Strategies in Foreclosure

DEEDS IN LIEU OF FORECLOSURE

THE "DEED IN LIEU" PURCHASE PRICE

Warning: During deed in lieu transactions, you should always be prepared to pay at least an approximation of the property's true value. The courts are very careful in making sure lenders do not take unfair advantage in these circumstances. If the borrower thinks he is cheated in this kind of deal, he can reclaim the property or cloud your title to it with a lawsuit.

You can actually afford to pay more for a deed in lieu than the property is worth. The savings in the costs of foreclosure (trustee's fees, advertising, and the cost of money tied up, for example) can make it worth your while to do so. Payment of more is also often sensible if you're faced with prospects of a decline in the property value (such as through waste) during the foreclosure period.

PROTECTIVE MEASURES

To protect yourself from a claim of unfair advantage, the deed in lieu must be carefully worded. An acknowledgement by the borrower that he has received fair consideration should be included. Appropriate phrasing for this purpose is best obtained from the title company expected to insure your ownership. The entire transaction, in fact, should be conducted in concert with a title company, to be certain you have an insurable title.

Though not always practical, you should try to have the borrower represented by an attorney during the transfer. A borrower's later complaint that he has been taken advantage of will then be more difficult to sustain.

You should also purchase a preliminary title report before accepting a deed in lieu. If time is short, a title company will sometimes give an oral run-down on the property and follow with a written report. A preliminary title report is necessary because your purchase by deed in lieu compels you to assume all the property's encumbrances, including liens junior to your position. A borrower in foreclosure usually incurs a series of such items, sometimes without realizing it. Tax liens, judgements, and other involuntary liens are common, and all of them become part of your purchase price under a deed in lieu.

The deed in lieu transaction often occurs in a hurried atmosphere. A cashier's check is exchanged over a table for a deed in lieu drafted only minutes earlier. The property's owners usually sign the deed just before the exchange, and their signatures are notarized at the same time. This poses a logistical problem, since getting everybody together in front of a notary is not always convenient, especially if you must meet during a notary's normal business hours. To get around the problem, the meeting sometimes occurs in the evening in the presence of a friend who happens to be a notary. If so, make sure the notary has no interest in the transaction, because the title company will otherwise refuse to insure your purchase.

The above type of exchange leaves you vulnerable to any encumbrance or deed previously recorded on the property. An unscrupulous seller might, for instance, borrow against the property minutes before selling it to you. If the new encumbrance is recorded before your deed, you will have to assume responsibility for its payment. If there is the slightest chance of this, back off and insist that you be protected with an escrow and title insurance. Even if you don't think another recording will be slipped in ahead of you, your deed in lieu should still be recorded as quickly as possible, just in case.

WHAT TO DO IN CASE OF WASTE

All foreclosures involve waste, or loss in the value of the security, in one form or another. Some types are much worse than others, however, and require special precautions.

TROUBLE SPOTS FOR WASTE

Agricultural property runs the highest risk of waste. If the property is an orchard, you can be certain it will be stripped of all the crop, no matter how immature. Watering or irrigation will be without regard for future production, barely enough to provide a retrievable crop. The same applies to weed control and the use of pesticides.

If the security is rental income property, unscrupulous borrowers have been known to "clean out the rents." This occurs when, to the infinite though fleeting delight of the tenants, each is offered a substantial discount on their rent if they pay in advance. These agreements are unenforceable against a successful bidder at a foreclosure sale. They do stand up against a person who purchases the property (as by deed in lieu of foreclosure) before the foreclosure sale. But even when your foreclosure invalidates such agreements, you probably will have to pacify the tenants to some extent. As a practical matter, it makes no difference if the borrower commits fraud in instances such as this; no one is going to be able to recover money damages from him if he is insolvent.

Deferred maintenance of buildings is a common form of waste, and so is lack of erosion control, and dumping rubbish on the property. If the property is abandoned by the borrower, waste may take the form of vandalism or outright theft — sometimes by the borrower: The fixtures can be stripped, and squatters can move in leaving you with a sticky, even impossible, unlawful detainer action to remove them.

COUNTER MEASURES AGAINST WASTE

If the property is abandoned before you complete your foreclosure, you should consider taking action to protect it. If it's a house, this may be your chance to be magnanimous by offering to let impoverished friends or relatives stay there, rent free. You may also want to maintain the property, at least sufficiently to prevent major damage.

The decision whether to maintain is sometimes not easy. Without judicial consent, the cost of maintenance cannot be added to your loan. And if you maintain the property at too high a level, it may be so attractive to others that you will be outbid at the foreclosure sale and thereby lose the additional amount invested.

Maintenance during foreclosure requires the consent of the court if you want to add the cost to your TD. To do otherwise exposes you to a number of problems explained in the Rents and Profits section of the appendix on Clauses. If you want to add the cost of maintenance to your TD, you must ask the court to appoint a receiver, who then manages and protects the property during the foreclosure period. The procedure is expensive but is routinely employed when the size of the numbers make the cost worthwhile.

TAX LIEN REDEMPTION RIGHTS

STATE "POSTPONED PROPERTY TAX" REDEMPTIONS

In order to protect a lien for property taxes which were postponed as a result of the Senior Citizens Property Tax Postponement Act of 1977, the state of California has a right of redemption similar to that held by junior TD lenders — if the notice of the lien is recorded *after* a TD's notice of default, and at least 30 days *before* the TD's foreclosure sale date. Unlike a junior TD, the state's right of redemption is not automatically severed by completion of the foreclosure; it extends into perpetuity beyond the foreclosure sale, unless appropriate notice of the pending sale is given. The form of notice is defined by CC 2924b, and it must be given to the state's Controller not less than 25 days beforehand. If the state does not then redeem before completion of the foreclosure sale, its right of redemption for the lien is severed.

REDEMPTIONS FOR FEDERAL TAX LIENS

The U.S. has a right of redemption for the collection of federal taxes, and it also extends beyond the foreclosure sale. In this case, to be valid the tax lien need only be filed more than 30 days before the sale. (Reason, incidentally, to be wary of sale postponements which might validate the lien.) Again, the right of redemption can be severed by giving (the Internal Revenue Service) notice of the sale in accordance with CC 2924b, at least 25 days beforehand.

To limit redemption, the notice of sale must be *received,* within the time limit, by the district director of the Internal Revenue Service whose jurisdiction covers the place of sale. Delivery of the notice to some other Internal Revenue Service office may or may not accomplish the task, depending on whether the notice is forwarded to the appropriate office in time. Most trustees are well acquainted with this and already know which office must be given notice. Those who don't know the district boundaries can easily learn them by calling an IRS regional office and asking the local Chief of Special Procedures.

The U.S. right of redemption expires 120 days following the trustee's sale, if you give proper notice. During the 120-day period, the property will be virtually unmarketable. If you find yourself the successful bidder in this type of situation, you may be able to extricate yourself by offering to purchase a waiver of the federal tax lien. If you offer the IRS as little as $100 for the waiver, they'll usually accept it if it's in their best interests to do so.

SCHEDULING THE SALE FOR TAX REDEMPTIONS

Normal foreclosure procedure described in the Foreclosure Chapters allows a minimum of 21 days between expiration of the first three months and the sale date. But severence of any tax lien redemption right requires at least 25 days notice, and the mechanics of giving notice lengthens the time span even more. To accommodate potential tax lien notices, most trustees therefore publish a delayed foreclosure date which allows for 25 days advance notice, just in case it becomes necessary; or they schedule the sale on a 21-day basis, and cry a postponement on the sale date in order to match any 25-day notice requirement.

If you're racing the clock to beat an anticipated bankruptcy or TRO (see also this appendix), delays such as the foregoing, even for a few days, can be fatal. By planning ahead, you can eliminate the problem completely. Trustees usually check for tax liens by asking for an update of the title information (called an "FTL date-down") as of the expiration of the first three months of foreclosure. But if you ask for a special date-down earlier, as of 29 days before the 21-day scheduled sale date, you'll probably have enough time to meet any 25-day notice requirements that may be revealed; and if you think a date-down 29 days beforehand won't give you enough time, a still earlier search (35 days ahead, for instance) can be requested — except that you then run the risk that subsequent valid tax liens may be filed within the allowed 30 days before sale.

COURT ORDERS RESTRAINING FORECLOSURE

Almost any borrower can obtain a court ordered restraint of an impending foreclosure sale of his property. If you play your cards right and prepare ahead of time, this may cause only a temporary delay in your foreclosure. (You sometimes also can take consolation from the fact that the borrower's attorney will then be unable to collect his fee from his client.) But if the borrower is successful in getting a "permanent" injunction against the foreclosure sale, you can expect mounting legal expense, loss of time while under the jurisdiction of the court, rising depreciation, waste, taxes, insurance, and all the other costs attendant upon delay. Whatever potential buyers you have lined up for the property will also be lost. Worst of all, you may also have to pay the borrower's attorney's fees.

THE TEMPORARY RESTRAINING ORDER (TRO)

The petitioner before the court (borrower) starts the fracas with an application for a "temporary restraining order," otherwise known as a "TRO." The petitioner's attorney files a complaint with the court giving whatever reason for a delay that comes to mind. The lender is supposed to be notified that the petition is to be filed so he can enter his arguments against it. Notification is not necessary, however, if the lender cannot be contacted — a circumstance which usually results in a fortuitous breakdown of the telephone company's equipment. Even if you are able to argue against the petition, a judge will probably grant the TRO, since reaching a clear understanding of the situation generally takes more time than is immediately available.

The TRO is effective if served on the trustee or beneficiary prior to the time the property is knocked down to the successful bidder at a foreclosure sale. It is ineffective if not served. (See Choice of the Sale Location, in the Foreclosure Redemption Chapter for possibilities in this regard.) If service is successful, the sale is stopped in its tracks and must be postponed until the court can hear the issue some 14 or more days later.

COURT HEARING FOR THE RESTRAINING ORDER

Within a given time period (14 to 20 days after the TRO, depending on the county of jurisdiction), the court must hear arguments on whether the restraint should be continued until a trial can be held, and, if so, under what terms.

If the court decides to grant a restraining order, it may or may not require the borrower to post a bond protecting you against loss caused by the delay. As additional protection, the bond requirement may be accompanied by directions to keep up your TD's payments during the injunction period. The bond requirement may also work to your advantage if the borrower's financial condition limits the chances it will be obtainable; the larger the bond required, the less chance he will be able to comply.

PREPARATIONS FOR COURT

The aforementioned court hearing is critical because you and your attorney have, in a practical sense, only this one time to put a stop to the affair.

Fortunately, you will be given time to prepare for a petition for a restraining order if you are alert to the warning signs. Conversations with the borrower give clues; large properties with good equity can expect a petition automatically; small properties not worth fighting over are immune; large properties with a small, or even a negative equity, are still susceptible to a petition — the borrower usually has an exaggerated view of the property's value and he can always convince some attorney that a TRO is the only way to prevent an oppressive lender from trying to steal it.

Preparations for the restraining order hearing should commence well ahead of the anticipated TRO. Correspondence with prospective purchasers of the property should be retained, and so should communications with the borrower. Phrasing used in correspondence can be employed with an eye to its later use as evidence. An appraisal may be in order, impressively detailed. Sending through a few buyers to make an offer for the property may provide evidence the borrower will never solve his problems because he is too greedy about the price. Selection of a good attorney, expert on the subject and known to the court, should also be done beforehand — it saves time later and gives you a chance to coordinate your actions with the arguments the attorney expects to use.

On the assumption you will defeat the restraint, preliminary thought should be given to the most desirable new sale date after the hearing. When the TRO stops a foreclosure sale, the trustee must cry a postponement. Unless you step in and assert your views, the trustee may postpone the sale as much as a month longer than needed. The best sale date to try for is one day after (or even the same day as) the anticipated date of the TRO hearing. Otherwise, even if you are successful in court, the borrower may find enough time to rush into bankruptcy and stay the sale again. (The borrower's attorney is certain to advise such a move, since it will be his best chance for recovering his fee.)

BENEFICIARY ARGUMENTS AT COURT

You should calculate the comparative merits of buying the borrower off, versus the success of your arguments in court. You can expect the court to be predisposed in favor of the borrower, and therefore a vigorous defense will be needed. In spite of earlier evidence to the contrary, the borrower can also be assumed to be a superior explicator — otherwise he would not have been able to ensnare you, his lawyer, and various others in his problems. No matter how honest he may have appeared in the past, he becomes a consummate liar on the grounds that "I have no choice but to save myself."

The injunction is supposed to be based on errors in the foreclosure, but protecting both borrower and lender from loss will dominate any hearing for continuation of the restraint. Your arguments to prevent continued restraint should therefore include evidence that the borrower's interest in the property is not worth saving; that the security's value is so low you cannot hope to recoup the amount due unless you continue the foreclosure; that the mounting costs of the property will cause extraordinary losses; that the buyers you have lined up will be lost; that the borrower is unrealistic or insincere in his proposed attempts to solve the problem; and that severe waste and/or vandalization will ensue if there is further delay.

ESTABLISHING THE POST-TRO SALE DATE

In some cases, you may have difficulty getting the foreclosure trustee to hold the sale one day after the TRO hearing, as suggested earlier. Before establishing a new sale date, trustees like to have on hand a "conformed" copy of the court order releasing the TRO; but a conformed copy requires getting the judge's signature and that can take days, even weeks.

To get around the above problem, you can try to convince the trustee he should settle for oral confirmation of the court order from the court clerk. If you expect the trustee will refuse to act without written authority, you should ask your attorney to have a previously prepared order of release on hand at the time of the TRO hearing, and ask for the judge's signature directly on his issuance of the release. Because the order for release may require amendment, your attorney should be prepared to alter or add to the proposed court order's wording during the hearing, so you can snag the judge for his signature before he disappears.

WHAT TO DO WHEN DOCUMENTATION IS MISSING

Before processing a foreclosure, trustees require the originals of the note, deed of trust, and any assignments connected with the TD's ownership. If you don't have the original deed of trust or assignments, the trustee will accept, instead, certified copies provided by the county recorder from the picture taken when the documents were recorded. The note portion of a TD is not ordinarily recorded, however, and its loss requires other measures to satisfy the trustee. The usual procedure in this instance is purchase (with the trustee's assistance) of a "lost instrument bond," which the trustee accepts in lieu of the original note.

Purchase of a lost instrument bond can be expedited if you provide the trustee with a photocopy of the original note, plus corollary evidence such as escrow documents. (In fact, some trustees will dispense with the bond requirement if a beneficiary of known character presents such evidence and accompanies it with a sworn statement as to its authenticity.) If you don't have photocopies of the signed note and related escrow documents in your file, additional copies usually can be obtained through the escrow which handled the transaction; escrows commonly make photocopies of all such documents before dispersing them among principals to a transaction.

STATUTORY CHANGES

See Foreclosure in the Supplement at the back of the book.

See Foreclosure in the Supplement at the back of the book.

See Foreclosure in the Supplement at the back of the book.

APPENDIX K

Escrow Instructions

Most escrow forms used for private TD investment are relatively simple affairs, drawn by others because TD investors seldom feel confident enough to interject their own requirements. As a consequence, TD escrows tend to serve first the needs of others interested in the transaction, and only secondarily those of the investor. If you wish to receive equal treatment, you'll have to introduce your own complications — and be fairly precise about it while doing so.

The escrow instructions you should ask for will vary, depending on whether you're purchasing a TD already in existence or making a new loan. The instructions suggested by this appendix are therefore divided into two parts: Part I covers instructions needed when you're involved in the purchase of an existing TD. Part II describes variations from Part I which are necessary to escrow a new loan.

Part I: Investor Requirements — Purchase of an Existing TD

THE PURCHASE PRICE INSTRUCTION

The custom in the sale of existing trust deeds is that once the dollar purchase price is established, further collections by the TD seller are applied toward reduction of the amount paid by the buyer. The operative phrasing is, "all future payments of principal and interest are to be paid or credited to the buyer." The custom is a weak one, however, and you must be sure the wording is entered in the escrow instructions.

251

A pegged purchase price instruction such as the foregoing contributes greatly to an efficient escrow. Any delay in completion of the transaction is then at the expense of the TD's seller. The TD's interest earned during escrow accrues to you, whether you've deposited money in the escrow or not. The seller is thereby motivated to get things moving toward an early close — it's his clock that's running.

HOW TO HANDLE PAYMENTS COLLECTED DURING ESCROW

If you've arranged to purchase a TD for a fixed dollar amount, as suggested above, you'll be entitled to credit for all payments received subsequent to the agreement date. During escrow, this is usually accomplished by having the escrow collect the borrower's checks and then pass them on to the TD buyer at the escrow's close — instead of passing them on to the TD seller and reducing the buyer's purchase price. But if you're to accept checks collected during escrow in lieu of reduction of the purchase price, you need to be sure that the checks will clear the bank. This leads, then, to the following instruction: ". . . hold from the seller's account an amount equal to the sum of all the borrower's checks surrendered to the buyer. Said sum is to be released to the seller on the buyer's confirmation that the checks have cleared. The withheld sum is to be automatically released to the seller at the end of _____ days unless the escrow receives a written instruction to the contrary from the buyer."

OWNER'S OFFSET STATEMENT REQUIREMENT

An "owner's offset statement" is a fundamental requirement of every TD purchase and should always appear as part of the escrow instructions. The statement is a form signed by the current owner of the property (the borrower). It contains assurances that the owner concurs with the information you have previously been provided about the trust deed's terms, the status of payments, and the balance owed. To make certain there have been no undisclosed amendments to the note and to cinch down everybody's understanding, you might also ask that a copy of the TD's note be attached to the offset statement and reference made to the attachment in the body of the statement. If the note has unusual payment terms susceptible to misunderstanding, a copy of the note's amortization schedule can also be attached. Because the escrow officer needs to track the note's payments, the offset statement should also instruct the borrower to pass the payments through the escrow during the period of its existence.

If you think the property owner will agree to them, you should also try to have assurances included in the offset statement that he is owner of the land, that he received full and valid consideration for his obligation under the note,

252

that there have been no advances, and that there are no unstated offsets, claims, or defenses against the note. By his acknowledgement of these conditions, the borrower may be prevented from later raising "personal defenses" to foreclosure. (For more on this, see Note's Endorsement later in this appendix.)

STIPULATING SENIOR LIEN TERMS

The expected details of any senior TD should be dictated into the escrow. To be sure that your understanding of these details comply with the actual TD, instructions should be given which require your initialed approval of a copy of the senior deed of trust and note, front and back. As explained in the chapter on Investigation of the TD, senior liens may carry elements, such as release clauses and due on sale clauses, which can either destroy the security for a junior, or enhance it. Normal title reporting practice may not uncover such clauses, and — even if he recognizes the significance — the TD's seller cannot be expected to pass such information on to you unless you ask for it.

BENEFICIARY STATEMENT REQUIREMENTS

The present condition of a TD senior to the one you are buying is confirmed with a "beneficiary statement" signed by the senior lender. All TD lenders are legally required to respond to authorized requests for such statements. (See also the chapter on Administration.) To expedite lender response, most escrows accompany their request for a "beny" with a preprinted form requiring only a few blanks and the lender's signature to be filled in. In doing so, the escrow may omit confirmation of some of the senior TD's terms or dilute the response by posing questions incompatible with some peculiarity in the trust deed. You therefore should require the form of beneficiary statement be submitted for your approval before it is sent to the senior beneficiary.

TITLE INSURANCE ENDORSEMENTS

A "title insurance policy" which assures you of your claim on the TD's security is a basic requirement in all TD escrows. An escrow for the purchase of an existing trust deed will not usually need a new title policy. Instead, a title policy issued to the TD's previous owner is deposited in escrow along with an appropriate endorsement transferring the protection to the TD's new owner.

A number of forms of title policy endorsements are available, but only one type is sensible if you have much at stake. It's called a "104A" endorsement when applied to a CLTA policy form and a "104" endorsement when applied to an ALTA form. (See Title Insurance Alternatives, later in Part II of this appendix, for title policy forms.) With the 104A endorsement, you are assured, among other things, that the person selling the TD is, in fact, the owner, and is competent to sell it; that the borrower has not filed bankruptcy; and that no unpaid tax, bond, or property assessments are outstanding except those named in the endorsement. Expanded coverage of the endorsement can also be purchased which verifies the present owner of the property.

Unless you are alert, a "104.1" endorsement will be used. The 104.1 is the form most commonly employed, because it's cheaper (by about $100), and because it causes less trouble. However, the 104.1 form only assures you that you have been placed in the shoes of the previous beneficiary. Unless expanded coverage is purchased, no examination is made for such items as bankruptcy, unpaid taxes, bond, or property assessments.

The entire subject of title policy endorsements is complex and you should not hesitate to carry questions about them to your preferred title officer. This is one place where truly expert opinion is a bargain.

THE RIGHT FORM OF NOTE ENDORSEMENT

You also need to specify the form of endorsement used by the TD seller for transfer of the note. The seller's endorsement on the back of the note, plus his recorded assignment of the deed of trust, provides the conclusive evidence needed for your ownership of the TD. Methods by which the note endorsement is accomplished vary, however, so you must make your wishes known.

Misinformation about note endorsements is the norm in real estate and it survives because people in the business who should know better underrate its importance. They pay only nominal attention to the subject, erroneously believing that title insurance will be proof against limitations in the form of transfer. As a consequence, most TD buyers don't bother to stipulate the form of endorsement to be used.

The best form of endorsement (from the investor's standpoint, anyway) is one called a "special endorsement;" that is, an endorsement which says "Pay to the order of (the investor)," and then is followed by the seller's signature. No other wording is added. An alternative form is called an endorsement "in blank," in which the back of the note is simply signed by the seller and that's all. The former is more desirable because it restricts the note's current ownership to the party named. The latter method becomes bearer paper, of which anyone in possession can claim ownership. Both forms make you a "holder-in-due-course" and are equally effective for purposes of collecting.

Some investors try to add words of guaranty or warranty to the endorsement. But additional wording is unnecessary. Unless you are acquiring a "purchase money" TD (see the Fundamentals Chapter), the seller of a TD is automatically liable for the debt if the borrower defaults in his payment (a valuable collection device, incidentally — often forgotten by lenders trying to salvage their investment in a troubled loan). The seller's endorsement also carries with it an implied warranty of the validity of the instrument. It also implies that he knows of nothing which would undermine its value. Only when the endorsement bears the words *"without* warranty," or *"without* recourse," is the TD seller relieved of these promises.

WHEN INSPECTION AND APPROVAL OF DOCUMENTS IS NECESSARY

If the escrow officer is of unknown character, instructions should be entered which require your approval of all papers or documents deposited in the escrow. Cautious escrow officers routinely submit documents for approval in any case, not wanting to risk a lawsuit over whether the documents satisfy the instructions. But some escrow officers are willing to take on responsibility, especially if it's to their advantage to force the escrow to a close. Instructions which require your initialed approval of each document will do much to prevent such independence.

FIRE INSURANCE REQUIREMENTS

If the TD's security includes structural improvements of any consequence, you need to be insured against their loss by fire and other hazards. According to the terms of all TDs, the borrower is obligated to supply the insurance. (See Insurance in the chapter on Administration.) To be sure the borrower has complied satisfactorily, you must include the insurance requirement among the escrow instructions.

Your instructions should call for delivery of a complete copy of the insurance policy in your hands at the close of escrow. The policy should name you first payee in the event of loss. (Or second payee if your loan is a 2nd TD.) Usually the TD seller already has a copy of the insurance policy in his possession, and all that's required is delivery of the policy along with the insurance company's endorsement substituting you as insured.

THE BROKER'S COMMISSION INSTRUCTION

Sometimes brokers try to insist on conducting the escrow themselves because they fear an independent escrow will reveal the amount of their commission to the TD buyer. (Although the broker's commission is paid by the seller, TD buyers often become dissatisfied with the deal upon learning the amount taken off by the broker.) Commission instructions given an independent escrow may therefore require special wording which mollifies the broker by authorizing the commission payment, yet hides the amount from the TD buyer: "The seller herein will pay a commission to the broker by separate written instructions." This creates a sort of subescrow from which the buyer is excluded, and the broker's privacy is preserved.

255

"REQUEST FOR NOTICE" INSTRUCTION

Instructions for issuance of a "request for notice of default" should be made part of your escrow if there are senior lien holders. The procedure is commonly employed whenever there is a transfer of TD ownership and any competent escrow office will have appropriate request forms on hand. Recording the forms will entitle you to notice of the senior's recording of a default within 10 days, instead of 30 days, as otherwise required by law — a valuable edge in some situations. (For more on the subject, see Default Notifications in the First Three Months of Foreclosure Chapter.)

California CC 2924e allows junior TDs secured by one to four residential units to also require senior TDs' notification if the senior payments are past due. Because of complications in the law, the requirement is useless and escrow instructions initiating the procedure would serve little purpose. To implement the request, the junior lender must send the senior TD a detailed "request for notice" in a form dictated by the statute. The request must also be accompanied by payment of $40, plus the property owners' written agreement to the procedure. Once the request is lodged with the senior, the junior will be entitled to notice only if the senior payments are more than four months past due. And if the senior fails to comply with the requirement, he can be socked with a penalty and damages so minor only the smallest senior lenders would notice the cost.

THE TAX SERVICE REQUIREMENT

Later management of your trust deed investment may be eased by an instruction for the purchase of a "tax service." The tax service is actually an insurance policy which notifies you when the property owner fails to pay his real property taxes. The cost of the service is negligible and should be no obstacle to either party. If the seller of the trust deed has already purchased the service, it can be assigned to you at no additional cost.

BUYER'S UNILATERAL WAIVER — A TIME SAVER

Inclusion of an escrow provision which permits you to waive an earlier requested instruction may later prove useful. Alterations of the escrow, even if waiver of only a minor requirement, normally delay the process because they need the written consent of both parties. An escrow instruction which states that "Any requirement of this escrow, necessary to the buyer alone, may be unilaterally waived by the buyer" saves time when the instruction is for your benefit alone — and, as explained elsewhere, saving time will often save the deal.

Part II: Investor Requirements — Loan Escrow

All the escrow requirements described in Part I for the purchase of an existing TD also apply to loan escrows. Except: No offset statement confirming the trust deed is required of the property owner, since you are dealing with him directly. No decisions are required regarding the type of endorsement, since no transfer of the note's ownership is involved. Nor is assignment of the beneficial interest in the deed of trust necessary. In exchange for elimination of these complications, loan escrows take on a few steps of their own — mostly born of the opportunity to make your investment safer.

THE INTEREST ACCRUAL DATE

Escrow instructions for any new loan you enter into should call for the start of interest before the close of escrow — commencing with the date you *anticipate* funding (setting aside) the money for the loan. Many loan escrows are worded so that interest accrues only when the loan money is paid to escrow, rather than when you set it aside in your own books for payment; it is hoped your greed for additional interest will thereby compel you to prematurely deposit the balance due, and thus lock you more securely to the deal. But the accumulation of interest from the date of your funding, coupled with your refusal to deposit the loan money until the end of the escrow, has a magical effect on everybody connected with the transaction. The "carrot and stick" incentive spurs everybody to be far more willing to promptly comply with your escrow requirements.

A CURE FOR CANCELLATIONS

One of the most aggravating things that can occur in an escrow is to have a borrower cancel out after the property has been appraised, negotiations are completed, credit reports obtained, and escrow papers drawn.

To diminish the chances of this occurrence, you can include instructions that the *borrower* deposit money to the escrow as part of its opening. This is the same opening deposit strategy employed against TD investors as described in the Escrow chapter, and it glues the deal together just as effectively. The trick will not work every time, since it may only be partially enforceable should the loan fall under the Truth-in-Lending laws (discussed later).

CHOOSING THE BEST TITLE INSURANCE

Escrows for new loans require the issuance of new title insurance assuring you of your security claim on the borrower's property. Two types of insurance are available. The most common, and the one which a non-institutional lender will be offered, is the CLTA form. This is the same type of title insurance issued to the borrower on his purchase of the property. The other form is called ALTA, sometimes referred to as "lender's insurance."

ALTA insurance provides additional protection from such off record risks as encroachments, mechanics liens, and prescriptive easement rights — in addition to the risks covered by CLTA insurance. Naturally, ALTA insurance is more expensive, but you should ask for it whenever possible.

Title companies resist issuing ALTA insurance to noninstitutional lenders because such lenders do not uniformly request it. The title companies' experience tells them that private lenders only call for such coverage in high risk situations, while institutional lenders require it as a matter of practice.

Some lenders try to entice borrowers by offering to settle for only a preliminary or other summary form title report, explaining that it is faster and less expensive than the full title policy. But they fail to explain that when title insurance is requested, a complete policy is never issued until after the escrow closes in any event. Furthermore, a preliminary report is always collected during escrow — whichever approach is used. Full title insurance doesn't slow the escrow one bit and often costs not much more than a preliminary report.

RENTERS' OFFSET STATEMENT REQUIREMENT

When making a new loan you should consider requiring a renters' offset statement if the security is to be income property. Like the owner's offset statement described in Part I, the renters' statement attempts to confirm the accuracy of the information you've received — in this case, the condition of any agreements between the property owner and his tenants. Purchasers of existing TDs have little opportunity to require this statement because they are dealing only with the existing TD lender; neither the property owner nor his tenant has an incentive to cooperate in completing the form.

The chief purpose of a renter offset statement is to flush out any hidden agreements between the owner and tenants, especially any deals the owner may have made with the tenants to reduce their rent in exchange for its prepayment. Lenders who are careless with this procedure run the risk of a swindle by borrowers who milk the property through rent collections six months or more ahead of its due date, and then go into foreclosure immediately after the loan is made.

The escrow officer probably will not have a renter's offset statement form on hand and you will have to provide it. A simple expression in the tenor and format of the owner's offset statement described in Part I is adequate. Some escrows have copies of forms used in similar transactions. If so, and if the escrow officer is the cooperative type, you may be permitted to adapt the previously used form for your own purposes.

TRUTH-IN-LENDING IRRITATIONS

If you regularly make new loans secured by real estate and your borrower is an individual who expects to use the loan proceeds for non-commercial purposes, the transaction will probably fall under the requirements of Regulation Z — the Truth-in-Lending law. Appropriate provisions in the escrow instructions will then be required. Namely, that you will submit papers to the borrower disclosing information about the loan in a manner prescribed by the law. And that the borrower will provide signed acknowledgements of receipt of the papers.

Loans for business, commercial, or agricultural purposes are exempt from coverage under the Truth-in-Lending Act. But the exemption's definition contains grey areas which can lead to violation of the law. A loan for purposes of investment in a partnership organized for personal or family purposes may, for example, be nonbusiness and subject to the Act. To avoid risk of violation in such instances, compliance with the disclosure requirements of the law is the safest approach. Furthermore, even if the commercial nature of the loan is clear, you'd be smart to protect yourself and enter escrow instructions requiring the borrower to sign a statement specifying the exact business use anticipated.

Under Regulation Z, the borrower also has a right to rescind the loan if it is to be secured by his personal residence. If the borrower does rescind, all his payments made to the escrow or lender are returned intact, less certain costs such as for credit report and document preparation. The money must be returned within 10 days. The borrower can waive his right of rescission in certain emergency situations if he signs a statement describing the emergency.

Unless you expect to do a large volume of loans subject to Truth-in-Lending, you're better off turning over the details of compliance to someone else. If a loan broker is handling the transaction, he should provide the disclosure for you; it's part of his job. Some escrows also offer the service. Absent such assistance, your escrow officer will probably be able to recommend a "loan processor" who will do the work at relatively little cost.

If you wish to delve further into Truth-in-Lending — perhaps to check on your loan processor's work — the basic of the law can be found in a publication entitled "Truth-in-Lending." You can get a copy by writing the Federal Trade Commission at Box 36005, San Francisco, CA 94102. It's free. Another source of information is the California Department of Real Estate's "Reference Book" (see the appendix on Information Sources), which has several pages on the subject.

Supplemental Checks

Filtering Questions

NEW LOAN

property value, source of evaluation, 30-31, 66-67
loan ratio, 28-29, 55-58
terms wanted, 29-30
credit check required, 34
too eager, 34
property location, 32, 38, 39
source of loan payment, 34-35
existing encumbrances:
>who, 34
>amount
windshield appraisal, 17
security complications, 31-32
broker's authority, 21, 35
military, 33
farmer. *See* Foreclosure; Bankruptcy
hotels, 31
co-ops, 31-32

EXISTING TD

See also New Loans, all items
property sale price vs TD amount, 35
current balance
payments current
price wanted, 29-30
payment terms
payment history
manufactured TD, 201
variable interest rate, 33
subordination clause, 33

Supplemental Checks

Investigation — New Loan

See also **ALL PREVIOUS CHECK LIST ITEMS**

COPIES, FRONT AND BACK

property owner's title policy
senior deed of trust, plus addenda
senior note
power of attorney

DOCUMENT REVIEW, ALL DOCUMENTS

See also Escrow — Danger Points
compare signatures, 62
name spellings, 62
power of attorney authority, 64
power of attorney expiration, 64
encumbrances in title policy, 61, 74
all legal descriptions, 61, 67, 152-153
security priorities, 242
senior encumbrances. *See* Senior TD Review

SENIOR TD REVIEW

See also Existing TD — Document Review check list:
prepayment privilege
loan balances
See also Escrow — New Loan Instructions check list:
prepayment penalty
due on sale
future advances
dragnet
abnormal payment terms, 60
past payment pattern, 60
acreage release clause, 59-60, 172-174
blanket encumbrance, 59, 59-60, 88-89, 184

ABOUT THE BORROWER

See also Bankruptcy Prospects; Credit Report
guarantors, 54, 164-166
additional security, 162-163
homestead. *See* Escrow — Danger Points

Investigation — New Loan *(continued)*

Investigation — Existing TD

See also NEW LOAN INVESTIGATION, all items

BROKER COMPETITION, 44-45
BID QUESTIONS, 25, 44
USURIOUS, 195, 200-202
TD SELLER'S COPIES, FRONT AND BACK

> prior assignments
> deed of trust
> deed of trust addenda
> note
> note endorsements
> borrower credit application
> borrower credit report
> title policy

DOCUMENT REVIEW

> *See also* New Loan — Document Review, all items
> *See also* Escrow — New Loan clauses:
> > prepayment penalty
> > due on sale
> > future advances
> > dragnet
> prior assignments, 63
> title policy, 61, 63
> inconsistencies of any kind, 62-63
> comparison all legal descriptions, 66
> recorder mailing address, 235
> property address deed of trust
> loan balance vs payment terms, 60, 63
> amount of title insurance, 74
> note endorsements, 63-64, 102, 254-255
> prepayment privilege, 60, 168
> subordination clause, 180-182
> power of sale clause, 163-164

Supplemental Checks

Appraisal

COPIES OF
> location maps
> prior appraisals
> surveyor's (metes and bounds) **drawing**
> *See also* Title Company Assistance

ASSESSOR'S MAP, 57, 235-236

SUBDIVISION MAP, 152-153

PRIOR APPRAISALS, 76-77, 77-78

TITLE COMPANY ASSISTANCE, 230

LOCAL BROKER VALUATIONS, 67, 68

EASEMENTS, 154-157, 235, 240

ZONING, 78-79, 236

SET BACK LIMITATIONS, 78-79, 157

HOMESTEAD. *See* Escrow — Danger Points

LEGAL ACCESS. *See* Easements

VISUAL INSPECTION
> farm land. *See* Agricultural
> industrial building. *See* Industrial
> neighborhood, 39, 71
> property lines, 69-70, 153, 157
> natural water course, 67, 70
> buildable terrain, 67, 70
> usable access, 71
> prescriptive easement, 71, 155
> encroachments, 71, 157-158
> square footage, 72
> waste, 125, 224, 242-243
> weeds and brush, 71
> landscaping, 71
> quality of construction, 71, 79
> mechanics liens, 72, 158-160
> utility meters, 71
> rental verification, 72
> photographs, 69

Supplemental Checks

Appraisals *(continued)*

Supplemental Checks

CHECK LIST

Escrow

BROKER ESCROW DECISION, 84
ESCROW OFFICER DECISION, 84-86, 259
DECISION DELIVERY OFFSET STATEMENT, 87-88
TIME LIMIT ON ESCROW SIGNUP, 86-87
SMALL OPENING DEPOSIT, 83-84
EXISTING TD INSTRUCTIONS

NEW LOAN INSTRUCTIONS

Escrow *(continued)*

Supplemental Checks

Supplemental Checks

Foreclosure *(continued)*

INDEX

INDEX

INDEX

SUPPLEMENT TO
SMART TRUST DEED INVESTMENT

in California

January, 1991

by

George Coats

Barr-Randol Publishing Company

Box 4486 • **Covina, CA 91723**

SUPPLEMENT

TRUST DEED PROFITS

TDs have suddenly become more profitable in the past few years. With the demise of so many S & L's, and tighter lending requirements of others, real estate borrowers are turning more and more to non institutional lenders for money. Private TD rates of return have risen accordingly.

The relatively unregulated market place of private TD investment has become very popular. Rock solid, risk free, TDs — especially those secured by commercial or industrial properties — now often go to private investors in spite of the higher cost of doing so. The number of loan brokers to serve the demand has more than tripled, and the volume of private lending in California has risen to well over 6 Billion dollars a year.

The more lively market has also resulted in a remarkable safety increase on formerly marginal loans. Investors who lend to borrowers with flawed credit but ample security rarely experience a loan which reaches a foreclosure sale. Recording a notice of default invariably triggers multiple refinancing offers to solve the debtor's problems. The defaulted loan is paid off within months, with an accompanying prepayment penalty and rates of return ranging up to 30%.

Affects page 2.

INVESTING THROUGH A LOAN BROKER

LENDER/PURCHASER DISCLOSURE STATEMENT

State law requires that you be provided a "Lender/Purchaser Disclosure Statement," if a real estate broker arranges your investment. (The "purchaser," in this case, refers to purchaser of a TD.) The statement is exact as to its form and is dictated by the State. It provides all the information about the investment, not just that which suits the purposes of the borrower or his broker. Most important, it includes a written estimate of the value of the security (The better brokers will back the estimate up with an outside appraisal).

The document deserves close examination for it contains much valuable information. It often provides answers to questions you forgot to ask. You'll also learn things you didn't know were important.

Valuable though the disclosure may be, it has its negative aspects. Some parts of the form are obscure and not easily understood. Because of its daunting appearance, the very person the form intends to protect, the amateur investor, will give it little attention. Difficulty in filling out the form also virtually eliminates an exceptionally valuable source of TD investment, the broker who only occasionally arranges a loan as opportunity presents itself. And in final analysis, the form does little to ensure the accuracy of the information; putting it in writing won't deter the broker (or property owner) bound to commit fraud.

Affects pages 15 - 17.

TD INVESTIGATION

TRUTH-IN-LENDING DISCLOSURE

Compliance with Federal Truth-In-Lending disclosure (p.259) has become so complicated it is almost impossible to avoid an error. Worse, recent court decisions now also permit rescission of some loans for even the most trivial errors in the disclosure.

Borrowers on owner occupied residential properties have a right of a rescission which can last up to three years from consummation (creation) of the loan. It grants the borrower return of all the interest and loan fees, as well as attorney fees paid in extracting the rescission from the lender. In order to rescind, the borrower must pay the balance of the loan, however.

Lenders aware of the risk generally try to ignore it. Despairing of being able to do anything about the problem, they hope it will go away. And most of the time it does go away because of borrower's general ignorance of the rescission right. Also, the requirement that the borrower be prepared to pay the balance of the loan tends to reduce the risk. Attorneys who specialize in representing borrowers have lately discovered the joys of this area of the law, however. They are increasingly using it to stop foreclosure, or at least deflect it for a while.

Only loans made to a real person (not a partnership, etc.), the proceeds of which is for personal (nonbusiness) use are subject to the disclosure requirement. Loans of four or fewer installments are excluded. Lenders who have made no more than 5 residential loans or 25 total loan's subject to the law in the previous or current calendar year, are exempt.

Only loans secured by owner occupied residential are affected by the right to rescind. Other recipients of the disclosure are subject "only" to penalty.

If you invest through a mortgage loan broker, he should automatically provide you with evidence of satisfaction of (or exemption from) the disclosure requirement. The ethics of the profession (but not the law) require it. Many don't do so, leaving it up to the lender to provide the disclosure if needed.

Purchase of an existing TD will not exempt you from a borrower's rescission defense. If you buy an owner occupied residential TD, your best protection is a copy of a borrower-signed statement as to the loan proceeds' personal use. The original lender's statement as to the 5 or less exemption, above, is common alternative, but relatively useless because it is so easily challenged.

Computer software programs designed to fulfill the disclosure requirements are now available, but they are impractical unless you invest in a very large volume of TDs. Very few escrows are capable of the task. You can fill the disclosure yourself (see Sources of Information, this supplement), but unless you're experienced in doing so, the TD probably won't be worth the effort

Affects pages 259 and 263.

HAZARDOUS WASTE

The newest risk to stalk real estate investors is liability for "hazardous waste" on their properties. Because of liability for its cleanup, as well as harm to people who come into contact with it, the subject has caused near hysteria among many in the business.

No property with human activity is safe from potential hazardous waste. Houses (insulation) and farm land (chemicals) can be tainted. Even neighboring properties can cause a hazard as a result of migration of waste.

Real estate lenders are supposed to be exempt from liability for hazardous waste, but as usual there are all sorts of exceptions to the exception. If the lender exercises some measure of "control" over management of the property, however remote, it's possible he too may be liable. If the lender forecloses on the property, he may be assuming responsibility for the waste. Even lenders with no liability can suffer its effects by being joined in whatever litigation intended to sort out who is responsible.

There is probably no way you can completely eliminate this risk to your investment. You can, however, do much to reduce it. Most important, is inspection of the security for possible hazardous waste. If the loan is large enough, you may find it profitable to hire an expert who specializes in this type of investigation. And it is possible to shelter yourself to some extent by requiring an indemnity agreement, separate from the TD, which compels the property owner, guarantor, or whoever, to protect you. A whole separate subclass of lawyers specializing in this area of the law has sprung into being, bearing such advice — assuming you're able to afford the cost.

Affects pages 65 - 74, and 80.

ESCROW

HOMESTEAD WARNINGS

A homestead filed ahead of a deed of trust isn't senior to the TD's security, as previously reported. Because a TD is voluntarily signed by the owners of the property, it is free of a homestead claim.

Exemption aside, many lenders continue to regard homesteads as basis for rejection of the loan. At the very least it should be considered a red flag calling for closer examination of the character of the borrower.

Homestead exemptions still apply to involuntary (judgement lien) claims against the property. Also, the amount of the exemption increases, as of January 1, 1991, up to $100,000 in some circumstances.

Affects page 89.

THE INTEREST ACCRUAL DATE

Interest accrual before the close of escrow is now prohibited in certain new loans — unless the borrower is paid in the form of cash, or by check or other form of draft which can be cashed in California at a federally insured bank.

This seemingly pointless exercise of legislative control actually has a purpose. In the past, some lenders have paid their borrowers with loan funds drawn on a distant bank located out of state or even in a foreign country such as Hong Kong. Delay in transfer of the funds a month or more was possible by selection of the right bank, giving the lender continued use of the money while accruing interest on the loan.

Few private TD investors are likely to encounter a loan which is subject to this statute. The only reason for its mention here is to clarify its limits. The described interest accrual restriction is exactly the sort of thing seized upon by half-informed individuals who'll try to convince you of the statute's application to all loans.

Affects page 257.

INSURANCE REQUIREMENTS

California law now forbids requirement of insurance exceeding the replacement "value" of the property's structures.

Literal interpretation of the law can be misleading. Replacement, for this purpose, means constructing a new building under an always more expensive current building code. Dependent on the age of the property's structures, replacement cost will generally exceed appraised value by a substantial margin.

Nevertheless, 2nd trust deed investors may run into a surprise, here. If the replacement cost of building improvements relative to the land is disproportionately small, a junior lienholder will not be able to demand insurance protection sufficient to cover his loan. He must consider the investment an unimproved property loan because he won't be able to exact recovery from insurance proceeds in event of a fire.

Affects pages 55 - 56, 96 - 97, and 255.

OWNER'S OFFSET STATEMENTS

Reader feedback indicates pages 252-253 have been taken to mean that owner's offset statements are a mandatory requirement in the purchase of an existing TD. This is an error. Requirement of an offset statement should instead be based on the circumstances surrounding the deal.

The owner's offset statement is a valuable — sometimes essential — tool in verifying the current condition of a TD as well as for affirmation of the obligation. But insistence on the statement in every TD purchase can put you out of business. The property owner has no obligation to sign the statement and therefore may simply refuse to do so (pages 87-88). Also, presentation of the statement for the owner's signature may trigger payoff of the loan before you manage to purchase it.

An offset statement presented for signature often is the first the property owner learns that the TD has been put up for sale (page 61). Because the owner may feel vulnerable when obligated to a new lender of unknown character, he may come in and pay off the loan and put an end to the transaction. Or the owner may be struck with the thought that he too might bid for the TD. And if he offers as little as a couple hundred dollars over your price, the TD seller may decide to dump you, regardless of your prior agreement.

If you sense when the foregoing is a possibility (and you generally can), you should consider corollary evidence in lieu of the offset statement. Loans collected by an independent agency, such as a bank, often may be confirmed by requesting the agent's statement showing the current condition of the account. Comparison between the claimed loan balance and the balance amortized according to the terms of the note (page 63) may also provide supporting evidence. And file correspondence plus escrow and other documents connected with the owner's purchase of the property, often can be substituted for owner affirmation of the obligation. Whether and to what extent you are able to accept such alternative evidence depends much on the nature of the people you are dealing with.

TD ADMINISTRATION

MILITARY PERSONEL

Borrowers who qualify under the Soldiers' and Sailors' Civil Relief Act (pages 125 - 126) can be charged no more than 6% per annum after entering active service. Loans bearing a higher interest rate must automatically be reduced to 6%, without application by the borrower. The lowered rate of interest continues only during the borrower's period of active duty.

An exception to the rule is made in cases where the borrower would not be inconvenienced financially by his entry in active service. To qualify for the exception, however, the lender must receive judicial consent.

If the lender is unaware of the borrower's exemption, or otherwise fails to reduce the interest rate, the borrower may sue for refund of the overcharge.

Benefits of the Act are extended only to servicemen who incurred their obligation before they entered the military.

Affects pages 125 - 126.

TRANSFER OF COLLECTION

Upon transfer of collection of a 1 - 4 residential trust deed, the borrower must be notified of the event by both the former and new loan servicers. If the loan is in foreclosure, the trustee handling the affair must also be notified. Absent proper notice, a borrower's continued payments to the TD's previous owner are valid against the obligation. If you buy an existing TD, you must be sure its seller concurrently notifies the borrower else you may have a difficult time trying to collect its payments.

Affects pages 90, 93 - 95, and 251.

LATE CHARGES

With the exception of financial institutions regulated by other means, and certain loans negotiated by loan brokers, all single family, owner occupied, loans must allow a 10 day grace period before late charge. Other loans may still include a late charge as short as one day after delinquency.

Loans negotiated by loan brokers are now restricted to a late charge fee not more than 10% of the delinquent installment, $5 minimum. Late charges on such loans are now also allowed on past due balloon payments, on a formula basis.

Affects pages 97 and 166.

ANNUAL INTEREST REPORT

If you're in a "trade or business" and collect $600 or more interest from an individual during a calendar year, and your collection is incident to the business, the IRS requires your report of the collected amount. The report must be on their form 1098, by February 28 of the next year. A copy must also be given the borrower by January 31. You can get copies of the form direct from the IRS by calling 1-800-424-FORM, or from one of their local offices. Most CPA offices will also provide copies, if asked.

The form requires the borrower's social security number. If the borrower refuses to provide the number, you must make the report anyway with comment as to the borrower's refusal.

Few private TD investors fall under this requirement of the law. If you're very active in the business, however, you'll need to pay attention to it. Failure to comply carries a fine of $50 per incident, $100 if you willfully refuse...

Affects page 98.

BENEFICIARY STATEMENTS

The penalty for failure to deliver a beneficiary statement now can be collected only if proven intentional by the lender, thus stripping the effectiveness of this section of the code.

Lenders may now claim a fee of up to $60 for a beneficiary statement or demand. Permission is no longer required in the TD for doing so. Nothing in the code requires that payment of the fee precede issuance of a statement or demand.

If you understate the amount due in a beneficiary statement or demand, and a sale escrow of the security closes based on the amount, you won't be able to collect the shortage from the new owner of the property. You'll have to try to collect the remainder from the former borrower as an unsecured loan. If the loan is purchase-money (pages 239 and 240), you won't be able to collect even that much, due your limitation to the security as a source of enforcement.

Affects pages 98,99.and 108

RECONVEYANCE

Substantial changes, long past due, have occurred in the rules governing reconveyance. Careless disregard of the borrower by some lenders, once the debt is paid, has caused terrible problems in the past.

Although the new rules look good and sound good, attempts at enforcement will be impractical in unexpected ways. The following should therefore be regarded only as an outline. To really know the process, you'll have to consult a trustee or an attorney with a detailed knowledge of the subject.

Upon receipt of final payment, the beneficiary has 30 days to deliver a request for reconveyance (p.104) to the trustee. Before doing so, however, the borrower's payment of the trustee's fee (page 105) and related expenses may be required. Delivery to the trustee of the request for reconveyance must be accompanied by the original documents (page 248) evidencing the debt.

The trustee then has 21 days to record the reconveyance. A copy of the reconveyance is sent to the beneficiary. The trustee must not record the reconveyance, however, if the beneficiary receives written request from the trustor that the document be delivered elsewhere (such as to an escrow). The trustee retains the original note unless the trustor requests otherwise (in writing).

If after 60 days from final payment of the loan the trustee has not performed as instructed, the beneficiary must execute a subreconveyance (see page 106) on written request from the trustor.

Violation of the above entitles the trustor to a $300 statutory penalty, plus actual damages and attorney's fees. If the violation is willful, it may be a misdemeanor punishable by a $50 to $400 fine, and/or imprisonment.

If reconveyance hasn't been accomplished 75 days after payoff of the loan, the trustor may request that a title company issue and record an equivalent document called "release of the obligation." Ten days advance notice of the action is required, in writing, to the trustee, trustor, and beneficiary of record. Improbable though it may seem, the title company must assume liability for its actions in this case, an event so remote as to make this provision useless.

Affects pages 8, 103-106, 108, 172-174.

FORECLOSURE

WHEN TO START

The subject of whether the borrower should be obligated to pay when due is receiving much attention these days. Previous cautionary recommendations regarding the start of foreclosure (page 101) should be regarded obligatory, and some embellishments have been added.

Late charge provisions now are treated as an automatic grant of an equal grace period for payment due dates.grace period for payment due dates.

Unless you're trying to squeeze in ahead of bankruptcy (page 118), or have some other objective (page 112), immediate foreclosure continues not to be very smart. The previously recommended 10 day wait before declaration of default is wiser.

If you anticipate a contested foreclosure (page 113), a 30 day wait may be in order.

In due course, more firm guidelines must, of necessity, be provided. Until then, check your timing with a reliable (and realistic — some trustees are so cautious they will see a lawsuit in anything you do) trustee or attorney when planning a foreclosure.

Affects pages 101, 112, 118, 119, and 166.

NOTICE OF DEFAULT

Notices of default must now be exact in the description of the breach on which the foreclosure is based. The shotgun approach described in page 119, is no longer enforceable.

As of January 1, 1991, all notices of default must follow a form dictated by CC 2924c The form calls for an express statement of the amounts due as of a given date. It warns that defaults in any other loan covenants will also be added to the amount due. And it informs the trustor that at any time on written request he is entitled to an itemization of the amounts necessary to cure the defaults.

By the time of this reading, every trustee should have thousands of the form on hand.

Affects pages 119 - 120.

FORECLOSURE NOTIFICATION REQUIREMENTS

Important correction: Copies of the notice of default must be mailed to the designated parties within one month of the recording, not 30 days as previously stated (affects pages 121 and 256).

A number of additions have been made to foreclosure notice requirements. If a "postponed property tax lien" has been filed against the security (affects pages 121 and 244), a copy of the NOD must be sent to the state Controller, in addition to a notice of sale. Also, State taxing agencies which file a lien against the security, before your NOD is recorded, are entitled to a copy of both the NOD and notice of sale (affects page 129). And all trustor notices must be sent by ordinary first class mail as well as by the previously required registered/certified mail (affects pages 121-122, 129).

You won't be able to get a "10 day letter" report, separate from the TSG, these days. Most title companies now insist on purchase of the full TSG before issuing a letter report. There never was a fee structure for a separate report. Desire to cooperate (compassion for the borrower?) was the only incentive for providing a separate 10 day letter (affects page 123).

FORECLOSURE REINSTATEMENT PERIOD

The reinstatement period (see page 114) for monetary default foreclosures has been changed. The right to reinstate formerly expired three months after the NOD was recorded. The reinstatement period now extends past the first three months following NOD, right up "until five business days prior to the date of sale."

The reinstatement period can also be revived if the foreclosure sale is postponed. If, at the time of a scheduled sale, postponement is declared to a date more than five business days later, a new – window period – right of reinstatement may be created. Postponement, for example, made in compliance with the newly required seven day wait after relief of stay (see Postponements, this supplement) may cause a short term revival of the right to reinstate.

Nothing else in the foreclosure time table has been changed. A wait of three months is still required before publication of the notice of sale can begin, and publication once-in-each-of-three-successive-weeks must occur before the sale is held. The reinstatement period has simply been expanded and the redemption period shortened accordingly.

Saturday is included when counting the required number of business days to expiration of the reinstatement period. Therefore, a sale scheduled on Monday – count five business days back – would result in a fifth business day falling on the previous Tuesday, and the last chance for reinstatement occurs the day before, on Monday.

The new reinstatement period rules don't include nonmonetary default rules. Foreclosures based purely on waste or on failure to provide insurance, for instance, are still subject to the old three-months-after-recording reinstatement period. But defaults recorded exclusively for nonmonetary issues are rare (page 119). Mixed monetary and nonmonetary defaults are more likely, and their divergent applications are certain to require future sorting out.

Affects pages 114, 123, and 204-205.

TENANT SECURITY DEPOSITS

If you're the successful bidder on a rental property foreclosure, you become jointly responsible for tenant security deposits with the property's previous owner. If you include the deposits in your bid price at the foreclosure sale, you're entitled to demand their reimbursement from the former owner (under assignment of rents clause, page 176). As a practical matter, you'll find any collection of the amount difficult, however. You won't know the amount of the deposits to add to the bid price until after the foreclosure, when you're able to talk to the tenants. Some of the tenants are certain to inflate the amount of their claimed deposit. And almost all will deny responsibility for repairs, etc., normally deducted from the deposit.

RENT CONTROL FORECLOSURES

Eviction of a tenant occupying a foreclosed rent controlled property is prohibited unless allowed by local ordinance — thus giving tenants rights which are senior to those of the property's lenders.

Affects page 140.

FORECLOSURE SALE POSTPONEMENTS

Foreclosure sales no longer may be rescheduled to the day after a relief of stay as suggested on page 247. In order to give borrowers' attorneys time for more mischief, no sale may be conducted sooner than seven calendar days after a relief of stay brought about by legal action such as a TRO or bankruptcy. A relief of stay received on Monday, for example, now requires a minimum wait – count seven days commencing Tuesday – until after the following Monday before the foreclosure sale may be held.

Exception to the seven day delay is allowed if the court waives it. A borrower who repeatedly files bankruptcy as a device to avoid paying his debts would be a likely cause of the waiver.

Affects pages 204-205, 247-248.

POST FORECLOSURE BANKRUPTCY

A major struggle is occurring over the question of whether a borrower who files bankruptcy gains the right to redeem an earlier foreclosed security. Taken in its most extreme form, the bankruptcy code has been interpreted to give the borrower a right of redemption extending as much as three years past a previous foreclosure sale – effectively destroying the foreclosed property's marketability during the interim. Other interpretations, on the other hand, have completely eliminated such bankruptcy right of redemption.

Currently, the right of redemption survives, but only against a beneficiary who ends up the successful bidder at a foreclosure sale. If an outside bidder gets the property, or if the successful beneficiary later borrows against or sells the property, the right of redemption is supposed to expire.

Some title companies continue to reflect the possibility of bankruptcy right of redemption as an exception in title insurance policies issued beneficiaries who end up with the property. Most consider the subject a dead issue, however, and don't bother with the exception.

Current opinion aside, consult an experienced title officer or bankruptcy attorney for the latest on the subject. Bankruptcy law wanders all over and can sometimes intrude in wondrous ways.

Affects pages 205 and 208.

OTHER APPROACHES

1911 ACT BONDS

1911 Act bonds are no longer generally available. A few of the bonds can still be found, but current subdivision practice utilizes other methods of financing off-site improvements. In due course the law is sure to be rediscovered, however, and this remarkable form of investment will once again become available.

Affects pages 142 and 143.

CLAUSES

FIRE INSURANCE

A borrower has the right to demand fire insurance proceeds be applied to reconstruction of the security. But if the borrower does so, the lender has the right to retain the money and control its disbursement as the work progresses. Also, if the borrower was in default on the loan at the time of the fire, the lender has the right to keep the insurance, whatever the borrower's intentions.

You'd be wise to consult a knowledgeable attorney in such situations. You may have more rights than might be apparent.

Affects page 175.

NOTE BALLOON NOTICE

Having exhausted the varieties of borrower notification, an inspired state legislature labored mightily and came up with the notice-of-a-notice. All purchase-money notes, secured by 1 - 4 residential (whether or not owner occupied) now must contain a notice of the right to receive notice (pages 99 and 100) of any balloon payment. Borrowers who are not purchase-money are considered bright enough to not need double warning of their balloon payment obligations. To ensure the uselessness of the law, provision was made that failure to include the notice would not affect collection of the note.

The form of notice is relatively simple. Any escrow agent claiming knowledge of the job will automatically include the wording in all balloon payment notes — whether or not required by the law.

Add to page 161 of the Clauses Appendix.

USURY

The Federal Reserve Bank of San Francisco's telephone numbers have been changed. To find the federal discount rate used in calculation of usury limits, you must now call 415/974-2230 or 213/683-2511/2512.

Affects page 196.

PURCHASE-MONEY EXEMPTION

Even though a TD between a buyer and seller of a piece of property is sold to another person at the instant of its creation, it still is "purchase-money." Because it is purchase-money, it is exempt from usury (pages 9 - 10). Lenders not otherwise exempt from usury have long used the device to invest their money at rates otherwise considered usurious.

When investing in a TD by this method, you must be especially careful that your participation not be "prearranged." Some investors go too far, even to the point of dictating the terms of the TD to be purchased. In doing so, they run the risk of usury. The substance of your participation must be as an investor entering into purchase of a TD created independent of your presence.

Affects pages 198 and 199.

INFORMATION SOURCES

A whole new array of sources of information helpful to trust deed investors has sprung up in recent years.

NEWSLETTERS

Bob Bruss, the real estate columnist, publishes *California Real Estate Law,* a newsletter aimed at real estate brokers. Most of the newsletter also applies to TD investors. If you want to keep up on the latest do's and don'ts affecting your investment, Bruss' newsletter is the way to go. Bruss manages to get so excited about changes in the law, and reports them in such a "can't wait to tell you" fashion that even routine events sound fascinating. Costs $48 Write 251 Park Rd., Burlingame, CA 94010.

The Paper Source (800-542-2270) is a great newsletter, national in scope, written especially for TD investors. It has a "Marketplace" section offering TDs for sale as well as news and articles. Many of the articles are contributed by subscribers of enormous experience, providing fascinating insights to the business. Regardless of the state of origin, 90% of the articles in the newsletter are useful to Californians. This publication essential reading if you plan to stay in TD investment very long.

The Real Estate Investor's Monthly is a newsletter written by Jack Reed (415-820-6292). Reed describes various techniques for making money in real estate, including TD investment. In doing so, he ranges all over, drawing on a tremendous array of contacts. His style of writing is also probably the most blunt and direct reporting you'll ever encounter. No persiflage, here. If you want a glimpse at the bare bones of the world of real estate, stripped of all fabrication, this is it.

The Distress Sales Report (405-523-6115) specializes in various forms of forced sales, and how to make money from them. Most of the newsletter relates to TD foreclosure, the rest being directed at other matters such as probate and tax sales. John Beck, its author, is an attorney with lots of experience on the subject of foreclosure. Occasionally he includes a detailed analysis of some specific part of the process, such as the twists and turns in foreclosure brought about by a due-on-sale clause. No other publication comes even close to this kind of reporting on the real world of foreclosure.

BOOKS

Invest in Debt, written by Jimmy Napier, is a small book on trust deed investment which can be purchased by special order from its author (800-544-4488). The book elaborates in great detail on the subjects of yield calculation (pages 185 - 193) and ways to boost TD yield (pages 144 - 147). *Smart Trust Deed Investment in California* also covers these subjects but in much more spare language. Napier's book should satisfy your needs if you want more detail on these very important areas of TD investment.

Leigh Robinson publishes a book, *All About Escrow,* of direct use to TD investors, especially beginners in the business. Leigh also publishes two other books, *Landlording* and *The Eviction Book for California,* related to the management of rental properties. Although not directly connected to TD investment, the latter two are written with such grace and charm that they make interesting reading even if you don't own rentals. All three books are generally available in bookstores. They can also be purchased at Express, Box 1639, El Cerrito, CA 94530-4639.

California Real Property Financing is a two-volume set of law books published by CEB (pages 233 - 234) which are valuable as a reference. If you ever get into a fracas, or want to second guess your attorney, you'll want these books in your library.

The CEB (415-642-6810) now has direct sales outlets for their books in Berkeley, Westwood, and downtown Los Angeles.

Affects pages 230 - 234.

CALCULATORS

Texas Instruments' *Financial Investment Analyst* and Hewlitt Packard's *Business Analyst* HP-19B are the newest and best for yield calculations. They both are much simpler to operate than their earlier counterparts and practically eliminate the need for yield tables.

Affects pages 236 and 187 - 188.

APPRAISAL

Record Data Inc. (800-321-1890) will assist in the appraisal of properties located anywhere in the U.S. No longer need you be concerned about property valuations biased by the interests of other parties (page 32). They will review any appraisal for its accuracy, or provide you with their own appraisal, complete with color photos, maps, and a list of comparable sales. They can make feasible investment in a TD outside your area — if the TD is profitable enough to warrant the cost of their services.

The organization also supplies title searches and title insurance. If later you find yourself in trouble, they'll also refer you to an attorney presumed capable of handling your case.

Affects pages 32, 65 et. seq., and 231 - 232.

ATTORNEY

Tele-Lawyer is an attorney service which provides legal advice over the telephone at the rate of $3 per minute. Payment may be made by credit card, in which case you must call 800-442-5529 for the service. If you call them at 900-446-4529, you can have their charge tacked on your telephone bill.

The service's charge is based on actual discussion time. Your call is supposed to be directed to an attorney experienced on the particular area of law questioned. If he doesn't have the answer, he'll research the matter at no charge and call you back.

The service's attorneys will not appear in court on your behalf, nor do they recommend you to other attorneys for that purpose (though they will counsel you on how to go about finding a good attorney).They do not involve themselves with litigation — which is important because it tends to ensure honest advice, untainted by the prospect of higher fees generated by getting you into court.

Affects page 227.

TRUTH-IN-LENDING ASSISTANCE

See also "Investigation," earlier in this supplement.

If you're of a mind to prepare your own Truth-In-Lending (aka Regulation Z) disclosure, forms may be purchased from 1st Tuesday (800-235-5522). If you know a cooperative real estate licensee, you may also be able to get the form via the California Association of Realtors.

The Truth-In-Lending form calculations are the most difficult part of the disclosure. Delphi Information Sciences (213-452-7575) provides the calculation over the phone and then sends a backup calculator tape of the figures. The cost is $18. If you do a large enough volume of business, TRW Loan Services (714-998-5500) will also provide the service, including completion of the form.

SECURITY LIMITS

PURCHASE-MONEY LIMITATIONS

The limits on borrower liability in "third party" purchase-money trust deeds, described on page 240, should have received greater explanation. The exemption has far more significance than implied by a brief, single paragraph, buried in the appendix section.

Purchase-money mortgages are commonly divided into two classifications: "Vendor" purchase-money (financing carried back by the seller of the property), and "third party" purchase-money (purchase financing provided by others, such as a savings and loan).

In California and many other states, vendor purchase–money TD collections can be enforced only against the security; the borrower has no further obligation in the loan. Unlike most other states, California also extends the exemption (CCP 580b) to certain third party purchase-money TDs: Those secured by dwellings built to house "not more than four families," occupied in whole or part by owners of the property.

Perhaps 80% of the real estate loans in California fall in the latter category.

By limiting borrower liability to only the security in such mortgages, California law (subject to exceptions below) in effect amends the payment terms of the bulk of real property loans within the state. Lenders in California, instead of requiring payment according to the terms of the note, must accept alternative forfeiture of the security as a form of satisfaction of the debt—even if the security is worth less than the amount of the loan.

The above purchase-money lenders must therefore accommodate themselves to the fact that, as a practical result, the borrower who wishes to do so should be allowed to escape his debt and walk away free simply by surrendering the security (see Deed In Lieu of Foreclosure, pages 117, 242-243). The only other alternative is foreclosure at significant cost in both time and money (pages 55-56) while giving the borrower continued free use of the property.

All real estate lenders, purchase-money or otherwise, are to a degree limited to the same choice described above (One Action Rule, page 239). But those not subject to purchase-money restrictions at least can threaten attachment of the borrower's other assets (Judicial Foreclosure, page 115) if the loan payments are not continued. Restricted purchase-money lenders, on the other hand, conceivably may not even be entitled to report a foreclosed property as defaulted because the debt, by law, has been satisfied through forfeiture.

Lenders presented with a borrower's voluntary surrender of the security often persist in foreclosure anyway. They are not required to accept a borrower's deed to the property and have only to return it to sever the attempted transfer. Sometimes this is necessary because foreclosure is the only way the lender can eliminate junior encumbrances and obtain clear title to the property (page 242). Some lenders use foreclosure to try to bluff the borrower into continuing his payments. And some lenders, especially large organizations, have an elitist view which disregards anything the borrower might propose, calling for blind pursuit of foreclosure as the only solution to a default in payment.

That borrowers don't give up their property and walk away from the debt more often, can only be attributed to ignorance. Made aware they have the option of forfeiture in settlement of their debt, many would easily find reason to do so. Residential loans with negligible net equity are common, especially among institutional lenders. A borrower in possession of a house with a net market value of $120,000 (after allowance for sales commission, escrow, title insurance, etc.) against an outstanding loan of $118,000, for example, has – absent personal liability – little incentive to keep the property. If he suddenly decides he doesn't like his neighbors, or he's transferred elsewhere to another job – nevermind whether he can keep up his loan payments – he would most likely jump at the chance to dispose of his obligation by handing over the property. Dependent on the lender's reporting practices, the borrower may not even suffer damage to his credit standing (page 239).

See also pages 117, 239, 240, 242-243.

ANTIDEFICIENCY EXCEPTIONS

The foregoing "purchase-money limitation" in trust collection, as well as the similar "one-action rule" (page 239), are called "antideficiency" laws (i.e., they prohibit lenders from collection of deficiencies in the security).

Neither of the above antideficiency limits are applicable when the debt is subject to overriding federal law, such as in federally insured FHA and VA loans.

Nor do antideficiency limits generally apply in the event of false conduct on the part of the borrower. "Intentional" or "bad faith" waste (pages 242-243), rent skimming (pages 176-178, 243), and fraud, are all conditions which – if they can be proven – allow lender collection for damages from other borrower assets in addition to the TD's security.

Waiver of antideficiency by the borrower may also create an exemption in some instances. A borrower may, for example, waive safety of his other assets from deficiency collection, in exchange for a TD alteration such as extension of time for payment.